Reinventing the Curriculum

Also Available From Bloomsbury

England's Citizenship Education Experiment: State, School and Student Perspectives, Lee Jerome
Literacy on the Left: Reform and Revolution, Andrew Lambirth

Reinventing the Curriculum

New Trends in Curriculum Policy and Practice

Mark Priestley and Gert Biesta

BLOOMSBURY
LONDON • NEW DELHI • NEW YORK • SYDNEY

Bloomsbury Academic
An imprint of Bloomsbury Publishing Plc

50 Bedford Square   1385 Broadway
London   New York
WC1B 3DP   NY 10018
UK   USA

www.bloomsbury.com

Bloomsbury is a registered trade mark of Bloomsbury Publishing Plc

First published 2013
Paperback edition first published 2014

© Mark Priestley, Gert Biesta and Contributors, 2013

All rights reserved. No part of this publication may be reproduced or transmitted in any form or by any means, electronic or mechanical, including photocopying, recording, or any information storage or retrieval system, without prior permission in writing from the publishers.

Mark Priestley, Gert Biesta and Contributors have asserted their rights under the Copyright, Designs and Patents Act, 1988, to be identified as Authors of this work.

No responsibility for loss caused to any individual or organization acting on or refraining from action as a result of the material in this publication can be accepted by Bloomsbury or the author.

British Library Cataloguing-in-Publication Data
A catalogue record for this book is available from the British Library.

ISBN: HB: 978-1-4411-3764-7
PB: 978-1-4725-9600-0
ePUB: 978-1-4411-3481-3
ePDF: 978-1-4411-4868-1

Library of Congress Cataloging-in-Publication Data
Reinventing the curriculum: new trends in curriculum policy and practice/edited by Mark Priestley and Gert Biesta.
  pages cm.
Includes bibliographical references and index.
ISBN 978-1-4411-3764-7 (hardcover) – ISBN 978-1-4411-3481-3 (epub) –
ISBN 978-1-4411-4868-1 (pdf) 1. Curriculum planning. 2. Curriculum change.
3. Curriculum planning–Scotland–Case studies. 4. Curriculum change–Scotland–
Case studies. I. Priestley, Mark. II. Biesta, Gert.
  LB2806.15.R45 2013
  375'.001–dc23
                                                    2013006861

Typeset by Newgen Imaging Systems Pvt Ltd, Chennai, India
Printed and bound in Great Britain

Contents

List of Contributors   viii

1   Introduction: The New Curriculum *Mark Priestley and Gert Biesta*   1
    Introduction   1
    Emerging curricula   2
    The book   6

2   The Origins and Development of Curriculum for Excellence: Discourse, Politics and Control *Walter Humes*   13
    Introduction   13
    Background and rationale   14
    Values and discourse   19
    Process and development   23
    Discussion   26

3   Capacities and the Curriculum *Gert Biesta and Mark Priestley*   35
    Introduction   35
    The idea of capacities in the Scottish Curriculum for Excellence   37
    The student as a learning outcome: Capacities and competences   38
    Five critical questions   42
    Concluding remarks   46

4   The Successful Learner: A Progressive or an Oppressive Concept? *Jenny Reeves*   51
    Introduction   51
    The origins and evolution of the learner   52
    Localizing the discourse – how Scottish policymakers made sense of 'the learner', 2004–10   60
    Conclusion   68

5   Confident Individuals: The Implications of an 'Emotional Subject' for Curriculum Priorities and Practices *Kathryn Ecclestone*   75
    Introduction   75

	Confidence as a high-stakes educational and social goal	77
	Changing the subject	84
	The effects of an 'emotional' subject on curriculum priorities and practices	87
	Conclusions	93
6	Responsible Citizens: Citizenship Education between Social Inclusion and Democratic Politics *Gert Biesta*	99
	Introduction	99
	Citizenship education in Scotland: The socio-historical context	100
	Characterizing citizenship and citizenship education	102
	Is the responsible citizen a democratic citizen?	111
	Conclusions	114
7	Effective Contributors: Evaluating the Potential for Children and Young People's Participation in their Own Schooling and Learning *E. Kay M. Tisdall*	117
	Effective contributors	117
	Children and young people's participation	119
	Understandings of participation	121
	What do we know about children and young people's participation in Scottish schools?	124
	Moving forward?	129
	Conclusion	133
8	Emerging International Trends in Curriculum *Claire Sinnema and Graeme Aitken*	141
	Commonalities in national curricula	141
	The goals of curriculum policy reform	142
	Commonalities in the emphases of recently revised national curricula	146
	Discussion	156
9	Developing the Teacher – or Not? *Ian Menter and Moira Hulme*	165
	Introduction	165
	Curricular and pedagogical reform	165
	Linking curriculum and pedagogy: The Scottish case	169
	Re- or de-professionalization?	180
	Conclusion	181

10	Teachers as Agents of Change: Teacher Agency and Emerging Models of Curriculum *Mark Priestley, Gert Biesta and Sarah Robinson*	187
	Introduction	187
	Defining and theorizing teacher agency	188
	Achieving agency (1): The role of values and beliefs	191
	Achieving agency (2): The role of relationships	197
	Concluding comments	203
11	High-Stakes Assessment and New Curricula: A Queensland Case of Competing Tensions in Curriculum Development *Bob Lingard and Glenda McGregor*	207
	Introduction	207
	Contextualizing the development of the New Basics in Queensland	212
	The New Basics: Producing new workers and new citizens	215
	Changing contexts: From New Basics to Queensland Curriculum, Assessment and Reporting (QCAR) Framework	218
	The National Schooling Agenda: National Curriculum and NAPLAN	220
	NAPLAN 2008, the masters review and the conservative restoration in Queensland schooling	222
	Conclusion: From New Basics to teaching and learning audits and discipline-based curriculum	224
12	A Curriculum for the Twenty-First Century? *Gert Biesta and Mark Priestley*	229
	Introduction	229
	Wider sociopolitical trends shaping the curriculum field	230
	Conclusion: A curriculum for the twenty-first century?	234
Index		237

List of Contributors

Graeme Aitken is the Dean of Education at the University of Auckland, New Zealand. His research has focused on teaching effectiveness, and on curriculum development and design. He aims, through his work, to offer insights into practice that help decision-making by policymakers, schools and teachers in the best interests of learners and learning.

Gert Biesta (www.gertbiesta.com) is currently Professor of Educational Theory and Policy at the University of Luxembourg, having previously worked in the Netherlands and the UK. He has published widely on the theory and philosophy of education and educational research and is particularly interested in relationships between education and democracy. His research has focused on citizenship education, teaching and teachers, curriculum theory and practice, and adult and vocational education. Recent books include *Good Education in an Age of Measurement* (2010) and *The Beautiful Risk of Education* (2013), both with Paradigm Publishers USA.

Kathryn Ecclestone is Professor of Education at the University of Sheffield, UK. Her research explores the effects of policy on everyday assessment and teaching, curriculum content and knowledge, and attitudes to learning in post-compulsory education, with a particular interest in the impact of government intervention in 'emotional well-being' on educational goals, activities and outcomes. Books include *The Dangerous Rise of Therapeutic Education* (2009) and *Transforming Formative Assessment in Lifelong Learning* (2010). Kathryn is a member of EdExcel/Pearson's expert group on assessment and is on the editorial boards of *Studies in the Education of Adults* and *Assessment in Education*.

Moira Hulme is a Lecturer in Educational Research at the School of Education, University of Glasgow, UK. She has undertaken research commissioned by the Scottish Government, General Teaching Council of Scotland and Learning and Teaching Scotland (now Education Scotland). Recent studies include teachers' response to draft curriculum guidance, professional culture among new entrants to the teaching profession and pupil participation in Scottish schools. Moira is convenor of the Teacher Education and Development Special Interest Group of the British Educational Research Association.

Walter Humes is currently Visiting Professor of Education at the University of Stirling, UK. Prior to his retirement in 2010, Walter Humes held professorships at the Universities of Aberdeen, Strathclyde and West of Scotland, UK. His publications include work on teacher education, educational leadership and management, history of education and policy studies. He is co-editor of *Scottish Education*, a 1,000-page text on all sectors of the Scottish educational system, the 4th edition of which will be published by Edinburgh University Press in 2013.

Bob Lingard works in the School of Education at The University of Queensland, Australia, where he researches in sociology of education. He has been Chair of the Governing Board of the Queensland Studies Authority, is currently on the Governing Board of the Authority and is Chair of the Board's Curriculum Committee. Bob is Editor of the journal, *Discourse: Studies in the Cultural Politics of Education*. His most recent books include *Boys and Schooling* (Palgrave, 2009), co-authored with Wayne Martino and Martin Mills, *Globalizing Education Policy* (Routledge, 2010), co-authored with Fazal Rizvi, and *Changing Schools* (Routledge, 2012), co-edited with Terry Wrigley and Pat Thomson. In 2013, Routledge will publish his Selected Works as *Politics, Policies and Pedagogies in Education*.

Glenda McGregor is a Senior Lecturer in the School of Education and Professional Studies at Griffith University, Brisbane, Australia, where she is Convenor of the Graduate Diploma of Education (Secondary) programme. For many years she has worked closely with the Queensland Studies Authority in the development of curriculum in that state and was also a member of the advisory committee for the development of the Australian Curriculum in History. Her research interests include sociology of youth, alternative schools, pedagogy and curriculum and, social justice and education. She is currently working on two major research projects on alternative and democratic models of schooling funded by the Australian Research Council.

Ian Menter (AcSS) is Professor of Teacher Education and Director of Professional Programmes in the Department of Education at the University of Oxford, UK. He previously worked at the Universities of Glasgow, the West of Scotland, London Metropolitan, the West of England and Gloucestershire, UK. Before that he was a primary school teacher in Bristol, UK. His most recent publications include *A Literature Review on Teacher Education for the 21st Century* (Scottish Government) and *A Guide to Practitioner Research in Education* (Sage). His work has also been published in many academic journals.

Mark Priestley is Professor of Education in the School of Education, at the University of Stirling, UK, where he is Director of the Curriculum and Pedagogy research programme. His main research interests concern the school curriculum, and especially the processes of curricular change. He was recently principal investigator of the Economic and Social Research Council funded *Teacher Agency and Curriculum Change* research project (RES-000-22-4208), and is currently Chair of the Editorial Board of the *Scottish Educational Review*.

Jenny Reeves is Honorary Senior Researcher in the School of Education at Stirling University, UK. She has worked in the field of teacher professional development, with a particular interest in leadership and management, for most of her career. Her research interests centre around the sociocultural dynamics of practice-focused professional development and organizational learning.

Sarah Robinson is currently employed in a post-doctoral position in the School of Business and Social Sciences at Aarhus University, Denmark. She is carrying out research in Entrepreneurship Education in Higher Education. Her research interests stem from policy enactment – in schools and educational administration – and in the practices that result. Sarah was previously a team member for the Economic and Social Research Council funded *Teacher Agency and Curriculum Change* research project (RES-000-22-4208) at the University of Stirling, UK.

Claire Sinnema is a Senior Lecturer at The University of Auckland, New Zealand. Her research focuses on the improvement of teaching and learning in the context of curriculum implementation, teacher professional learning, teacher evaluation, pedagogy and school leadership. It is also concerned with the role of policy in such improvement. She was recently a principal investigator for the New Zealand Ministry of Education funded *Monitoring and Evaluating Curriculum Implementation* project and has served on several national policy advisory groups.

E. Kay M. Tisdall is Professor of Childhood Policy and Programme Director of the MSc in Childhood Studies (www.sps.ed.ac.uk/pgtcs), at the University of Edinburgh, UK. She is Co-Director of the *Centre for Research on Families and Relationships* (www.crfr.ac.uk). She undertakes research, teaching and policy work centred on children's rights generally and children's participation in particular. Recent publications have been in the journals *Children's Geographies*, *International Journal of Children's Rights* and *Social Policy & Society*.

Introduction: The New Curriculum

Mark Priestley and Gert Biesta

Introduction

This is a book about the school curriculum. Ostensibly it is a book about a particular curriculum development, Scotland's Curriculum for Excellence (CfE), often described 'as the biggest educational reform in Scotland for a generation', which 'aims to transform education in Scotland' (Ipsos Mori,[1] 2012). However, the book has far wider significance, with contributions from a range of writers drawing on international perspectives about newly emerging curriculum developments. It comes at a time when writing about the curriculum is beginning to experience a renaissance after two decades when the field of curriculum studies had become fairly moribund (Moore, 2006; Edwards, 2011). The book has been written in response to new, emerging trends in curriculum policy and practice. These are at one level exciting, as they herald the re-emergence of an interest in school-based curriculum development, for example. However, they are simultaneously problematic because they come at a time when education systems arguably lack the capacity for such approaches following a period of extreme prescription in curriculum policy, and when there is a decreased prominence of the field of curriculum studies, which might otherwise inform the development of such capacity. A related issue lies in the formulation of curriculum policy, which has been criticized in some quarters for being theoretically agnostic and ill-informed (Priestley and Humes, 2010), overtly instrumental (Yates and Collins, 2010) and lacking in rigour (Wheelahan, 2010). It is worthwhile to briefly trace some of the policy trajectories that led to the emergence of the new curricular models that are the focus of this book.

The launch of the National Curriculum in the United Kingdom[2] in 1988 marked a seminal moment in the history of the school curricular policy. This new curriculum was hailed by its protagonists as being radical and visionary. The speech of June 1987 by education minister Kenneth Baker to the Society of Education Officers, for example, referred to the radical reforms that may 'be unwelcome to those who value what is traditional and familiar' (cited in Lawton and Chitty, 1988, p. 2), and it is clear that the initiative represented a new direction in many respects. It heralded hitherto unprecedented levels of government control over the content of the curriculum, and the ensuing years were to see a creeping extension of this control into matters of teaching methodology. In terms of its objectives-based and linear structure it was the first of its kind, and was subsequently copied in other countries (see, for example, the New Zealand Curriculum Framework; Ministry of Education, 1993).

Nevertheless, this did not represent an end of history moment, to draw upon Fukuyama's contemporaneous analogy. Many educationalists were united in their condemnation of what they saw as a foolhardy, ill-considered and retrogressive step. Kelly, for example, was overtly critical of the whole approach, alleging that 'the National Curriculum has sprung fully formed from the head of Mr. Baker, like the goddess Athene from the head of Zeus' (1990, p. 66). Lawton described the curriculum reforms as 'multiple change which has sometimes bordered on chaos' (1996, preface). Such criticisms seemed to be borne out in practice, as the National Curriculum lurched from crisis to crisis, most notably the major climb-down of the 1993/4 Dearing Review. Kelly's (1990, p. 130) prediction that the 'inadequacies [of the 1988 model] are likely to result in the early breakdown of the National Curriculum', has indeed come to pass in many respects. Moreover, this pattern of continual crisis and reactive innovation has been mirrored elsewhere to some extent. For example, in Scotland, 5–14 did not embed fully in schools, especially in the secondary sector (Swann and Brown, 1997), and in New Zealand, a highly contentious attempt to frame school subjects around the competency-based Unit Standards was dropped under the *Achievement 2001* initiative (see Priestley and Higham, 1999).

Emerging curricula

In recent years, this already complex situation has seen the emergence of an apparent curriculum turn, at least across the Anglophone world. Many educational systems have witnessed a nativity of a new model of curriculum. These curricula have idiosyncratic features, but also share much in common, reflecting a culture of policy-borrowing (Priestley, 2002; Rizvi and Lingard, 2009). In many ways, such developments can be seen as a renaissance. First, there is an apparent rebirth of progressive education, including child-centred approaches. For example, CfE makes much of the need for schools to develop approaches to active learning (although this concept is rarely explicitly spelled out) and emphasizes the role of teachers as co-learners, and as facilitators of student learning. Within CfE there is an implicitly constructivist philosophy of learning. In New Zealand this philosophy is made yet more explicit, through the development of models for enquiry learning (e.g. see Aitken and Sinnema, 2008; Sinnema and Aitken, this volume; for a critique of the turn towards learning, see Biesta, 2006, 2010). Secondly, in policy rhetoric at least, the new curricula explicitly place the teacher at the forefront of curriculum development, heralding an apparent [re]turn to teacher autonomy and teacher agency in curriculum-making (see, for example, Priestley, Robinson and Biesta, 2012). However, such developments are only part of the story.

The new curricula are widely claimed by critics and advocates alike to be a response by education systems to pressures associated with globalization, particularly in respect of economic competitiveness and citizenship (e.g. HMIE, 2009; Yates and Young, 2010). They tend to be framed around capacities or core/key competencies. Thus, for example, Scotland specifies that the curriculum will enable young people to develop four capacities, becoming: *successful learners, confident individuals, responsible citizens* and *effective contributors*. New Zealand has adopted slightly different language in its key competencies, although the message is similar. Here learners will develop competency in: *Thinking; Using Language, Symbols and Texts; Managing Self; Relating to Others;* and *Participating and Contributing*.

At first glance, the use of such terminology suggests a progressivist approach to the curriculum, redolent of the sorts of process curriculum advocated by the likes of Stenhouse (1975) and Kelly (1999). Such a discourse shift is accompanied by a growing popularity in policy circles and among practitioners for active forms of pedagogy, more associated with progressive models of education. These include cooperative learning, critical skills pedagogies and formative assessment. However, some writers have critiqued these trends.

Yates and Collins (2010), for example, see it as 'a fascinating rapprochement of . . . a child-focused developmentalism and an economic instrumentalism' (p. 92). Whether such a rapprochement is evidence of a deliberate, unholy alliance between progressive educators and neo-liberal politicians is open to debate. It may be, as Wheelahan (2010) suggests, that such adoption is simply part of a long-standing process whereby neo-liberal discourses have assimilated progressive language while maintaining technical-instrumental goals for education (see also Biesta, 2010), a process described by Bernstein (1990) as a 'new pedagogic Janus' which 'recontextualises and thus repositions within its own ideology, features of apparently oppositional discourses' (p. 88).

Other writers suggest that key competencies/capacities have more sinister overtones relating to indoctrination. For example, Watson (2010) suggests that CfE 'is concerned with setting out not what children are expected to know, but how they should be' (p. 99). She adds:

> To criticise such laudable aims would be like giving motherhood and apple pie a good kicking but whose values underpin this? Who says what counts as a responsible citizen? An effective contributor? etc. . . . Despite the veneer of self-evident goodness these are not . . . unproblematic constructions of self-hood. (Ibid.)

There is clearly a fine line between the convergent notion of educating for capacity implied by Watson, and more divergent approaches advocated by progressive educators; nevertheless, regardless of one's view on these issues, it is apparent that there is a strongly instrumental (towards economic and civic goals) slant to the new curricula, heavily influenced by publications from supra-national organizations such as the OECD (2005) and the European Union (2006). The pervasive role of such organizations in driving states' education policy, as a driver for economic development via international comparative testing (e.g. PISA), has also been noted by critics (see, for example, Hopmann, Brinek and Retzl, 2007).

A second area casting doubt on the progressive credentials of the new curricula lies in their structure. Curricula such as CfE have retained a structure more redolent of their curricular ancestors such as Scotland's 5–14 Curriculum, the 1993 New Zealand Curriculum Framework and the UK National Curriculum. There is a continued adherence to the articulation of the curriculum in terms of assessable outcomes, set out by subject area in hierarchical levels. While such outcomes tend to be less prescriptive (or more vague depending on one's outlook) in terms of content, and while each level tends to cover a longer period of schooling than was previously the case, they are still overtly framed as assessment standards, with all of the implications contained therein for assessment-driven teaching (see, for example, Scotland's *Building the Curriculum 5*; Scottish Government, 2011). Such outcomes tend to be phrased as short statements of what students are able to experience in their learning and/or do as a result of such learning.

The following examples from the science curriculum in New Zealand (Ministry of Education, 2010) and Scotland (Education Scotland, no date) illustrate this approach.

> Students will recognize that there are life processes common to all living things and that these occur in different ways. (Level 4, Life Processes, New Zealand Science Curriculum)
>
> I can sample and identify living things from different habitats to compare their biodiversity and can suggest reasons for their distribution. (Third level, Biodiversity and Interdependence, Scotland's Curriculum for Excellence)

The comparative lack of specification of knowledge/content in these outcomes has laid the new curricula open to charges that they have stripped knowledge out of the curriculum (see, for example, Young, 2008; Wheelahan, 2010; Yates and Collins, 2010). Moore and Young (2001) suggest that this new emphasis on generic skills is especially problematic at a time when 'we are (or soon will be) in a "knowledge society" and . . . more jobs require people to be "knowledge workers"'. They suggest further that 'government policy documents have been remarkably silent about what this knowledge is' (p. 445). Related to this point, these writers, often drawing upon Bernstein's (2000) work about the development of academic disciplines, also point to the tendency of the new curricula to fail to differentiate between theoretical and everyday knowledge, thus potentially depriving students of access to 'powerful knowledge' necessary for modern life (Young, 2008; Wheelahan, 2010; Rata, 2012). Again the argument here is that this model is driven by a narrow instrumentalism based upon economic imperatives – in other words, soft skills required for the workplace rather than the sorts of 'powerful knowledge' required to critically engage with the world.

Alongside the above-described focus on generic skills and key competencies, lies the renewed emphasis on the centrality of the learner. Here, again, there have been critiques of curricular policy, framed largely by new discourses on learning – what Biesta (2010) has termed the 'learnification of education' – rather than an overtly progressive philosophy of learning. This critique centres upon the emphasis in such discourses on technical processes, and a lack of attention to questions of educational purpose. According to Biesta (2009), this tendency reflects an unproblematized acceptance that learning is a good, and a failure to address educational questions such as 'what are we learning?' and 'why are we learning it?'

Finally, we should acknowledge that the new curricula are being implemented in a climate characterized by increasingly pervasive regimes of accountability and cultures of performativity, despite policy rhetoric that constructs teachers as agents of change and professional developers of the curriculum. Performativity has been widely claimed to have a number of serious consequences, especially pertinent in an era when teachers are being required to re-engage with school-based curriculum development. Biesta (2004, 2010) has highlighted how a culture of measurement drives out a concern for what constitutes good education, instead substituting short-term instrumental goals that encourage a detachment from big picture ideas, as teachers distance themselves from their personal values in order to 'play the game' (Gleeson and Gunter, 2001). This game can take the form of fabrication of the school's image – careful impression management and discourses of excellence (Keddie, Mills and Pendergast, 2011) and the concealing of 'dirty laundry' (Cowie, Taylor and Croxford, 2007), as well as more serious corruption and cheating (Ball, 2003; Sahlberg, 2010).

The book

It is against the backdrop of this complex terrain – curriculum in 'crisis' (Wheelahan, 2010), accelerating cycles of policy innovation, a moribund state of affairs in curriculum studies and the emergence of new curricular models – that this book was conceived. We take, as our point of departure, Scotland's Curriculum for Excellence. We draw upon CfE to illustrate some of the common features of the new curriculum approach. The early chapters in the book explore CfE as a case study, providing a genealogy of the new curriculum, and offering a critique of some of its features, particularly the framing of the curriculum around the four capacities. In the latter part of the book, chapters explore the implications of some of these features for educational practice and curriculum making in general.

Chapter 2, by Walter Humes, provides an introduction to the book by examining the origins and development of CfE from a number of perspectives. It sets the initiative against the background of previous reforms of the Scottish Curriculum (Standard Grade, 5–14, Higher Still) and the insights they gave into the management of change. Humes refers to global pressures to reform the curriculum in line with an ideological position which favours a particular view of the relationship between schooling, economy and society. This genealogy of CfE provides fascinating insights into the composition and remit of the review group charged with producing the principles which would subsequently underpin the reform programme, and spotlights the 'political' role of key agencies in the reform process (e.g. Her Majesty's Inspectorate of Education, Learning and Teaching

Scotland), as well as documenting the emergence of key documentation as the curriculum unfolded between 2004 and 2011.

Chapter 3 by Gert Biesta and Mark Priestley examines the framing of CfE around the idea of capacities as part of a wider trend in curriculum policy and practice where the purposes of education are no longer articulated in terms of what students should *learn* but in terms of what they should *become*. The chapter explores this wider trend and asks what it means for our understanding of curriculum and for the design of educational processes and practices more generally. The chapter looks at the history of the Scottish Curriculum for Excellence and its decision to utilize the language of 'capacities', and discusses how the idea of 'capacities' functions within the CfE. From here it turns to the wider trend to turn the student into the intended outcome of education and discusses different manifestations of this, ranging from traditions of *paideia*, *Bildung* and liberal education to a focus on capacities and competencies. Against this background it raises questions about the potential risks of focusing the curriculum (too) strongly on questions of becoming and being.

In Chapter 4, Jenny Reeves takes a critical look at the notion of the *successful learner*. Since the term 'successful learners' first appeared in the context of the CfE in 2004, its meaning has continued to evolve in guidance to teachers and schools being issued through the curriculum agency *Learning and Teaching Scotland*. Reeves's chapter starts by examining the relationship between the particular meanings coalescing around the term 'learner' in Scotland and the wider international discourse of developmentalism associated with lifelong learning and personalization. In considering the move from good pupil to successful learner, she provides a critical focus on what are arguably three key characteristics of the latter as: a person with an agentive orientation to the world; a master of pedagogic tools and techniques relating to the self; and a product armed with core transferable skills that can be customized and applied, particularly in the economic field.

Chapter 5 focuses on the idea of the *confident individual*. Kathryn Ecclestone provides a critical view of recent changes to curricular policy framed around, as discussed previously, the downgrading of knowledge and the development of a dispositions-based curriculum in its place. She suggests that changes to the Scottish Curriculum lie in the broader context of social policy in a growing number of countries, where developing the emotional well-being of individuals and communities has become a key concern of government. In a context where there has been virtually no challenge to this goal or its educational effects, this chapter evaluates how emotionally focused targets, their underlying rationales, and the interventions they lead to, change beliefs about desirable educational goals, outcomes and subject content in new and profound ways.

In Chapter 6, Gert Biesta offers a critique of the notion of the *responsible citizen*. Over the past two decades the question of citizenship education has emerged as a major theme on the agenda of politicians and policymakers, and schools in many countries are now required to play a major role in the development of good citizenship. This chapter focuses on an analysis of the idea of responsible citizenship in CfE, in order to highlight the range of choices available to curriculum developers and educators within this domain. Biesta argues that the idea of the responsible citizen runs the risk of individualizing the question of citizenship, seeing it more as an issue of social integration and inclusion, and 'good behaviour' more generally, than as a vehicle for the reinvigoration of democratic processes and practices.

Kay Tisdall examines the notion of the *effective contributor* in Chapter 7. Her chapter looks at this capacity through the lens provided by the agenda of children and young people's participation in their education. Children's rights and, specifically, the *United Nations Convention on the Rights of the Child* have given renewed impetus to recognizing and promoting children and young people's participation in their own learning and schooling. Scotland should be a leader of the devolved nations, as it was the first in the United Kingdom to place children's views in their own schooling squarely in statute, with the *Standards in Scotland's Schools etc. Act 2000*. Tisdall questions whether this is the case, and whether Scotland's schools are indeed capable of developing effective contributors as they are currently configured. The chapter concludes by suggesting ways forward for policy and practice, to place schools in the vanguard of promoting children and young people's meaningful participation. This chapter concludes the first section of the book.

The latter part of the book from Chapter 8 onwards takes more of an international perspective on curriculum policy and development. In Chapter 8, Claire Sinnema and Graeme Aitken provide a detailed analysis of commonalities in curriculum policy across Anglophone nations. The authors employ a theoretical framework that analyses curricular policy in terms of *goals* – improving teachers' practice, ensuring equity and maintaining relevance and coherence – and *emphases* – the development of competencies for lifelong learning, values education, participation and pedagogy. The chapter challenges assumptions about the extent to which these emphases actually support the reform goals. Their analysis includes discussion of two unique cases – Australia and the United States – where education has been traditionally devolved to state legislatures, but where there have been recent moves to extend federal jurisdiction into curricular policy.

In Chapter 9, Ian Menter and Moira Hulme provide an analysis of the role of teachers in implementing this sort of curriculum. The chapter reviews the connections between curriculum reform and the reform of teachers' work, especially over the last ten years, providing an analysis of links between pedagogical and curriculum policy. Although the central focus is on Scotland, there is considerable reference made to parallel developments elsewhere in the United Kingdom and internationally. The authors draw on their empirical work (including involvement in a major consultation with teachers and others in Scotland) and the United Kingdom (including studies of teacher engagement in enquiry and responses to pay restructuring). The main theme that emerges from the chapter is the question of whether teachers are being reprofessionalized and empowered by the reforms, or whether they are actually being drawn into and subjected to new forms of management and control.

In Chapter 10, Mark Priestley, Gert Biesta and Sarah Robinson further develop these themes. They draw upon an ethnographic study conducted in three schools over the course of a year. The chapter presents a theoretical model for understanding teacher agency, posing the question of whether teachers are able to be agents of change and professional developers of the curriculum. The chapter explicitly examines two key facets of teacher agency: [1] the organizational structures within which teachers work, and specifically the relational resources afforded to teachers by these structures as they engage with their work; and [2] the impact of teachers' beliefs and aspirations on their ability to achieve agency, especially the manner in which teacher beliefs frame their professional discourses about education in general and the curriculum in particular.

The final chapter in this section takes a look at a parallel case to CfE, the example of the Queensland New Basics programme. In Chapter 11, Bob Lingard and Glenda McGregor provide a detailed genealogy of curriculum policy development in Queensland. They outline the historical trajectory of the curriculum in a state which has traditionally enjoyed relative autonomy from federal government control. An interesting feature of Queensland lies in the absence, until recently, of externally set terminal examinations. The chapter draws upon empirical research, considering how policy aspirations in respect of school-based curriculum development may be eroded by an excessive focus on teacher accountability through high-stakes assessment. The authors document how the New Basics programme developed in the early years of the millennium, but has subsequently been undermined in the face of increasing dirigisme from a central government now developing a national curriculum, poor performance in PISA tests and political nervousness about what these might mean in educational terms.

The book concludes with a final chapter which draws together these complex threads. In this chapter, Gert Biesta and Mark Priestley consider the implications for curricular policy and practice of the insights generated by the contributing authors. They review the prospects of the particular approach exemplified in CfE, indicating strengths and weaknesses and wider lessons to be learned for curriculum development and innovation in other contexts and settings.

Notes

1 The quotation in question is taken from the Ipsos Mori website. This organization has recently undertaken research for the Scottish Government. It is interesting that this CfE truism has become an oft-repeated claim about CfE, rarely subject to critical analysis, and cropping up in multiple places, including policy websites such as www.scotland.gov.uk/Publications/2010/05/20152453/4, and government-funded quangos such as www.scotlandscolleges.ac.uk/curriculum/curriculum-for-excellence/curriculum-for-excellence.html.
2 This did not apply to Scotland, where curriculum policy has traditionally been developed independently of the rest of the United Kingdom. In Scotland, the early 1990s witnessed the development of a softer version of the National Curriculum, known as the 5–14 Curriculum. 5–14 shared many features with its English counterpart – notably the setting out of content into hierarchical levels articulated as outcomes – but took the form of non-statutory guidelines, being far less prescriptive in terms of content.

References

Aitken, G. and Sinnema, C. (2008), *Effective Pedagogy in Social Sciences/Tikanga ā Iwi: Best Evidence Synthesis Iteration*. Wellington: Ministry of Education.
Ball, S. J. (2003), 'The teacher's soul and the terrors of performativity'. *Journal of Education Policy*, 18, 215–28.
Bernstein, B. (1990), *The Structuring of Pedagogic Discourse: Class Codes and Control*, volume 4. London: Routledge.
— (2000), *Pedagogy, Symbolic Control and Identity* (rev. edn). Oxford: Rowman and Littlefield.
Biesta, G. J. J. (2004), 'Education, accountability, and the ethical demand; can the democratic potential of accountability be regained'. *Educational Theory*, 54, 233–50.

— (2006), *Beyond Learning: Democratic Education for a Human Future*. Boulder, CO: Paradigm Publishers.

— (2010), *Good Education in an Age of Measurement: Ethics – Politics – Democracy*. Boulder, CO: Paradigm Publishers.

Cowie, M., Taylor, D. and Croxford, L. (2007), '"Tough, Intelligent Accountability" in Scottish secondary schools and the role of Standard Tables and Charts (STACS): a critical appraisal'. *Scottish Educational Review*, 39, 29–50.

Education Scotland (no date), *Curriculum for Excellence: Successful Learners, Confident Individuals, Responsible Citizens, Effective Contributors*. Online at www.educationscotland.gov.uk/Images/all_experiences_outcomes_tcm4-539562.pdf (accessed 04/10/12).

Edwards, R. (2011), 'Whatever happened to curriculum theory?' *Pedagogy, Culture and Society*, 19, 173–4.

European Union (2006), *Key Competences for Lifelong Learning*. Online at http://europa.eu/legislation_summaries/education_training_youth/lifelong_learning/c11090_en.htm (accessed 15/10/12).

Gleeson, D. and Gunter, H. (2001), 'The performing school and the modernisation of teachers', in D. Gleeson and C. Husbands (eds), *The Performing School: Managing, Teaching and Learning in a Performance Culture*. London: RoutledgeFalmer, pp. 139–58.

HMIE (2009), *Improving Scottish Education*. Online at www.hmie.gov.uk/documents/publication/ise09.html (accessed 26/01/12).

Hopmann, S. T., Brinek, G. and Retzl, M. (eds) (2007), *PISA zufolge PISA – PISA According to PISA. Hält PISA, was es verspricht? Does PISA Keep What It Promises?* Vienna: Lit Verlag.

Ipsos Mori (2012), *Education and Training*. Online at www.ipsos-mori.com/offices/scotland/specareas/education.aspx (accessed 16/10/12).

Keddie, A., Mills, M. and Pendergast, D. (2011), 'Fabricating and identity in neo-liberal times: performing schooling as "number one"'. *Oxford Review of Education*, 37, 75–92.

Kelly, A. V. (1989), *The Curriculum: Theory and Practice* (4th edn). London: Paul Chapman Publishing.

— (1990), *The National Curriculum: A Critical Review*. London: Paul Chapman Publishing.

Lawton, D. (1996), *Beyond the National Curriculum*. London: Hodder and Stoughton.

Lawton, D. and Chitty, C. (eds) (1988), *The National Curriculum*. London: The Institute of Education.

Ministry of Education (1993), *The New Zealand Curriculum Framework*. Wellington: Learning Media.

— (2010), *Science Curriculum Achievement Aims and Objectives*. Online at http://nzcurriculum.tki.org.nz/Curriculum-documents/The-New-Zealand-Curriculum/Learning-areas/Science/Science-curriculum-achievement-aims-and-objectives#level%204 (accessed 15/07/10).

Moore, A. (2006), 'Introduction', in A. Moore (ed.), *Schooling, Society and Curriculum*. Abingdon: Routledge, pp. 1–14.

Moore, R. and Young, M. (2001), 'Knowledge and the curriculum in the sociology of education: towards a reconceptualisation'. *British Journal of Sociology of Education*, 22, 445–61.

Organisation for Economic Co-operation and Development (OECD) (2005), *The Definition and Selection of Key Competencies: Executive Summary*. Online at www.oecd.org/pisa/35070367.pdf (accessed 13/09/12).

Priestley, M. (2002), 'Global discourses and national reconstruction: the impact of globalization on curriculum policy'. *The Curriculum Journal*, 13, 87–104.

Priestley, M. and Higham, J. (1999), *New Zealand's Curriculum and Assessment Revolution*, Occasional Publication no. 8. Leeds: School of Education 14–19 Research Group.

Priestley, M. and Humes, W. (2010), 'The development of Scotland's Curriculum for Excellence: amnesia and déjà vu'. *Oxford Review of Education*, 36, 345–61.

Priestley, M., Robinson, S. and Biesta, G. J. J. (2012), 'Teacher agency, performativity and curriculum change: reinventing the teacher in the Scottish Curriculum for Excellence?', in B. Jeffrey and G. Troman (eds), *Performativity Across UK Education: Ethnographic Cases of its Effects, Agency and Reconstructions*. Painswick: E&E Publishing, pp. 87–108.

Rata, E. (2012), 'The politics of knowledge in education'. *British Educational Research Journal*, 38, 103–24.

Rizvi, F. and Lingard, B. (2009), *Globalizing Education Policy*. London: Routledge.

Sahlberg, P. (2010), 'Rethinking accountability in a knowledge society'. *Journal of Educational Change*, 11, 45–61.

Scottish Government (2010), *A Curriculum for Excellence: Building the Curriculum 5: A Framework for Assessment*. Edinburgh: Scottish Government.

Stenhouse, L. (1975), *An Introduction to Curriculum Research and Development*. London: Heinemann.

Swann, J. and Brown, S. (1997), 'The implementation of a National Curriculum and teachers' classroom thinking'. *Research Papers in Education*, 12, 91–114.

Watson, C. (2010), 'Educational policy in Scotland: inclusion and the control society'. *Discourse: Studies in the Cultural Politics of Education*, 31, 93–104.

Wheelahan, L. (2010), *Why Knowledge Matters in Curriculum: A Social Realist Argument*. London: Routledge.

Yates, L. and Collins, C. (2010), 'The absence of knowledge in Australian curriculum reforms'. *European Journal of Education*, 45, 89–101.

Yates, L. and Young, M. (2010), 'Editorial: globalisation, knowledge and the curriculum'. *European Journal of Education*, 45, 4–10.

Young, M. (2008), 'From constructivism to realism in the sociology of the curriculum'. *Review of Research in Education*, 32, 1–28.

The Origins and Development of Curriculum for Excellence: Discourse, Politics and Control

Walter Humes

Introduction

This chapter examines the origins and development of Curriculum for Excellence (CfE) from a number of perspectives. It sets the initiative against the changing context of Scottish politics, as well as international trends in educational policy deriving from a particular view of the relationship between schooling, economy and society. The experience of previous reforms of the Scottish Curriculum (Standard Grade, 5-14, Higher Still) is noted, especially the insights they provided into the management of change. Consideration is given to the composition and remit of the review group charged with producing the principles which underpin the reform programme, leading to an examination of the various discursive shifts apparent in subsequent documentation. The 'political' role of key agencies in the reform process (e.g. Her Majesty's Inspectorate of Education, Learning and Teaching Scotland) is analysed in terms of what they reveal about leadership and control. Reactions, both positive and negative, by teachers, headteachers, educational administrators, academics and other stakeholders, are analysed. Finally, an assessment of the ambitions of CfE, its political significance and what it reveals about the culture of Scottish education is offered.

Background and rationale

In attempting to explain the origins and development of any curricular reform, it is necessary to take account of a range of interacting forces at work, including:

- the political and ideological climate, both national and international, at the time the reform is initiated
- the experience of earlier reform programmes, their achievements and limitations
- the intentions and conceptual coherence of the new programme
- the effectiveness of the agencies and individuals charged with promoting it
- the support offered to teachers in engaging with the proposed reform, including documentation, teaching resources and professional development opportunities
- the responsiveness of government and officials to feedback from schools and local authorities as the reforms are promoted and implemented.

In the case of Scotland's Curriculum for Excellence, the political context is especially important. Scottish education has always been distinctive from provision in the rest of the United Kingdom (Humes and Bryce, 2008), and is generally regarded as a key indicator of national identity. National political consciousness was heightened with the re-establishment in 1999, after more than 300 years, of a Scottish Parliament in Edinburgh, with a range of devolved powers. It should be noted, however, that even before devolution educational policy in Scotland had developed separately in accordance with a set of beliefs about the 'democratic intellect' (Davie, 1961). These beliefs take the form of a story or 'myth', shaped by history but not always supported by historical evidence, to the effect that Scottish society is considered to be relatively egalitarian and meritocratic, that ability and achievement, not rank, should determine success in the world, that public (rather than private) institutions should be the means of bringing about the good society, and that, even where merit does justify differential rewards, there are certain basic respects – arising from the common humanity of all men and women – in which human beings deserve equal consideration and treatment (Humes and Bryce, 2008).

It was not surprising that all political parties in the new Scottish Parliament should see education as one of its main fields of interest. In December 2000, five national priorities for education were approved under the following headings: *Achievement and Attainment*; *Framework for Learning*; *Inclusion and Equality*;

Values and Citizenship; Learning for Life. Furthermore, an enquiry into the future of the teaching profession was commissioned by the Labour/Liberal Democrat administration. The recommendations of the enquiry report, *A Teaching Profession for the 21st Century* (Scottish Executive, 2000), formed the basis of the McCrone settlement of 2001, covering salaries, promotion, staff development and conditions of service. In March 2002, a national debate was launched to canvass public views on future policy: the title of the Scottish Executive's response to the debate introduced the word 'excellence' into official discourse (Scottish Executive, 2003). These developments served as the backdrop to the work of the review group set up in 2003 to consider the form and content of the Scottish Curriculum.

The new political position of Scotland made it possible for greater divergence from educational provision in other parts of the United Kingdom. At the same time, however, there were global pressures, which tended to push educational systems in the direction of greater convergence. International studies of educational achievement, particularly those conducted by the Organisation for Economic Cooperation and Development (OECD), made political leaders extremely sensitive about their country's position on tables comparing results in language, science and mathematics (see OECD, 2007). Global economic pressures, linked to technological developments and changes in patterns of employment, led to an international emphasis on skills, enterprise and adaptability. Sahlberg (2011) has referred to a Global Education Reform Movement influencing the thinking of politicians in many countries and driving policy in uniform directions. Traditional conceptions of knowledge were seen as too narrow and rigid to cope with the demands of rapidly changing work environments. Any country which did not take account of this perspective ran the risk of placing its young people at a disadvantage in a highly competitive world. New approaches to management in the public sector, emphasizing improved efficiency, defined targets and clear lines of accountability, also tended in the direction of convergence across educational systems (see Bush, 2003; Seddon, 2008). Scottish education was, therefore, trying to set its distinctive agenda during a period when there were countervailing forces pushing educational systems in a uniform direction. Curriculum for Excellence arrived on the scene at a moment when it had to negotiate tricky political and ideological terrain which was, at the same time, both national and international.

CfE seeks to provide a coordinated approach to learning for the whole age range 3–18. In this it differs from previous reform programmes which dealt with more restricted stages: Standard Grade, based on the Munn Report of 1977, covered the third and fourth years of secondary school; the 5–14 programme, initiated following a 1987 policy document, offered curricular guidelines covering primary education and the first two years of secondary; and Higher Still (later National Qualifications), partly based on the Howie report of 1992, focused on the upper secondary school. In retrospect, these three programmes revealed a number of issues which perhaps explain the way in which CfE was approached. First, there was a problem of progression and continuity between the different stages, which lacked a common set of concepts and principles to underpin pedagogic practice: this pointed to the need for a more comprehensive approach to the curriculum as a whole. Secondly, it had taken nearly 25 years to introduce the earlier reforms, with extended development phases before implementation could proceed. There was a perception that schools were in danger of falling behind developments in the outside world and that updating of the form and content of the curriculum needed to proceed at a brisker pace. And thirdly, there were mixed messages about the role of teachers in initiating change: often they were expected simply to follow central directives, leading to charges that they were being 'de-professionalized'. Effective change, it was argued, required schools to engage in a process of self-evaluation and teachers to be given freedom to exercise their professional judgement, based on their detailed knowledge of their pupils and the environment in which they worked (see Macbeath, 1999).

The report of the curriculum review group, published in 2004, which marked the formal beginning of the CfE programme, sought to address these issues (Scottish Executive, 2004). Members of the group were appointed on the traditional patronage model used to control entry to the Scottish policy community (Humes, 1986; MacPherson and Raab, 1988), a well-established system of recruitment to public service in Scotland.[1] The group was asked to identify the purposes of education from 3 to 18 and the principles for the design of the curriculum, taking account of the views expressed during the national debate, evidence from research and international comparisons. Their report argued for a curriculum that would:

- make learning, active, challenging and enjoyable
- not be too fragmented or over-crowded in content
- connect the various stages of learning from 3 to 18
- encourage the development of high levels of accomplishment and intellectual skill
- include a wide range of experiences and achieve a suitable blend of what has traditionally been seen as 'academic' and 'vocational'

- give opportunities for children to make appropriate choices to meet their individual interests and needs, while ensuring that these choices lead to successful outcomes
- ensure that assessment supports learning. (Scottish Executive, 2004, p. 10)

The main reason offered for listing these particular features was that 'We need a curriculum which will enable all young people to understand the world they are living in, reach the highest possible levels of achievement, and equip them for work and learning throughout their lives' (ibid., p. 10). This resonates with some of the characteristics of Sahlberg's Global Education Reform Movement alluded to above.

Other important features of the document included the centrality of four key capacities which all young people should develop (discussed below), the contribution which schooling should make towards democracy and social justice, and the rights and responsibilities of individuals within Scottish society, including the need to understand and respect diverse cultures and beliefs (see Biesta, 2008). There was also encouragement of cross- or interdisciplinary approaches to learning, with less emphasis on traditional bodies of knowledge, a point that was later to become a source of contention.

Following the original report, a research and review process was initiated in 2005, involving representatives from different sectors of education as well as inspectors, civil servants and staff from Learning and Teaching Scotland (LTS). The research dimension of the process appears to have been limited. Literature reviews relevant to different subject areas were undertaken and a short summary document was produced (Christie and Boyd, 2005). However, only passing reference was made to research in the 2006 document, *A Curriculum for Excellence: Progress and Proposals* (Scottish Executive, 2006a), with a stronger emphasis on reviews of existing curriculum guidelines and on engagement with teachers and other stakeholders. Constructing a new curriculum was seen as a developmental project, signalled in the 'building' metaphor used in the title of five key documents published between 2006 and 2011 (Scottish Executive, 2006b, 2007; Scottish Government, 2008, 2009, 2011a). These focused on particular aspects of the reform: how the various curriculum areas could promote the four capacities (*Building the Curriculum 1*); active learning in the early years (*Building the Curriculum 2*); a framework for learning and teaching (*Building the Curriculum 3*); the development and application of skills (*Building the Curriculum 4*); and guidance on assessment strategy for CfE (*Building the Curriculum 5*). The underlying framework of eight curricular areas (expressive arts, health and well-being, languages, mathematics, religious and moral education, sciences, social studies and technologies) was set out in the first of these documents and, although subject to some qualification through later references to interdisciplinary studies and cognitive transfer across subjects, remained the structural basis of subsequent proposals. Draft 'experiences and outcomes', outlining in detail the nature and intended result of learning across the eight main areas of the curriculum were published in stages between 2007 and 2008, leading to the final version in 2009 (Education Scotland, no date). As well as emphasizing the responsibility of all teachers for literacy and numeracy (and also health and well-being), these set out in tabulated form the learning experiences pupils should encounter at different stages of their careers. The draft 'experiences and outcomes' were subject to research evaluation and underwent some revision as a result (Scottish Government/University of Glasgow, 2009). Some teachers felt that the descriptors were vague, lacking specificity in relation to what should be taught. Greater prescriptiveness would, however, have run counter to the intention of giving teachers more professional autonomy in deciding what to cover in their classrooms. Having been used to a high degree of central direction in the past, it was not easy for teachers to adjust to the degree of freedom and independent judgement that the new approach was intended to encourage. This highlighted the difficulty of enabling teacher agency in a culture that had previously relied heavily on central direction (see Priestley, Robinson and Biesta, 2012). Reports of staff development events offered to teachers to promote CfE suggested that those leading them were not always well equipped to explain the shift in professional thinking that was required. While they were comfortable addressing operational issues to do with the timeline for implementation, they were less comfortable dealing with issues that required a theoretical understanding of the reconceptualization of professionalism on which the programme depended. Part of the reason for these difficulties will become clear when some of the key documents are subjected to discourse analysis in the next section.

Proposals on assessment came quite late in the process, a feature which subsequently attracted criticism on the grounds that teachers needed to know the likely shape and demands of new national qualifications before they could form a clear idea of the kind of curriculum that might serve as a suitable preparation. Delaying arrangements for assessment presumably arose from a desire to avoid a situation where examinations were the determinant of curriculum content and the learning experience.

Values and discourse

In the original CfE report produced by the review group in 2004, the central ideas are described in terms of *values, purposes* and *principles*. Instead of adopting a traditional 'aims and objectives' model of curriculum, the report starts from a statement of 'the values upon which . . . the curriculum should be based' (Scottish Government, 2004, p. 7). An appeal is made to the words that are inscribed on the mace of the Scottish Parliament – *wisdom, justice, compassion* and *integrity* – which are taken to encapsulate the values on which Scottish society is based. At the same time reference is made to the importance of respecting 'diverse cultures and beliefs' (ibid., p. 11). There is no extended philosophical justification for the particular values which are highlighted: they are asserted rather than argued for. Gillies (2006) is critical of the extent to which an adequate rationale is provided: the result is that 'the stated curriculum values, though worthy, [lack] coherence and force' (Gillies, 2006, p. 25). While he welcomes the recognition of the fundamentally political nature of state education, and the link to the aspirations associated with the new Scottish Parliament, he suggests that a much more carefully argued case is needed to support some of the report's assertions. He notes that the word 'excellence' in the title is not explained in the text and comments that 'if it is a curriculum for "excellence" why is the term not defined in the document, and why is its elevated status not argued for in the document?' (ibid., p. 35). Similarly, Priestley and Humes observe that '*A Curriculum for Excellence* does not offer much in the way of extended justification for either its terminology or its recommendations. In this sense it should be regarded as a broad framework document, designed to form the basis of subsequent policy development, rather than an extended rationale' (Priestley and Humes, 2010, p. 351).

With regard to *purposes* – a softer term than aims or objectives – there is a clear statement of the importance of promoting four key capacities: successful learners; confident individuals; responsible citizens; effective contributors (Scottish Executive, 2004, p. 12). These capacities quickly became a kind of mantra in Scottish education, regularly cited at conferences and CPD events, and were subject to little in the way of critical interrogation. It might be asked, for example, how crucial are the particular combinations of adjectives and nouns. Would it make much difference if the capacities were given as effective learners, responsible individuals, successful citizens and confident contributors? And are the capacities to be regarded as equally important, or should 'successful learners' be seen as the fundamental one on which the others depend? The fact that these questions were not asked when the proposals were first made suggests that one rather double-edged achievement of the initial CfE document was the power of its 'discursive capture' of subsequent debate. The capacities were soon regarded as self-evidently desirable without the need for deeper exploration.

A similar absence of critical scrutiny can be seen in what the document says about curriculum *principles*. These are defined rather narrowly as 'the design principles which schools, teachers and others will use to implement the curriculum' (ibid., p. 8), indicating that the focus is to be on operationalizing the proposals rather than on any consideration of alternative educational philosophies. The intention is 'to assist teachers and their schools in their practice and as a basis for continuing review, evaluation and improvement' (ibid., p. 13). The recommended principles are: *challenge and enjoyment*; *breadth*; *progression*; *depth*; *personalization and choice*; *coherence*; and *relevance*. The precise meaning of these terms, some of which could be subject to various interpretations, is not defined.

Subsequent documentation can be considered under various discursive headings. First, there is a strong developmental thread, evident in the metaphor of a journey. A set of resources under the general heading of 'The Journey to Excellence' was produced by LTS (www.journeytoexcellence.org.uk) consisting of publications, videos and other materials designed to encourage teachers to reflect on five broad areas of excellence: learning and teaching; vision and leadership; partnership; people; culture and ethos. The Journey to Excellence website attempts to explain the concept of excellence. It is described as 'the furthest end of the quality spectrum. When we think of excellence, we think of an outstanding aspect, a model of its kind – the very best there is'. Reeves suggests that this strand of CfE discourse is potentially incompatible with the drive for school improvement in other official documents which seem to favour approaches which give more weight to hard managerialism, formal audit and tight quality control. While the intention of CfE is to move away from 'the requirement for conformity with centrally determined procedures and practices' (Reeves, 2008, p. 6), she feels this will not happen unless there is a major rethink of the most effective means of promoting school and teacher development. In other words, the success of curricular reform is dependent on parallel reforms in other aspects of educational policy. She concludes: 'Without creating the conditions for teachers to learn based on a sense of agency and efficacy, the effects of performance-based accountability may be the opposite of what is desired' (ibid., p. 14).

Secondly, there is a recurring emphasis on pedagogic discourse. The learner and the learning process are seen as central to the whole endeavour. In the *Progress and Proposals* document of 2006, for example, it is stated that: 'experiences and outcomes will be designed from the learner's point of view, using terms like "I have…" for experiences and "I can…" for outcomes' (Scottish Executive, 2006a, p. 12). The use of the first person is no doubt intended to mark a departure from teacher-dominated approaches and to emphasize the importance of personal engagement by the learner. However, as set out in the final specification of experiences and outcomes (Scottish Government, 2009b), the result is a certain artificiality, when the language employed in first-person statements is sometimes at odds with the verbal skills of some pupils. In this sense, the 'subjectivity' of the experience is somewhat misleading, an artifice designed by the curriculum planners, rather than a true reflection of the learning process. Simply using a form of words containing 'I' cannot guarantee that worthwhile learning is taking place. Similarly, other concepts such as 'active' learning suggest a commitment to progressive, learner-centred pedagogy but this term can be interpreted in a variety of ways and needs to be defined more precisely in relation to the understandings offered by social constructivist theories of learning. Maclellan and Soden (2008) argue that the conceptualization of learning should be based on the insights of psychological research, warning that 'without understanding of how learners construct knowledge bases through thinking and reasoning, and the teachers' role in facilitating such processes, it is unlikely that the intentions of *Curriculum for Excellence* can be fully realised' (Maclellan and Soden, 2008, p. 29). This may be considered a rather narrowly psychological perspective but it does highlight, once again, the limited extent to which CfE has been informed by insights from research.

A third discursive theme relates to skills – in the words of *Building the Curriculum 4*, 'Skills for learning, skills for life and skills for work' (Scottish Government, 2009) . Rather unusually for CfE documentation, an extended definition of a skill is offered:

> It is the ability, competency, proficiency or dexterity to carry out tasks that come from education, training, practice or experience. It can enable the practical application of theoretical knowledge to particular tasks or situations. 'Skill' is also applied more broadly to include behaviours, attitudes and personal attributes that make individuals more effective in particular contexts such as education and training, employment and social engagement. (Ibid., p. 31)

This emphasis on skills, evident in many of the 'outcomes' statements for different curricular areas, can be regarded as an attempt to counterbalance the traditional priority given to formal academic knowledge. Given the pace of technological and social change, adaptable 'thinking skills' are seen as more important than the ability to acquire large bodies of factual information, though in many contexts the two cannot be separated: 'knowing how' (procedural knowledge) may depend on having the relevant propositional knowledge ('knowing that'). The link with the economy and employment is explicit: three of the skills to be developed are 'personal learning planning and career management', 'working with others' and 'enterprise and employability' (ibid., pp. 13–14, 18). Most secondary schools now offer work experience programmes with a variety of public and private employers, as well as voluntary organizations. Many also have good links with local further education colleges where courses have a strong vocational element. The promotion of the right attitudes and dispositions, of the kind valued by employers, is seen as an important responsibility for schools and teachers. This argument may serve as a powerful motivator when the job market is strong and there are plenty of opportunities to make good use of the positive attitudes that have been developed. Its persuasive power may be weaker during periods of economic recession when jobs are scarce. Moreover, none of the documents address the problems that can arise when people find that there is a mismatch between the skills they have acquired and the limited opportunity they have to exercise them in certain jobs. The relation between education and the economy is complex: to portray it in terms of schools and colleges somehow remedying a 'skills deficit' in the workforce is simplistic.

As implementation approached, school leadership issues came to the surface as responsibility passed from those involved in the development process to those who had to make it happen on the ground (Scottish Government, 2011b, 2011c). As part of this, headteachers were expected to have a key role in the professional development of their staff, enabling enthusiasts to try out new ideas and providing incentives for those who had still to be convinced of the merits of the new approach. The 2011 Donaldson report on teacher education makes an explicit connection between 'the quality of leadership' and 'the ability and willingness of teachers to respond to the opportunities [CfE] offers' (Donaldson, 2011, p. 4). This could be viewed as a tacit acknowledgement that the aspiration to secure teacher engagement in the reform programme had had limited success and an attempt to shift responsibility from policymakers to headteachers. The same document illustrates another discursive thread – that relating to innovation: 'Curriculum for Excellence is much more than a reform of curriculum and assessment. It is predicated on a model of sustained change which sees schools and teachers as co-creators of the curriculum' (ibid.). In rather more extravagant terms, the Cabinet Secretary for Education and Lifelong Learning, Michael Russell, claimed at the Scottish Learning Festival in 2011 that 'Curriculum for Excellence is the big idea in Scottish education . . . CfE is well in advance of most other educational reforms worldwide.' In the management of the reform, however, there was some tension between representations of CfE as innovative and original on the one hand, and representations which suggested that it is merely an extension of existing good practice (see Priestley, 2010).

The discourse of CfE emerges as shifting and malleable. While the early policy documents contained broad aspirations designed to secure general assent, later documents drew on forms of discourse that were not entirely consistent with each other: appeals to teacher autonomy and professionalism; the promotion of learner-centred pedagogy; future-oriented portrayals of young people as workers and global citizens; an emphasis on tightly specified learning outcomes; the importance of leadership in managing change and implementing CfE. However, despite these internal tensions, one of the interesting features of the Scottish reform programme was the relative absence of highly charged party political debate about the overall direction of educational change, such as was evident in England during the same period (see Ball, 2006) or Australia (see Lingard and McGregor, this volume). Although there was a switch of political administration in Scotland in 2007, with an SNP government taking over from a Labour/Liberal democrat coalition, there was a high degree of continuity in terms of the substance of CfE policy (if not the day-to-day management of the project). One interpretation of this is that it testifies to the strength of the professional policy community in Scotland (inspectors, senior bureaucrats, top officials in educational agencies) and their ability to maintain at least the appearance of a high measure of consensus in the face of a changing cast of politicians. As will be seen, where serious criticism arose, it mainly took the form of grass-roots concerns about readiness rather than an ideological challenge directed at the underlying principles.

Process and development

The introduction of any major educational reform requires considerable management expertise, involving planning, communication, agreed timelines and action plans. Scotland has a well-established educational infrastructure, with national bodies responsible for curriculum, assessment and inspection. Existing lines of communication between these bodies and central government, at both ministerial and civil service levels, should have ensured that the management challenges of CfE were well handled. However, a number of difficulties arose. In the early stages LTS was given lead responsibility for taking the CfE programme forward, albeit with strong input from senior civil servants and members of the inspectorate. It was an organization in the middle of restructuring, following the appointment of a new chief executive in 2004. Reports suggested that this was a painful exercise, challenging existing practices and bringing in other new staff at senior level.[2] At various points in the development process criticism of the way in which the programme was managed surfaced in the press, sometimes from people who were well placed to know what was going on. One of the members of the original CfE review group, for example, Keir Bloomer, expressed a series of concerns about the way in which the reform was being developed and managed and in 2009 wrote that 'Curriculum for Excellence is a programme that is in real trouble' (Bloomer, 2009). Moreover, the Management Board itself was a rather unwieldy body containing representatives of a wide range of agencies with different interests. Given this background, it is perhaps not surprising that in 2011, a new organization, Education Scotland (ES), bringing together LTS and the inspectorate, was created (see Boyd, 2013, in press), and the management of CfE was redefined as a partnership between Scottish Government, Education Scotland and the Scottish Qualifications Authority.

It was intended that the development of CfE from the broad principles set out in the 2004 Review Group report should involve widespread consultation with teachers and other stakeholders, so that it was not perceived as another 'top-down' imposition from central policymakers. The aim was to draw on teachers' knowledge and expertise as the overall structure of the curriculum was devised and fleshed out in terms of pedagogy, subjects, cross-curricular themes and stages. Underlying this approach was a belief that if teachers were given more freedom to contribute to the process they would acquire a sense of 'ownership' of the new curriculum and feel that their professionalism was being recognized and respected. In the early stages, a three-year development programme (2004–7) to map the architecture of CfE was undertaken: this included engagement with practitioners. More substantial involvement followed when the draft experiences and outcomes, setting out a framework for recommended learning in each curriculum area and the kind of evidence that could be used to evaluate pupil progress, were released in stages in 2007 and 2008. As well as teachers, feedback from parents, employers, local authorities, colleges and universities was invited.

A research team from the University of Glasgow was commissioned to collect, analyse and report on teacher responses gathered via questionnaires, focus groups and staff involved in the trialling of curricular material (see Menter and Hulme, this volume). One important finding of this study was that 'those teachers who experienced fuller "engagement" with the draft curricular materials, through piloting them, tended to be more wholehearted in their disposition towards the new curriculum and its associated pedagogy, than those who had only been "consulted", through completing questionnaires, for example' (Baumfield et al., 2010, p. 57). The Glasgow study also reported significant variation in teacher attitude towards three specific themes: professional discretion and collaboration; pedagogy and assessment; learning across the curriculum. On the first theme, while some welcomed the greater autonomy of the new approach, others were uneasy about the removal of the 'safety blanket' of prescription. Similarly, there was a divide between those teachers who saw the pedagogical shift required by CfE as desirable, and consistent with the earlier Assessment is for Learning programme, and those who doubted the readiness of the profession to adapt and feared that the attainment agenda promoted by the inspectorate was inconsistent with the apparently progressive intentions of the new curriculum. The critics inclined to the view that although CfE employs educationally progressive language, it remains at heart a technical-rational form of curriculum. With regard to learning across the curriculum, the Glasgow research revealed that there was not a shared understanding of what constituted 'cross-curricular' or 'interdisciplinary' work in secondary schools, but teachers in primary and special schools were more receptive to 'integrated' approaches to learning.

In 2011 a report on inspectors' support for schools preparing for the implementation of CfE, carried out by George Street Research, a private market research organization, was published (see Buie, 2011). This followed a programme of some 400 events across the country aimed at increasing awareness of the new curriculum and addressing teachers' concerns. The findings were mixed. The most positive responses came from heads of primary and secondary schools and quality improvement officers in local authorities. Principal teachers in secondary schools were the least positive and were particularly critical of expectations relating to interdisciplinary work. The report, *Partnership Support for Curriculum for Excellence*, stated:

> Some secondary school staff... perceive their primary aim to be to ensure that pupils have the necessary knowledge and skills to pass specific exams and this can be seen to conflict with the implementation of interdisciplinary teaching

> within their school. This issue was raised time and time again throughout the focus groups and some principal teachers feel they have [had to create] very artificial or contrived scenarios to introduce interdisciplinary learning, (ibid., p. 6)

Teachers generally did value the opportunity for professional dialogue, but whereas 57 per cent identified group discussion with peers as the most valuable aspect of the exercise, the question and answer sessions with CfE specialists attracted only a 24 per cent positive response.

It is not entirely surprising that early reactions to the reform programme were variable. In any occupational context, the prospect of change is often unsettling and, in the particular context of teaching, it raised a series of questions about the extent to which the content of the curriculum should be specified, the pedagogic methods which teachers should employ, and the desired learning outcomes in terms of knowledge, skills and dispositions. Subject teachers in Scottish secondary schools are traditionally a professionally cautious group, slow to change and deriving much of their professional identity from their specialist discipline (Humes, 2001). The process of developing CfE was complicated by a number of factors: changes of personnel (government ministers, civil servants, education professionals); restructuring of key agencies, notably LTS, and the creation of Education Scotland; a new political administration following the election success of the Scottish National Party at the 2007 and 2011 elections; variable success in communicating both the vision and the operational requirements to both local authorities and schools. To make these points is not to deny the very considerable efforts that many individuals devoted to the process. They serve, however, to reinforce the complexity and challenge of any major curricular reform.

Discussion

CfE is a 'high stakes' policy in the sense that political and professional reputations – and indeed the reputation of Scottish education as a whole – depend on it being perceived as reasonably successful. This arises partly from the scope and ambition of the project, indicated by its application to the age range 3–18, as well as by the pervasive discourse of 'excellence'. The way in which the programme has been promoted qualifies it to be considered as an example of what the American political theorist Murray Edelman has called 'policy as spectacle', in which presentation is as important as substance (Edelman, 1988). Nearly ten years after the original proposals, some observers, while well-disposed to the basic ideas underlying the programme, remain to be convinced that it has been developed to the point where it has won the hearts and minds of the majority of teachers. Letters in newspapers and in the educational press still express complaints about the seeming vagueness of the 'transformational change' that is being recommended and the way in which the policy has been managed. Carole Ford, a former headteacher of Kilmarnock Academy, and also a former president of School Leaders Scotland, has complained about 'the gulf in opinion between the educational establishment and the professionals on the ground' with regard to the success of the initiative (Ford, 2011). She cites 'poor management' and 'poor communication' as features of the way the development was promoted and poses the question: 'Where is the solid evidential and intellectual basis for CfE developments?' Questioning the recommended approaches to literacy and numeracy, and to interdisciplinary learning, as well as doubting the wisdom of giving so much weight to 'confident individuals' as one of the key capacities (see also Ecclestone, this volume), she claims that 'much of CfE runs counter to teachers' experience, training and intuition'. Again, a primary headteacher, Niall MacKinnon, has argued that there are major contradictions between the engagement intentions of CfE, seeking to involve teachers in the curriculum development process, and the audit systems of inspection driven by a rigid attainment agenda (MacKinnon, 2011).

Any major educational change needs to be evaluated independently over a period of some years. A worrying feature of CfE is that no large-scale research programme to assess its impact has been commissioned by the Scottish Government and, so far, the amount of independent academic research has been limited, perhaps reflecting caution in relation to a policy that has so much political weight behind it. Any internal evaluation – for example one carried out by the inspectorate – would lack credibility, since those conducting it would in effect be passing judgement on a policy which they had helped to initiate and promote. Official reaction to small-scale research findings so far has not been encouraging. A study carried out by Mark Priestley and Sarah Minty into the implementation of CfE in one local authority came to the following conclusions:

> First, CfE has much to commend it, although its implementation has been far from smooth. There remains a risk that eventual implementation in many schools will not represent the sorts of transformational change envisaged by the architects of the new curriculum. Second, implementation is dependent upon the active engagement of professional and committed teachers. Our research

has convinced us that Scotland has a highly professional and motivated teaching workforce; however, such engagement has been rendered difficult for many by a lack of clarity and coherence in the documents that have guided implementation, and the lack of systematic processes for closing the implementation gap between policy and practice. (Priestley and Minty, 2012, p. 9)

The official response to this report was ill-judged. Instead of acknowledging that the research contained some positive findings (e.g. that more than half of the survey respondents reported that their school had made good progress in implementing CfE) and that a mixed picture was only to be expected at this stage of implementation, the government reaction was to try to present the study as out-of-date and unrepresentative of the country as a whole (see Johnson, 2012). When the researchers responded in defence of their report the result was that the episode received much more media attention that it might otherwise have had.

The relative lateness of information about the system of assessment which would accompany the new curriculum was noted above (see also Hepburn, 2012). During session 2011–12 concern was expressed about the readiness of schools to prepare their pupils for the National 4 and 5 examinations which would replace Standard Grade in 2013–14. One local authority decided to delay implementation by a year.[3] In response, and to forestall a bandwagon effect, a package of £3.5 million was announced to extend support to schools that needed help, together with an audit of what was happening across the country to be carried out by Education Scotland. One teachers' union, the Scottish Secondary Teachers' Association (SSTA), carried out its own audit to find out how the data were being collected and found that only 6 local authorities (out of 32) had sought information directly from principal teachers. The others had collected data from headteachers or education officials, leading to a claim by the union that non-teaching staff could not possibly know what the situation was at departmental and classroom level. Headteachers and educational officials would, it was alleged, be inclined to present a rosy picture in order to maintain good relations with senior members of the policy community, particularly the inspectorate. It is ironic that a reform programme which emphasized teacher engagement as a critical feature in the transformation that was being sought, should have failed to canvass the opinions of many of those at the sharp end of education.

What can be learned from the experience of CfE? It certainly bears out the suggestion by Stephen Ball that policymaking in education is often 'unwieldy and complex', and sometimes 'unscientific and irrational' (Ball, 1990, p. 3). This is not surprising given the scope and ambition of the reform. It was always unreasonable to expect a smooth series of transitions from conception through consultation, development, implementation and evaluation. All sorts of background factors came into play at various stages of the operation – changes of government and key personnel; restructuring of the key development agency (LTS) and its later amalgamation with the inspectorate; criticism of the management of the programme (including by some of those closely involved in its development); union concerns about the pace of change, the clarity of the proposals and the quality of the support available to teachers; press reports which inevitably focused on problems rather than achievements. All of these features are common to many policy initiatives and not confined to education. In addition, however, there were three other related factors which, with the benefit of hindsight, can be identified as having presented particular problems.

First, there were tensions between the reforming intentions of CfE and the institutional apparatus of Scottish education. This was not simply a matter of the seeming anomaly of powerful centralist forces seeking to liberate a teaching force that had been used to directives from above which had traditionally encouraged them to ask only 'How?' rather than 'Why?' questions. It also involved a fair measure of bureaucratic resistance from parts of the educational system that perceived themselves to be under threat from the proposed changes, particularly subject departments in secondary schools. Despite the self-perceptions of many teachers as 'radical' in political terms, when it comes to matters of professional self-interest they are inclined to adopt a conservative stance. The strength of teacher unions in Scotland, particularly the largest, the Educational Institute of Scotland, meant that the pathway to reform was never going to be easy. They often paid lip service to the official discourse, while finding ways of delaying the process. Furthermore, as Ball (1990) has observed, policy 'texts' are often subject to multiple interpretations and what is enacted may be quite different from what is intended. This was made easier by the inconsistency of statements by politicians, sometimes boasting about the 'transformational change' signalled by CfE, at other times saying that good teachers were already doing much of what was being recommended.

Secondly, attempts to convince teachers of the wisdom of the reform proposals were often not well handled. With any innovation, there are always a few enthusiasts, keen to become involved in pilots and the development of new materials. Convincing the majority of teachers of the benefits to be gained from new approaches to teaching and learning is a much harder task. The CfE programme cannot be faulted for the amount of documentation it produced or the range of information made available on the LTS (and subsequently ES) website. However, the production of material does not ensure that it will be read, understood and acted upon. One former inspector involved in the creation of the Journey to Excellence package of resources said he was sceptical about the impact it had. Furthermore, as noted above, the quality of some of the CPD presentations, explaining the thinking behind CfE, to teachers up and down the country was highly variable. Some speakers seemed ill-equipped to go beyond 'headline' points, relying heavily on centrally prepared Powerpoint presentations. This leads to the third, and most fundamental, point.

From the start, CfE was under-conceptualized: that is, it lacked a strong theoretical basis that had been carefully thought through and grounded in existing research on curriculum and curriculum change (Priestley and Humes, 2010). This was recognized in 2012 by no less a person that the former Senior Chief Inspector of Schools, Graham Donaldson, when he acknowledged that the success of the reform 'requires a deep understanding of the "why" of CfE as much as the "what" or the "how"' (Donaldson, 2012, p. 33). He also acknowledged that, while the four capacities could serve as powerful indicators of the desired direction of travel, they could easily be reduced to little more than slogans. Priestley and Humes (2010) refer to the 'lack of conceptual clarity' in what was proposed, drawing attention to switches between three different models of curriculum: curriculum as content; curriculum as process; and curriculum as product. This, they argue, led to tensions in the way the learning process was conceived, sometimes veering in the direction of 'an essentialist body of knowledge to be acquired and tested', at other times to 'a view of knowledge as being something constructed by learners' (Priestley and Humes, 2010, p. 358). Other aspects of the under-conceptualization of the programme include an inadequate account of how the four capacities relate to each other and a superficial view of both active learning and interdisciplinary approaches. The present writer (Humes, 2001) has commented on a tendency towards anti-intellectualism in Scottish education, particularly within the inspectorate and teachers' organizations. This leads to 'scepticism about what research can offer and a debased conception of professionalism' (ibid., p. 9). It is significant that, certainly in the early stages of CfE development, there was little input from academics, who might have been able to strengthen the intellectual basis of the reform programme, and even in 2012, official reactions to the research carried out by Priestley and Minty suggested a defensive response to a constructive academic contribution based on research findings. The absence of a properly independent evaluation strategy is also indicative of a mindset that fears open intellectual enquiry.

The fact remains, however, that CfE is happening and will remain centre-stage in Scottish education for the foreseeable future. Conscientious teachers are doing their best to make it a success in the interest of their pupils and there are certainly many examples of innovative work in various parts of the country which represent encouraging growth points for the future. Primary schools have found it easier than secondary schools to respond to the curriculum guidelines, partly because they do not have the same departmental structure, and partly because they are not so constrained by the need to prepare for examinations. What the experience of CfE shows, however, is that curriculum reform is not just a matter of reshaping the form and content of education. At every stage political, bureaucratic and managerial considerations come into play. These can be disguised to some extent by a disarming rhetoric of progressive pedagogy and professional engagement, but in the final analysis the policy decisions that are made owe as much to the differential power of the various stakeholders as to any 'purely' educational considerations.

Notes

1   The chair of the review group was a senior civil servant and two other members of the 18-strong group were also senior civil servants. Only three people working in schools were members (two headteachers and a principal teacher). Other members consisted of three representatives from local authorities, all at directorate level; two academics; a senior member of Her Majesty's Inspectorate of Education; the chief executives of LTS, at that time the key agency advising government on the curriculum, and the Scottish Qualifications Authority (SQA), the national body responsible for examinations; two representatives of parents' groups; the director of the Confederation of British Industry (CBI) Scotland; and the principal of an FE college.
2   Against this background, LTS's task in leading CfE was decidedly challenging. Traditionally, the inspectorate had been drivers of educational innovation in Scotland but they too were going through a transitional phase, following the embarrassment of the examinations crisis of 2000 (Paterson, 2000), in which a significant number of students had failed to receive their results in an accurate and timely fashion. Although direct responsibility for this was down to the Scottish Qualifications Authority, in the enquiries that followed HMIs came in for a fair amount of criticism and it was decided that their involvement in policy matters

should be scaled down. At critical phases this meant that senior civil servants took a leading role in CfE development, reporting to ministers and shaping the agenda of the CfE Management Board. While this situation had some advantages in terms of communication with government, the downside was that career civil servants were not education specialists and were sometimes impatient with the concerns that professionals raised (see Boyd, 2013: in press).
3   This was an embarrassment to the government but as the council concerned, East Renfrewshire, was the top performing local authority in the country, as judged by examination results, it felt confident enough to act independently.

References

Ball, S. J. (1990), *Politics and Policy Making in Education*. London: Routledge.
— (2008), *The Education Debate*. Bristol: Policy Press.
Baumfield, V., Hulme, M., Livingston, K. and Menter, I. (2010), 'Consultation *and* engagement? The reshaping of teacher professionalism through curriculum reform in 21st century Scotland'. *Scottish Educational Review*, 42, 57–73.
Biesta, G. (2008), 'What kind of citizen? What kind of democracy? Citizenship education and the Scottish Curriculum for Excellence'. *Scottish Educational Review*, 40, 38–52.
Bloomer, K. (2009) 'Well-rehearsed slogans won't replace vision and forward planning', *The Scotsman*, 9 July.
Boyd, B. (2013, in press), 'National Curriculum Support: from LTS to Education Scotland', in T. G. K. Bryce, W. M. Humes, L. D. Gillies and A. Kennedy (eds), *Scottish Education, 4th edition, Referendum*. Edinburgh: Edinburgh University Press.
Buie, E. (2011), 'Mixed feedback for HMIE on CfE support, report says', *Times Educational Supplement Scotland*, 23 September.
Bush, T. (2003), *Theories of Educational Leadership and Management* (3rd edn). London: Sage.
Christie, D. and Boyd, B. (2005), *A Curriculum for Excellence: Overview of recent research-based literature for the curriculum review*. University of Strathclyde.
Davie, G. E. (1961), *The Democratic Intellect*. Edinburgh: Edinburgh University Press.
Donaldson, G. (2011), *Teaching Scotland's Future: Report of a Review of Teacher Education in Scotland*. Edinburgh: Scottish Government.
— (2012), 'Whether CfE succeeds or sinks is ultimately up to you', *Times Educational Supplement*, 27 April.
Edelman, M. (1988), *Constructing the Political Spectacle*. Chicago: University of Chicago Press.
Education Scotland (no date), *Curriculum for Excellence: Successful Learners, Confident Individuals, Responsible Citizens, Effective Contributors*. Online at www.

educationscotland.gov.uk/Images/all_experiences_outcomes_tcm4-539562.pdf (accessed 04/10/12).

Ford, C. (2011), 'The trouble and truth about Curriculum for Excellence', *Times Educational Supplement Scotland*, 16 December.

Gillies, D. (2006), 'A Curriculum for Excellence: A question of values'. *Scottish Educational Review*, 38, 25–36.

Hepburn, H. (2012), 'Limited progress on assessment under CfE', *Times Educational Supplement Scotland*, 3 August.

Humes, W. (1986), *The Leadership Class in Scottish Education*. Edinburgh: John Donald.

— (2001), 'Conditions for professional development'. *Scottish Educational Review*, 33, 6–17.

Humes, W. and Bryce, T. (2008), 'The distinctiveness of Scottish education', in W. M. Humes and T. G. K. Bryce (eds), *Scottish Education, 3rd edition, Beyond Devolution*. Edinburgh: Edinburgh University Press, pp. 98–110.

Johnson, S. (2012), 'Scottish teachers "floundering" over Curriculum for Excellence', *The Telegraph*, 11 April.

MacBeath, J. (1999), *Schools Must Speak for Themselves*. Routledge: London.

MacKinnon, N. (2011), 'The urgent need for new approaches in school evaluation to enable Scotland's Curriculum for Excellence'. *Educational Assessment, Evaluation and Accountability*, 23, 89–106.

Maclellan, E. and Soden, R. (2008), 'Successful learners, confident individuals, responsible citizens and effective contributors to society: exploring the nature of learning and its implications for Curriculum for Excellence'. *Scottish Educational Review*, 40, 29–37.

McPherson, A. and Raab, C. D. (1988), *Governing Education: A Sociology of Policy since 1945*. Edinburgh: Edinburgh University Press.

OECD (2007), *Quality and Equity of Schooling in Scotland*. Paris: OECD.

Paterson, L. (2000), *Crisis in the Classroom*. Edinburgh: Mainstream.

Priestley, M. (2010), 'Curriculum for Excellence: transformational change or business as usual?' *Scottish Educational Review*, 42, 23–36.

Priestley, M. and Humes, W. (2010), 'The development of Scotland's Curriculum for Excellence: amnesia and déjà vu'. *Oxford Review of Education*, 36, 345–61.

Priestley, M. and Minty, S. (2012), *Developing Curriculum for Excellence: Summary of Findings from Research Undertaken in a Scottish Local Authority*. Stirling: University of Stirling.

Priestley, M., Robinson, S. and Biesta, G. (2012), 'Teacher agency, performativity and curriculum change in the Scottish Curriculum for Excellence?', in B. Jeffrey and B. Troman (eds), *Performativity Across UK Education: Ethnographic Cases of its Effects, Agency and Reconstructions*. Painswick: E & E Publishing, pp. 87–108.

Reeves, J. (2008), 'Between a rock and a hard place? Curriculum for Excellence and the quality initiative in Scottish schools'. *Scottish Educational Review*, 40, 6–16.

Sahlberg, P. (2011), *Finnish Lessons: What Can the World Learn from Educational Change in Finland?* New York: Teachers' College Press.

Scottish Executive (2000), *A Teaching Profession for the 21st Century*. Edinburgh: HMSO.

— (2003), *Educating for Excellence: Choice and Opportunity*. Edinburgh: Scottish Executive.

— (2004), *A Curriculum for Excellence: The Curriculum Review Group*. Edinburgh: Scottish Executive.

— (2006a), *A Curriculum for Excellence: Progress and Proposals*. Edinburgh: Scottish Executive.

— (2006b), *Building the Curriculum 1: The Contribution of Curriculum Areas*. Edinburgh: Scottish Executive.

— (2007), *Building the Curriculum 2: Active Learning in the Early Years*. Edinburgh: Scottish Executive.

Scottish Government (2008), *Building the Curriculum 3: A Framework for Learning and Teaching*. Edinburgh: Scottish Government.

— (2009), *Building the Curriculum 4: Skills for Learning, Skills for Life and Skills for Work*. Edinburgh: Scottish Government.

— (2011a), *Building the Curriculum 5: A Framework for Assessment*. Edinburgh: Scottish Government.

— (2011b), *Curriculum for Excellence Action Plan*. Edinburgh: Scottish Government.

— (2011c), *Curriculum for Excellence Implementation – Questions and Answers*. Edinburgh: Scottish Government.

Scottish Government/University of Glasgow (2009), *Curriculum for Excellence Draft Experiences and Outcomes: Final Report*. Edinburgh: Scottish Government.

Seddon, J. (2008), *Systems Thinking in the Public Sector*. Axminster: Triarchy Press.

3

Capacities and the Curriculum

Gert Biesta and Mark Priestley

Introduction

One of the cornerstones of the Scottish Curriculum for Excellence (CfE), and also one of its defining characteristics, is the fact that it proposes to organize all educational activity in relation to the promotion of four capacities: the successful learner, the confident individual, the responsible citizen and the effective contributor. The 2004 *A Curriculum for Excellence* document (Scottish Executive, 2004, p. 12) lists these four capacities as 'purposes of the curriculum'. On the one hand the capacities frame the overall *aspiration* of CfE. The authors of the document write: 'Our aspiration for all children and for every young person is that they should be successful learners, confident individuals, responsible citizens and effective contributors to society and at work' (ibid., p. 3). On the other hand the capacities are presented as the intended *outcomes* of education. 'By providing structure, support and direction to young people's learning, the curriculum should enable them to develop these four capacities' (ibid., p. 12).

For each capacity the documentation specifies both the particular *qualities that characterize* the successful learner, the confident individual, the responsible citizen and the effective contributor, and the things that successful learners, confident individuals, responsible citizens and effective contributors *are able to do*. The capacities are thus presented as a combination of what in the documentation is referred to as 'attributes' and 'capabilities' (see ibid., p. 11).[1] Thus we find a description of *successful learners* as having enthusiasm and motivation for learning; determination to reach high standards of achievement; and openness to new thinking and ideas, and as being able to use literacy, communication and numeracy skills; use technology for learning; think creatively and independently; learn independently and as part of a group; make reasoned evaluations; link and apply different kinds of learning in new situations. Of *confident individuals* as having self-respect; a sense of physical, mental and emotional well-being; secure values and beliefs; and ambition, and as being able to relate to others and manage themselves; pursue a healthy and active lifestyle; be self-aware; develop and communicate their own beliefs and view of the world; live as independently as they can; assess risk and take informed decisions; and achieve success in different areas of activity. Of *responsible citizens* as having respect for others; and commitment to participate responsibly in political, economic, social and cultural life, and as being able to develop knowledge and understanding of the world and Scotland's place in it; understand different beliefs and cultures; make informed choices and decisions; evaluate environmental, scientific and technological issues, and develop informed, ethical views of complex issues. And of *effective contributors* as having an enterprising attitude; resilience, and self-reliance, and as being able to communicate in different ways and in different settings; work in partnership and in teams; take the initiative and lead; apply critical thinking in new contexts; create and develop; and solve problems (ibid., p. 12).

CfE is not unique in formulating the overall purposes of education in terms of capacities. We can find a similar trend in other countries, sometimes also in terms of capacities (e.g. in the pre-2010 iteration of the English National Curriculum), and sometimes using related terms such as 'general capabilities' (Australia), 'cross-curricular skills' (Northern Ireland) or 'key competencies' (New Zealand) (see also Sinnema and Aitken, this volume). In this chapter we argue that to think of the purposes of education in terms of capacities, competencies or capabilities is part of a wider trend in curriculum policy and practice where the purposes of education are no longer articulated in terms of what students should *learn* but in terms of what they should *become* (see also Watson, 2010). What is significant here is that as a result of this the student shifts from being the *subject* in education – that is the one who is supposed to study, learn, master, acquire, evaluate, judge, etcetera – to being the *outcome* of education. In this chapter we explore and discuss this wider trend and ask what it means for our understanding of curriculum and for the design of educational processes and practices more generally. Our chapter is organized in the following way. We start with a brief look into the history of CfE and its decision to utilize the language of 'capacities', and discuss how the idea of 'capacities' functions within CfE. We then focus on the wider trend to turn the student into the intended outcome of education. Here we use the rise of the idea of competence-based education as a prime example of this trend. In a third and final step we raise a number of critical questions about this trend in order to evaluate the strengths and weaknesses of a capacities-based curriculum.

The idea of capacities in the Scottish Curriculum for Excellence

Given that Scotland is not unique in formulating the aims of education in terms of the promotion of personal qualities and attributes, one interesting question is why the developers of CfE decided to use the concept of 'capacities' rather than, for example, that of 'competences' or 'capabilities'. Interestingly, our enquiries with several members from the review group that developed the CfE documentation brought to light that the use of the notion of 'capacities' was not the result of a deliberate decision, but rather something that emerged from the work civil servants did. Moreover, it was a notion that was not necessarily endorsed by all members of the group. Apparently the discussion in the group had been about purposes and characteristics, but not about capacities (nor, for that matter, about competences).[2] While this indicates that there is no real point in raising deep questions about the term 'capacities' itself – the choice seems to have been rather arbitrary – the more general suggestion that educational purposes can and should be articulated in terms of qualities and attributes of the person does, of course, warrant further exploration.

Before we do so, there is one point we wish to make about the way in which the capacities function within the Scottish context. In terms of the purposes that should guide educational practice, CfE provides a very open and 'light' framework that explicitly aims 'to engage teachers in thinking from first principles about their educational aims and values and their classroom practice' (Scottish Executive, 2006, p. 4; see also our chapter on teacher agency in this volume) rather than to simply prescribe what they should 'deliver' and how this should be done. Yet this open framework is complemented by an extremely detailed list of 'experiences and outcomes' that aims to cover 'the totality of experiences which are planned for children and young people, including the ethos and life of the school and interdisciplinary studies as well as learning within curriculum areas and subjects' (Education Scotland, no date).

While the experience and outcomes framework is presented as being 'less detailed and prescriptive than previous curriculum advice' and therefore claims to provide 'professional space for teachers and other staff to use in order to meet the varied needs of all children and young people' (ibid.), the 317 pages of the experience and outcomes document nonetheless provide an extremely detailed grid of learning outcomes that stands in sharp contrast to the openness of the CfE framework itself. The joint existence of this open framework and the detailed Experience and Outcomes document thus sends a rather mixed message to teachers in that, on the one hand, they are encouraged to exercise judgement and be agents of change while, on the other hand, they are provided with a step-by-step 'manual' that seems to leave little room for their professional agency. This apparent tension has been noted by Priestley and Humes (2010), who see it as a hybridization of different, incompatible curriculum planning models. Notwithstanding such tensions between convergent and divergent frameworks, it is also clear that both approaches have their roots in a common strand of thinking about the purposes of education, and a particular framing of curriculum in terms of what young people should become. We explore these notions in the following sections of the chapter.

The student as a learning outcome: Capacities and competences

The idea that education should have an interest in and a focus on the formation of the person is, in itself, anything but new. We can find it, for example, in the Greek idea of *paideia* which emerged in classical Athens and stood for a broad process of cultivation of the person towards good character or 'virtue' (ἀρετή) and, more specifically, towards civic virtue. Among the subjects that were supposed to lead to such cultivation are rhetoric, grammar, mathematics, music, philosophy, geography, natural history and gymnastics. This set of subjects re-emerged in medieval times as the *trivium* (grammar, rhetoric, logic) and *quadrivium* (arithmetic, geometry, music, astronomy) which, together, constituted the seven liberal arts that were seen as the core of 'higher learning'. *Paideia* was conceived as the kind of education that would bring human beings to their true form, that is, towards achieving 'excellence' in what was considered to be distinctively human which, for philosophers such as Plato and Aristotle, was the ability for reason (man as a 'rational animal', in Aristotle's formulation). *Paideia* was, however, confined to free men (not women, nor slaves) in order to further their freedom as citizens. It thus stood in opposition to the education that was meant for manual labourers and artisans, the 'banausoi' (βάναυσοι). This was why *paideia* required free time – the literal meaning of the word 'schole' (σχολή) – rather than that it was connected to the domain of work and production (see, for example, Jaeger, 1945). It was only during the Enlightenment that the latter point shifted and education became conceived as a process that could bring about freedom rather than that it was confined to those who were already free (see Biesta, 2010a).

There is a clear, although not direct or uninterrupted line from the Greek idea of paideia to the idea of education as *Bildung*, an idea that emerged in Europe from the Renaissance onwards (see Klafki, 1986). While Bildung shares with *paideia* the idea of education as a process of cultivation, it became increasingly understood as a process of *self-formation* through the interaction of individuals with culture and society. This not only raised the question of which aspects of culture and society were worthy enough for 'real' or 'true' Bildung to occur. It also raised the question about the role of the individual in the process of *Bildung*. Here it was argued that *Bildung* is not a 'blind' process in which individuals simply adopt and adapt to existing cultural and social ways of doing and being, but that it has to be understood as a *reflexive* process, that is a process in which individuals establish a relationship *with* and develop a stance *towards* culture and society. In this regard *Bildung* emerged as a process that always involves the evaluation of existing culture and society (see Kron, 1989, p. 66). Both aspects returned in the work of twentieth-century authors such as Heinz-Joachim Heydorn and Wolfgang Klafki. Klafki not only highlighted more explicitly that *Bildung* had to be understood as a process of 'double disclosure' – that is the disclosure of both 'self' and 'world' (see Klafki, 1969). He also oriented *Bildung* more explicitly towards the idea of emancipation, thus adding an explicit political dimension to it (see Klafki, 1964, 1986; Heydorn, 1972).

Paideai and *Bildung* provide two influential examples of conceptions of education that focus explicitly on the formation of the person rather than on just the acquisition of (bodies of) knowledge or (sets of) skills. In the English-speaking world we can find similar ideas in the idea of 'liberal education' (see, for example, Van Doren, 1943; Mulcahy, 2008). The name 'liberal education' shows its historical connection with the 'liberal arts' that made up the curriculum for 'higher learning' in medieval universities. Over time it has developed into a distinctive conception of education that promotes the formation of the whole person, particularly through engagement with the humanities. In this way it still plays a role in contemporary discussions about education in schools and universities (see, for example, Nussbaum, 1997). Similar thinking is also evident in the notion of curriculum as development and process, most notable in the United Kingdom through the work of Stenhouse (1975) and Kelly (1999). This view of curriculum frames educational purposes and practices in terms of their 'likely contribution to the development of the pupil, and ... recommends that we see these purposes not as goals to be achieved at some later stage in the process, but as procedural principles which should guide our practice throughout' (Kelly, 1999, p. 76). There are clear parallels between the purposes framed within a process curriculum and the four capacities – notably a concern for the development of the person and a focus on practices to achieve this. There are also differences, most related to the question we pose of whether the student should be the 'subject' or 'object' of education.

These examples show that a focus on what the student should become *through* education rather than on what the student should learn *from* education is in itself not new. What, then, is new about more recent developments? The best way to show this is by looking briefly at what over the past 25 years has become the most prominent manifestation of this idea, which is the suggestion that education should focus on the development of *competences,* that is on what people should be able to do rather than (just) on what they should know or (just) on the skills they should acquire (see, for example, Lum, 1999; Argüelles and Gonczi, 2000; Chappel, Gonczi and Hager, 2000). The idea of what has become known as 'competence-based education' or 'competency-based education'[3] has its origins in the field of human resources management. The interest in competencies started in the 1970s, initially in order to distinguish the characteristics of more successful managers from those of less successful ones. Increasingly it became used for management training and the evaluation of performance (see Mulder, 2007, pp. 8–11). From the 1990s onwards the idea of competence became influential in the field of vocational and professional education, where it has remained an influential approach (see, for example, Barnett, 1994; Hyland, 1994; Hodkinson and Issitt, 1995). Over the past decade it has not only become a central idea in lifelong learning policies – particularly through the development of a European reference framework of 'key competences for lifelong learning' (European Council, 2006; see also Deakin Crick, 2008) – but has also become influential in discussions about school education, not in the least as a result of the work of the OECD's project on the Definition and Selection of Competencies (DeSeCO), which was conducted as part of its Programme for International Student Assessment (PISA) (see Rychen and Salganik, 2003).

Within the literature a relatively wide range of different definitions of the idea of competence can be found. Some definitions are brief and succinct – such as Eraut's definition of competence as '(t)he ability to perform the tasks and roles required to the expected standards' (Eraut, 2003, p. 117, cited in Mulder, Weigel and Collins, 2007) or Arnold et al.'s, definition of competence as 'the capacity of a person to act' (see ibid.). Other definitions are more elaborate, such as Deakin Crick's definition of competence as 'a complex combination of knowledge, skills, understanding, values, attitudes and desire which lead to effective, embodied human action in the world, in a particular domain' (Deakin Crick, 2008, p. 313). Rychen and Salganik (2003, p. 43) define competence as 'the ability to successfully meet complex demands in a particular context through the mobilisation of psychosocial prerequisites (including cognitive and non-cognitive aspects)' and as the 'internal mental structures in the sense of abilities, dispositions or resources embedded in the individual' in interaction with a 'specific real world task or demand'. The internal structures of a competence include dimensions of 'knowledge, cognitive skills, practical skills, attitudes, emotions, values, ethics and motivation' (ibid., p. 44). Two things are important about the latter definition. One is that competence goes well beyond the possession of knowledge and skills, involving 'the ability to meet complex demands, by drawing on and mobilising psychosocial resources (including skills and attitudes) in a particular context' (OECD, 2005, p. 3). The other is that, as Deakin Crick puts it, 'the site of a competence is at the *interface* between the person and the demands of the real world' (Deakin Crick, 2008, p. 313, emphasis added). This means that competencies are never formulated in the abstract, but always in relation to specific views about desirable abilities, capacities and attitudes in relation to specific domains of action and being.

The latter explains why the idea of competencies has taken such a flight in the field of vocational and professional education, because one could argue that adequate preparation for a particular job or profession is precisely about acquiring the knowledge, skills, attitudes and wider vocational or professional habitus that makes one capable of performing a job or profession successfully. (It is also for this reason that the turn towards competencies seems to address one of the often-heard complaints about vocational and professional education, which is that such education might give students knowledge and skills but doesn't prepare them properly for the workplace.) But the fact that competencies are about the interface between the person and the demands of the 'real' world also begins to show one of the more problematic aspects of the turn towards competencies, which is the fact that 'the world' never demands anything in itself, so that any demands that frame competence-based education are always the demands of particular individuals or groups based on their views about what a good or successful or desirable way of acting and being is. Whereas this might be relatively uncontroversial in the domain of work, it becomes more problematic when the discussion is extended to other spheres of life or to life in general (such as in the case of the capacities that frame CfE), because in that case the formulation of competencies that individuals should acquire becomes immediately an expression of what a good, successful or desirable way of living one's life is – which in modern liberal-democratic societies is precisely seen as something that people should be free to define for themselves rather than being defined for them by others.

Five critical questions

If this gives an indication of what might be at stake in the turn from curriculum as a description of the content of learning to curriculum as a description of what the student should be and become, we now wish to raise a number of critical questions.

A disjointed curriculum?

While a focus on competencies and capacities has the potential to address one of the often-heard complaints about education – which is that it gives students knowledge and skills but doesn't prepare them for the 'real' world, which can either be the world of work or the world of life more generally – one danger with a focus on competencies and capacities is the production of long and detailed lists of all the things that individuals apparently need to obtain and master in order to perform a particular task well or to be competent at their job or profession. The recent history of CfE clearly illustrates this danger, as the lack of specificity of the capacities, combined with their framing as competencies, has led to just such a spiral of specification (Wolf, 1995), and their incorporation into a much more technicist approach than was at first apparent. This specification can easily result in a disjointed 'tick-box curriculum' where teachers become too much focused on checking that all the different competencies and sub-competencies have been mastered rather than taking a more integral and integrative approach. That this is a real danger can, for example, be seen in teacher education in England, where teaching and assessment became strongly focused on making sure that students had obtained all the competencies on such lists, not in the least because the inspectors of teacher education required positive evidence from teacher educators that each of their students had met each of the competencies listed. This left teacher educators with relatively little time to focus on the bigger questions about what it means to be a good and effective teacher, and also pushed them in a direction where such questions were mainly approached in an analytical way, that is in terms of connecting the many different competencies, rather than in terms of more holistic strategies that would, for example, start from questions about educational purpose and the question as to what good education and good teaching look like (see Biesta, 2010b). The 'translation' of the open structure of the four capacities of CfE into the very detailed list of Experiences and Outcomes provides another example of the risk of a focus on what students should be able to do leading to a disjointed curriculum rather than an integrative one.

Necessary but not sufficient?

A second risk of a focus on capacities, competencies and capabilities can be articulated in terms of the difference between necessary and sufficient conditions for good or effective performance. The question here is not only whether individuals who have acquired all the capacities or competencies that are needed to perform a particular task will actually be able to perform the task – this, one could say, remains always an open question because the proof of the pudding of capacities or competencies remains in the eating. There is also the question whether good or effective performance of a task, job or profession just follows from the mastery of all the capacities or competencies that are necessary for doing so, or whether something *additional* is needed, such as the ability to judge which capacities need to be utilized in which particular situation. One can imagine, after all, that even teacher students in England who have provided evidence of having mastered all the different competencies that they are supposed to need in order to teach, may still not be good teachers if they cannot tailor their general competence to the always concrete and always unique situations in which they have to 'perform'. While the possession of capacities or competencies may therefore be a *necessary* condition for good or effective performance, it may not be a *sufficient* one. This problem is indeed recognized in the literature on competencies, where a clear distinction is made between competence and performance and where one of the ongoing questions is precisely about how competence 'translates' into performance (see, for example, Gilbert, 1978; Dubois, 1993). Some authors have tried to solve this problem by arguing that the ability to judge which competencies should be utilized in which situations is actually itself a competency – or, as Haste (2001) suggests, a 'meta-competence' (see also Deakin Crick, 2008). Others have argued that a clear distinction needs to be made between competence and judgement, where the first is about the ability to do and the second is about the ability to judge what to do when and for what purpose (see, for example, Biesta, 2012).

A new behaviourism?

A third risk – partially related to the previous points – lies in the fact that a focus on the competencies and capacities that students need to acquire and master may reintroduce behaviourist ways of thinking and doing into education. The danger here is that education focuses too much on the 'outside', so to speak, that is on performance and behaviour, and too little on the 'inside', that is on thinking, understandings, reflection and judgement. This is not only a problem with regard to the ways in which competencies and capacities are supposed to be *taught*, and here there is a real danger that too strong an emphasis on the 'outside' makes education into a process of behaviour modification rather than a process of building up critical understanding of the how and why of action and performance. It is also a potential problem with regard to *assessment*, particularly if assessment were only to focus on action and performance – that is on the behaviours – and not on the accompanying knowledge, understanding and judgement (see, for example, Smithers, 1999, on this problem in relation to the use of competence-based approaches in vocational education in England). In the literature we can thus find warnings that competence-based education pays too little attention to questions of knowledge and understanding and the formation of judgement and practical wisdom. This is partly related to a much older discussion about the risks of connecting education too much to 'real' or 'real life' situations. The risk here is that while such education may equip students to function well in the particular situations in which they learn their skills and competencies, it does not prepare them sufficiently for utilizing those skills and competencies in different situations. If, to put it differently, the focus is too much on learning concrete behaviour, there is a risk that what students learn cannot be transferred to other situations. (For an interesting discussion in relation to mathematics education, see Boaler, 1993.)

Adaptation or agency?

A fourth potential problem with focusing education on capacities and competencies stems from the fact that the formulation of such capacities and competencies is based on the requirements of already known practices and situations. Capacities and competencies are thus strongly orientated towards the *past* rather than towards the *future* or, to the extent that they are orientated towards the future, they are orientated towards a particular conception or view or vision of what the future will be (e.g. see OECD, 2005). When we think of competencies and capacities in relation to the domain of work this is perhaps inevitable, as the key challenge here is how to prepare students effectively for action in very specific situations (and much guidance for the development of competence-based education does indeed start with the requirement to describe in detail all the particular tasks that need to be performed). This already becomes a bit more of a problem when the particular field of work students are being prepared for does not just consist of routine operations but contains unpredictable elements. Then it becomes already more difficult to describe the exact competencies that students would need to acquire – which is one reason why in contemporary discussions about vocational and professional education there is much attention to such things as 'transferable skills' including the skill of learning itself.

This becomes a more serious problem, in our view, when competencies and capacities become connected to life in general rather than to the domain of work. One reason why this is so has to do with the fact that the formulation of competencies and capacities tends to be strongly linked to particular views of what a good or desirable life is. The OECD document on key competencies for modern life does indeed acknowledge that '(k)ey competencies are not determined by arbitrary decisions about what personal qualities and cognitive skills are desirable, but by careful consideration of the psychosocial prerequisites for a successful life and a well-functioning society' (ibid., p. 6). The difficulty here is that what counts as a successful life or a well-functioning society is open to interpretation and in our view should be open to interpretation – that is, in modern democratic societies people should have the opportunity to articulate their own views about what a good or successful life is, and it is unlikely that there will be total agreement about such a question. That is why a 'demand-led approach' that only asks 'what individuals need in order to function well in society as they find it' (ibid.) but does not engage with the question of what in individuals might want that is different from what society 'is' or 'demands', runs the risk of turning education into an instrument of adaptation rather than that it is able to promote the democratic agency of students. While education does have a task in engaging students with and preparing students for the existing world it has, at the same time a task in emancipating students from the existing world so as to foster critical democratic agency. To think of education entirely in terms of capacities or competencies runs the risk that it puts too much emphasis on the former – that is on education as socialization or adaptation – and too little on the latter – that is on education as emancipation and subjectification (for the latter term see Biesta, 2010b, chapter 1).

Normativity and values

All this shows that the formulation of capacities, capabilities and competencies is not a matter of factual description of the situations for which education should prepare children and young people, but inevitably implies *values* and (normative) *judgements*. This is already the case when the formulation of capacities, capabilities and competencies is focused on the domain of work. After all, the process here always starts with a judgement about what *good* performance is – which is a value judgement. It becomes even more of an issue when the formulation of capacities, capabilities and competencies is connected to the wider life in society, because in democratic societies people have very different views about what a good, desirable and flourishing life looks like. This not only raises the question how the values and normative judgements that inform the formulation of capacities and competencies can be made visible so as not to give the impression that there are no value-laden choices and judgements involved. It also raises the question of justification, which is always the double question of *how* particular points of view can be justified and of *who* should be involved in such processes of justification. And this is another way in which the question of whether education is orientated towards the student as object of instruction and intervention or as a subject of action and responsibility poses itself.

Concluding remarks

Starting from the observation that what is distinctive about CfE is the fact that it formulates the purposes of education in terms of personal capacities we have, in this chapter, explored the wider trend in curriculum policy and practice to articulate the purposes of education no longer in terms of what students should *learn* but in terms of what they should *become*. This is a process where the student is repositioned from being a subject in the educational process – that is as the one who is supposed to study, learn, master, acquire, evaluate and judge – to being the (intended) outcome of education. While we have argued that the question of what the student should become as a result of education is an important one and, moreover, a question with a long and respectable pedigree, the risk in the turn towards capacities and competencies in contemporary curriculum policy and practice is that the student ceases to be a subject in the educational process and rather becomes an object of other people's interventions. The key question, in other words, is whether the turn towards capacities and competencies can support emancipation and the development of critical and democratic agency, or becomes too easily a 'technology' that is focused on adaptation, adjustment and survival. To what extent the framework for the Scottish Curriculum for Excellence runs this risk is an important question that requires careful analysis, not only of the policies and frameworks but also of how these work out in practice. In this chapter we have tried to point both at possibilities and dangers of the turn towards capacities and competencies in order to provide tools for a critical analysis of this particular dimension of the new curriculum.

Notes

1 In the 2004 document, these were listed separately, but not named as such. Since 2012, the schematic diagram depicting the four capacities has included the labels 'attributes' and 'capacities' – see www.educationscotland.gov.uk/thecurriculum/whatiscurriculumforexcellence/thepurposeofthecurriculum/index.asp (accessed 21/10/12).
2 There is a similar story about the values that ended up on the mace of the Scottish Parliament. Whereas the *A Curriculum for Excellence* document refers to these values – wisdom, justice, compassion and integrity – as 'the values on which Scottish society is based' (Scottish Executive, 2004, p. 11), they were actually suggested by Michael Lloyd, the silversmith who designed the mace (see http://uruisg.blogspot.fi/2012/01/truth-about-wisdom-justice-compassion.html and http://uruisg.blogspot.fi/2012/03/here-goes-then.html; accessed 04/10/12).
3 Some authors make a distinction between 'competence' as the general concept and 'competency' as referring to specific abilities (see, for example, Mulder, 2007). Other authors use either or both concepts without making a specific distinction.

References

Argüelles, A. and Gonczi, A. (eds) (2000), *Competency Based Education and Training: A World Perspective*. Mexico City: Grupo Noriega Editores.

Barnett, R. (1994), *The Limits of Competence. Knowledge, Higher Education and Society*. Buckingham: Open University Press.

Biesta, G. J. J. (2010a), 'A new "logic" of emancipation: the methodology of Jacques Rancière'. *Educational Theory*, 60, 39–59.
— (2010b), *Good Education in an Age of Measurement: Ethics, Politics, Democracy*. Boulder, CO: Paradigm Publishers.
— (2012), 'The future of teacher education: evidence, competence or wisdom?'. *Research on Steiner Education*, 3, 8–21.
Boaler, J. (1993), 'The role of contexts in the mathematics classroom: do they make mathematics more "real"?'. *For the Learning of Mathematics*, 13, 12–17.
Chappel, C., Gonczi, A. and Hager, P. (2000), 'Competency based education', in G. Foley (ed.), *Understanding Adult Education and Training* (2nd edn). St Leonards, NSW: Allen and Unwin, pp. 191–205.
Deakin Crick, R. (2008), 'Key competencies for education in a European context'. *European Educational Research Journal*, 7, 311–18.
Dubois, D. D. (1993), *Competency-Based Performance Improvement: A Strategy for Organizational Change*. Amherst, MA: HRD.
Education Scotland (no date), *Curriculum for Excellence: Successful Learners, Confident Individuals, Responsible Citizens, Effective Contributors*. Online at www.educationscotland.gov.uk/Images/all_experiences_outcomes_tcm4-539562.pdf (accessed 01/08/2012).
European Council (2006), *Recommendation 2006/962/EC of the European Parliament and of the Council of 18 December 2006 on Key Competences for Lifelong Learning* [Official Journal L 394 of 30.12.2006].
Gilbert, T. F. (1978), *Human Competence. Enginieering Worthy Performance*. New York, NY: McGraw-Hill.
Haste, H. (2001), 'Ambiguity, autonomy, and agency: psychological challenges to new competence', in D. S. Rychen and L. H. Salganik (eds), *Defining and Selecting Key Competencies*. Gottingen: Hogrefe & Huber, pp. 93–120.
Heydorn, H. J. (1972), *Zu einer Neufassung des Bildungsbegriffs* [*For a New Understanding of the Concept of Bildung*]. Frankfurt am Main: Suhrkamp.
Hodkinson, P. and Issitt, M. (eds) (1995), *The Challenge of Competence. Professionalism through Vocational Education and Training*. London: Cassell.
Hyland, T. (1994), *Competence, Education and NVQs. Dissenting Perspectives*. London: Cassell.
Jaeger, W. (1945), *Paideia: The Ideals of Greek Culture*. New York, NY: Oxford University Press.
Kelly, A. V. (1999), *The Curriculum: Theory and Practice* (4th edn). London: Sage.
Klafki, W. (1964), *Studien zur Bildungstheorie und Didaktik* [*Studies in the Theory of Bildung and Didactics*]. Weinheim/Basel: Beltz.
— (1969), 'Zur Theorie der kategoriale Bildung' ['On the theory of categorical formation'], in E. Weber (ed.), *Der Erziehungs und Bildungsbegriff im 20. Jahrhundert* [*The Concepts of Education and Bildung in the 20th Century*]. Bad Heilbrunn: Klinkhardt, pp. 54–85.

— (1986), 'Die Bedeutung der klassischen Bildungstheorien fur eine zeitgemasses Konzept von allgemeiner Bildung' ['The significance of the traditional theory of "Bildung" for a contemporary conception of general education']. *Zeitschrift fur Padagogik*, 32, 455–76.

Kron, F. W. (1989), *Grundwissen Pädagogik. Zweite, verbesserte Auflage* [*Foundational Theory of Education*] (2nd rev. edn). München/Basel: Ernst Reinhardt.

Lum, G. (1999), 'Where's the competence in competence-based education and training?'. *Journal of Philosophy of Education*, 33, 403–18.

Mulcahy, D. (2008), *The Educated Person: Towards a New Paradigm for Liberal Education*. Lanham, MD: Rowman and Littlefield.

Mulder, M. (2007), 'Competence – the essence and use of the concept in ICVT'. *European Journal of Vocational Training*, 40, 5–21.

Mulder, M., Weigel, T. and Collins, K. (2007), 'The concept of competence in the development of vocational education and training in selected EU member states: a critical analysis'. *Journal of Vocational Education and Training*, 59, 65–85.

Nussbaum, M. C. (1997), *Cultivating Humanity. A Classical Defence of Reform in Liberal Education*. Cambridge, MA: Harvard University Press.

OECD (2005), *The Definition and Selection of Key Competencies. Executive Summary*. Paris: OECD. Online at www.oecd.org/pisa/35070367.pdf (accessed 21/10/12).

Priestley, M. and Humes, W. (2010), 'The development of Scotland's Curriculum for Excellence: amnesia and déjà vu'. *Oxford Review of Education*, 36, 345–61.

Rychen, D. S. and Salganik, L. H. (eds) (2003), *Key Competencies for a Successful Life and a Well-Functioning Society*. Göttingen: Hogrefe & Huber.

Scottish Executive (2006), *A Curriculum for Excellence. Progress and Proposals. A Paper from the Curriculum Review Programme Board*. Edinburgh: Scottish Executive.

Smithers, A. (1999), 'A critique of NVQs and GNVQs', in M. Flude and S. Sieminski (eds), *Education, Training and the Future of Work II. Developments in Vocational Education and Training*. London: Routledge, pp. 143–57.

Stenhouse, L. (1975), *An Introduction to Curriculum Research and Development*. London: Heinemann.

Van Doren, M. (1943), *Liberal Education*. New York, NY: Henry Holt.

Watson, C. (2010), 'Educational policy in Scotland: inclusion and the control society'. *Discourse: Studies in the Cultural Politics of Education*, 31, 93–104.

Wolf, A. (1995), *Competence-Based Assessment*. Buckingham: Open University Press.

4

The Successful Learner: A Progressive or an Oppressive Concept?

Jenny Reeves

Introduction

While 'the learner' is a term that has become familiar over the last few years in Scottish education, its origins lie in the discourse of developmentalism that emerged after the Second World War. Prior to 2004 the common term for referring to children in school was 'pupil', a word that has been studiously avoided in favour of 'learner' in the series of documents that support the introduction of the Curriculum for Excellence (CfE) in Scotland. This change in nomenclature signifies a major alteration in the relations between children and young people, their teachers and the curriculum. However, the nature of these new relations is far from clear cut given the disparate meanings that have become associated with 'the learner' over time. This chapter begins by exploring the history of 'the learner' as a concept. Tracing the movement of the term across different contexts the chapter highlights how different discourses concerning education and change have coalesced to create the term as a compendium encompassing disparate strands of meaning. In particular, it focuses on three characteristics of 'the successful learner': first, as someone with an agentive and autonomous orientation to the world; secondly, as someone committed to self-improvement; and thirdly, as someone who has mastered the skills of personal learning so that they can respond flexibly to a changing environment. The second part of the chapter examines how 'the learner' has been interpreted in the course of six years of policymaking in Scotland. This section analyses a suite of documents issued by central government agencies between 2004 and 2010. These texts were intended to help teachers implement CfE, a new curriculum based on a broadly constructivist and experiential approach to learning, for the education of children and young people from 3–18 years of age. The examination reveals some of the tensions and discontinuities that the move from pupil to learner can entail. The concluding section considers the implications of the case for the realization of the aspirations originally associated with 'the successful learner' and the problems of making these meaningful in the context of schools.

The origins and evolution of the learner

The evolution of the notion of the learner is complicated since, from a set of common origins, there were two distinct lines of development which later coalesced in the current discourse on lifelong learning. One evolved as a result of the influence of developmentalism within the education system, particularly in adult education. This strand was generally perceived by those involved in translating the discourse into classrooms as educationally progressive. The second line of development, where developmentalism was conceptualized as a means of achieving learning in organizational settings, had a major influence in business and commerce. This strand is associated with the rather more oppressive practices of performance management and quality assurance. Here, the discourse that gave birth to the learner derived from a belief that social affairs could, in response to research in the human sciences, be better and more humanely managed than they had been in the past (Lewin, 1948). Later, there was increasing disquiet at the ease with which the organizational learning discourse, shorn of its moral purpose, could be used to control and manipulate economic and social life (Rose, 1999).

Theories of cognitive development

In the decades following the Second World War, there were a number of educational debates centring around constructivist ideas of learning. These derived from the work of psychologists investigating change and development in children and adults. The publication, in the 1950s and 1960s, of Piaget's investigations appeared to lend empirical support to a pragmatist approach to education. In the United States this led to a revival of interest in enquiry, activity and reflection on experience as essential elements of learning (Dewey, 1973). After the successful launch of Sputnik in 1957, the resultant fear that Western democracies were being outstripped by the technological advances of state socialism highlighted the shortcomings of education and the need for reform became a priority. In this context, educationalists in the United States (Bruner, 1977) and the United Kingdom (Stenhouse, 1975) proposed fundamental changes to the curriculum and pedagogy in schools, based upon constructivist principles. At the same time the works of Russian developmental psychologists, in particular Vygotsky's research into the sociocultural mediation of learning in young children, were published in the West (Vygotsky, 1961, 1978). He identified the central role of language and social interaction in the cognitive development of the child as the means whereby concepts were abstracted from phenomena. These ideas were compatible with the earlier work of Mead in the United States, who proposed that the development of identity and practice was dependent on social interaction (Mead, 1934; Berger and Luckman, 1967). The result was a renewed focus on processes of knowledge use and creation. Constructivism/social constructivism was seen as a way for children and young people to master abstract concepts and habits of thinking, which would allow them to be flexible and creative in a world where change and innovation were constant features of social life. The means of achieving these outcomes was to switch to an educational process centred on the child, and her interaction with both the material world and the ideas and thoughts of others (Bruner, 1977).

A critique of conventional schooling also came from another branch of psychology concerned with the learning of people with mental and emotional problems. Carl Rogers, a leading practitioner of humanistic counselling therapy, published *Freedom to Learn* in response to what he described as a profound educational crisis. He wrote:

> ... we cannot rest on the answers provided in the past but must put our trust in the processes by which new problems are met. (1969, p. 303)

> A way must be found to develop a climate in the system in which the focus is not upon teaching, but upon the facilitation of self-directed learning. – Only thus can we develop the creative individual who is open to all of his experience; aware of it, and accepting it, and continually in the process of changing. (Ibid., p. 304)

These terms are almost exactly replicated in the current discourse on the need for lifelong learning (OECD, 2004). What a humanistic focus brought to the proposals for reform was a concentration on the need for the development of the 'whole person', or 'self', of every child. This was seen as part of an inward-looking reflection on experience, which developed self-awareness, confidence and resilience. The emphasis on a person's capacity for self-direction was in part derived from Maslow's work on motivation (1943) which posited self-actualization as a fundamental drive towards autonomy and agency. Concentration on the active participation of persons in self-direction also resonated with the pragmatists' concern that education should foster young people's ability to participate in a democracy. While humanistic psychology placed an emphasis on self-development it also brought to the table a number of group and one-to-one pedagogic strategies for achieving 'personal growth' which could be adapted for use in educational settings (Brandes and Ginnis, 1986; Jacques, 2004).

While these ideas generated relatively large-scale curricular projects in the secondary sector (Stenhouse, 1968; Bruner, 1977), they achieved little long-lasting influence on the curriculum. Child-centred approaches fared rather better in primary schools, for example, through the implementation of the recommendations for curriculum reform made in the Plowden Report (HMSO, 1967) in the United Kingdom. Even so, their hold was relatively tenuous. 'Progressive' ideas about self-directed and active learning were largely rejected with the introduction of the National Curriculum (HMSO, 1988), which reverted to a more transmissive approach to developing children's knowledge. There were, however, further revivals of constructivist teaching approaches in secondary education in the 1980s, for example, as 'student-centred learning' under the banner of the Technical and Vocational Education Initiative (Yeomans, 1996). This time the association between constructivism and schooling was about developing alternative curricula that would motivate underachieving pupils. It was less closely linked to accelerating cognitive development than it had been in the 1960s and 1970s although the development of generic thinking and study skills was supported by TVEI. The therapeutic version of developmentalism retained an influence in the maintenance of systems for pastoral care, pupil guidance and behavioural management. Child-centred approaches became associated with remediation, useful responses to underachievers who had proved 'unable' to benefit from the rigours of an academic curriculum.

However, constructivist reconceptualizations of learning became more firmly embedded in adult education. At much the same time as Rogers (1969) levelled his critique at schools in America, Jessup, in a paper entitled *The idea of lifelong learning*, asked why the British education system was so out-of-date:

> Each man must learn for himself; it is an individual, internal experience, and no one else can do his learning for him. However, at least in recent years, the didactic aspect of education and the role of the educator have been emphasized more than the learning aspect and the role of the educand. (1967, p. 15)

He went on to say that teaching methods in school should be based on participation and discovery, giving young people 'an appetite to continue learning' since 'schools create an aversion for learning that lasts a lifetime' (ibid.). In 1973, Knowles published *The Adult Learner*, in which he made a contrast between education, as an imposition by teachers aimed at controlling the development of the individual and learning, as the growth, development and fulfilment of capacities under the control and direction of the learner. He promoted what he called andragogy as an ethical approach to personal growth, whereby learning activities were planned and evaluated by the learner. He contrasted this to pedagogy where planning and assessment were exclusively the domain of the teacher (Knowles, 1984). Influenced by the work of Freire (2001), his use of the term 'learner' signalled emancipation from the oppressive dogma of formal 'schooling' signified by the use of the terms 'pupil' and 'student'. Andragogy also stood for the right to learn what was of practical relevance to the person at the centre of the education process. Thus, it also ran counter to the class-bound classification of subjects and the hierarchical relation of theory to practice typified by 'traditional' schooling. This 'anti-academicism' remains as an underlying thread of meaning associated with 'the learner'.

Political elements in the definition of the learner continued to be influential especially in those movements opposed to the marginalization and oppression of particular groups. For example, within the feminist movement, the use of education as the means of raising women's consciousness of their own oppression gave them 'voice' to counteract the powers ranged against them (hooks, 1994). At the same time, the practice of 'andragogy' critiqued the basis of formal education and challenged institutional control of what constituted legitimate knowledge and who had the right to define it. Some of these ideas about the status of 'the learner' were eventually given a measure of endorsement for children and young people under the United Nations Convention on the Rights of the Child (1989). In the United Kingdom, this led to a movement to promote the development of 'pupil voice' (McIntyre et al., 2005) in schools. This was both a recognition of children as full human beings with a right to participate in decision-making and, more prosaically, as members of the school community with useful things to say about their educational experiences.

Social psychology and action learning

The second line of development for constructivist/pragmatic approaches to learning also originated in the post-war era. Kurt Lewin's ideas about the means of changing social action (particularly in relation to racial conflict and prejudice) through the use of a new form of practitioner inquiry were extremely influential in the field of organizational development and management (Lewin, 1948). He proposed an approach to practitioner learning that he called 'action research' as the way to improving social practice. He claimed that change had to come through the collective involvement of those engaged in social action, because attempts at changing individuals outside their social context were ineffective. Action research, which is therefore fundamentally collaborative, is based upon a spiral of learning cycles consisting of three activities: first, planning; secondly, taking an action to carry the group towards its agreed objective and; thirdly, fact finding to evaluate the effect of this action and provide the chance for participants to learn from it. The learning resulting from the completion of the first cycle is then fed into the next phase of planning, making a decision about the next action step and so on. Lewin argued that the complexity of social action required that practitioners should be directly involved in the research. This was because any improvement in practice had to be tailored to the situation in which activity took place, if it was to prove viable. In effect, action research was firmly based on a constructivist argument. This set of ideas about the social dynamics of learning were popularized in a series of influential texts on organizational learning (Argyris and Schon, 1974; Senge, 1990). In adult education settings, the legacy was Kolb's (1984) conceptualization of experiential learning which underpinned approaches to work-based learning developed in the 1980s and '90s (Boud and Solomon, 2001).

Lewin's other major contribution to learning theory was his exploration of the effects of levels of aspiration. He found that setting goals for achievement that were either too high or too low decreased the motivation to learn and that the most successful students set goals which were just beyond their current capability. This was elaborated in the years that followed as goal theory (Locke and Latham, 1990) which provided the rationale for the development of performance management. Performance management uses a stripped-down process of action learning in one-to-one interviews between a worker and her supervisor based on target setting and review. This technique, the appraisal interview, has been widely adopted, often tied to financial incentives, as a means of improving employees' motivation and capability in both private sector and, more recently, public sector organizations (Armstrong and Baron, 1998). Performance management is seen as embedding ownership (responsibility) with the employee who internalizes the obligation 'to learn how to learn' to become more effective and efficient. The learner in this context masters the skills of 'self-management' and 'self-direction' towards the goals of the organization.

To summarize, the notion of 'the learner' is broadly underpinned by constructivist learning theories formulated by psychologists in the 1940s and 1950s, and adopted by educationalists and policymakers in the 1960s and 1970s in a pragmatist/constructivist amalgam expressed as 'student-centred learning'. These ideas found a relatively secure home in adult and continuing education, in part because they gave a justification for the rejection of traditional transmissive teaching approaches that were the bane of those whom schooling had failed. They were also adopted and adapted by those interested in organizational development and the improvement of commercial outcomes. Having become entrenched in adult education and associated with the use of work-based learning and performance management strategies, these ideas have returned full circle through the discourse of 'lifelong learning' (Organisation for Economic and Cultural Development [OECD], 1996, 2004) to their origins in child development and their application to schooling.

From these two trajectories, three dominant characteristics of the successful learner emerge:

- as someone who does rather than as someone who is done unto, the learner is an active agent who becomes increasingly autonomous as she learns;
- as a person who is continuously motivated by the goal of 'self-actualization' in a reflective and inventive process of continuous self-improvement; and
- as someone who can use and apply the skills of learning how to learn in a variety of contexts and respond flexibly to the requirement for change.

There is no clear endpoint embedded in these characteristics for being a 'successful learner' in terms of knowledge and understanding rather, being 'successful' consists in the acquisition and maintenance of certain dispositions and competences and their associated procedural tools.

More equivocally, there is also the theme of collaboration and social interaction as necessary for cognitive development, for inventing and establishing new practice and as the basis of critical political action. The tension between this collectivist interpretation of learning and the more individualized interpretation of learning favoured by classic views of pupils and students tends to have been resolved in the latter's favour. Collectivism is tamed by its conversion in lifelong learning discourse to 'communities of learning' and 'shared vision'.

Bridging the gaps

There are three more recent developments which have a bearing on the notion of the learner in Scotland. Arguably, these have all had an effect in reconciling the two major variants of the developmental discourse discussed above. The first of these is the penetration of quality assurance and performance management techniques; the second is the initiative *Assessment for Learning*; and the third is the promulgation of the idea of 'personalization' in the delivery of public services.

Since the introduction, 20 years ago, of the *Quality Initiative in Scottish Schools* (Reeves, 2008), the use of target setting, school and departmental development planning and the publication of outcomes, inspection reports and reviews have become entrenched within the education service. While the performance management of teachers has proved remarkably difficult to implement, this has not been the case in relation to pupils. Spurred on by the need to publish good results and corresponding improvements in data storage and retrieval, schools are increasingly engaged in tracking individual pupil performance. These developments offer both an improved capacity for diagnosis, targeted at the learning needs of individual pupils, as well as increased surveillance and control of children and young people. Through target setting and review during interviews with guidance staff and others, the techniques of performance management are an increasingly salient element in the work of schools. However, exactly who benefits from these practices is often unclear (Priestley, Robinson and Biesta, 2012).

Assessment for Learning was popularized by the publication of Black and Wiliam's pamphlet Inside the Black Box in 1998. This promoted constructivist teaching techniques that centred on pupils and teachers receiving frequent and timely feedback on learning where the purpose of pupils' learning activities was explicit and understood. Such formative feedback maximized the achievement of desirable learning outcomes through improving the accuracy of teaching responses and their relevance to pupils' learning needs. Formative assessment, through the constant adjustment of the interactions between pupils, teachers and the curriculum in the context of learning and teaching, was key to the success of the most effective teachers (Wiliam, 2007). One of the crucial techniques was for pupils to work collaboratively as peer assessors as well as engaging in self-assessment.

Black and Wiliam argued that the variability in pupils' attainment at classroom level was four times that of the variability of pupils' overall attainment at school level and that these differences were due to teacher quality. From their review of the research evidence, it followed that if a teacher were to consistently apply *Assessment for Learning* techniques in class she would add eight months extra learning per annum to her pupils' attainment. This thesis had an obvious appeal to policymakers. Labelling constructivist practices, such as questioning techniques, 'assessment' tapped into politicians' obsession with performance. *Assessment for Learning* subsequently influenced policies for school improvement throughout the United Kingdom. In Scotland it formed part of the *Assessment is for Learning* programme, widely seen as a precursor to the CfE, and it is cited as providing the pedagogical basis for its implementation.

The concept of 'personalization' in the delivery of public services championed originally by New Labour is the final development I want to consider. Leadbeater produced a pamphlet for the think tank Demos entitled *Personalisation through Participation*. He argued that 'personalization', where those using public services engaged with professionals to co-produce services tailored to their needs, was the way forward in the provision of public goods by the state.

> More personalised solutions, *in which the user takes responsibility for providing part of the service*, should enable society to create better collective solutions with a less coercive, intrusive state, a lower tax burden, a more responsible and engaged citizenry and a stronger capacity within civil society to find and design solutions to problems without state intervention. (Leadbeater, 2004, p. 88, my emphasis)

Leadbeater claimed that personalization, applied to education, would provide children with a greater repertoire of scripts for their education. The basic curriculum would be a common script for all but this could branch out in many ways and lead to different destinations. While *Personalisation through Participation* made great claims to be about fostering democracy and enabling service users to gain some control over how services are provided, Hartley (2007) makes the point that there was little in this document to indicate any real change in power relations. Indeed, Leadbeater's description of personalized learning takes us straight back to the performance management cycle so central to managerialist practice:

> – learners should be actively, continually engaged in setting their own targets, devising their own learning plans and goals, choosing from a range of different ways to learn. (Ibid. p. 71)

As Ranson observed (2008), pursuing a constructivist logic implies that pupils are released from the straitjacket of subject boundaries and given greater freedom to explore connections between fields. However, it also shifts the focus from measurable knowledge to 'monitoring the attributes and character of students as they engage in the learning process' (p. 215). Personalization seems to entail that this monitoring becomes the 'do-it-yourself' obligation on the person benefiting from state provision. Applied to children and young people, it places responsibility for learning with the learner, not simply as a matter of motivation or moral obligation but as a direct and continual engagement in a new form of managerial-clerical work. On the more positive side 'their own' choice of targets, plans and learning experiences might pave the way to greater autonomy.

Localizing the discourse – how Scottish policymakers made sense of 'the learner', 2004–10

This section tracks how the concept of the learner has been developed in the series of documents, published by the Scottish Government, to support the implementation of CfE between 2004 and 2011. The analysis that follows is illustrated in Figure 4.1, which shows how the original elements that framed the idea of 'the successful learner' in 2004, shown with bold lines in the centre of the diagram, developed over time to achieve a rather different balance and emphasis at the end of the period. The abbreviations used in the diagram are the same as those outlined in the text.

The policy thread begins in 1996 with the publication by the OECD of *Lifelong Learning for All* which marks the transition of the term 'lifelong learning' from its reference to adult education to its application to 'all learning endeavours over the lifespan' (OECD, 2004). What is important to note here is that the term 'learner' travels, as an integral part of the lifelong learning discourse and the meanings attached to it in non-compulsory adult education, into schools and other educational settings. The 2004 OECD briefing on lifelong learning emphasizes that its contemporary significance is systemic – it refers to learning across all sectors of education and in both formal and informal settings. Its other key features are:

- The centrality of the learner with the concentration on meeting learner needs rather than on the learner complying with what educational institutions are prepared to offer;

The Successful Learner 61

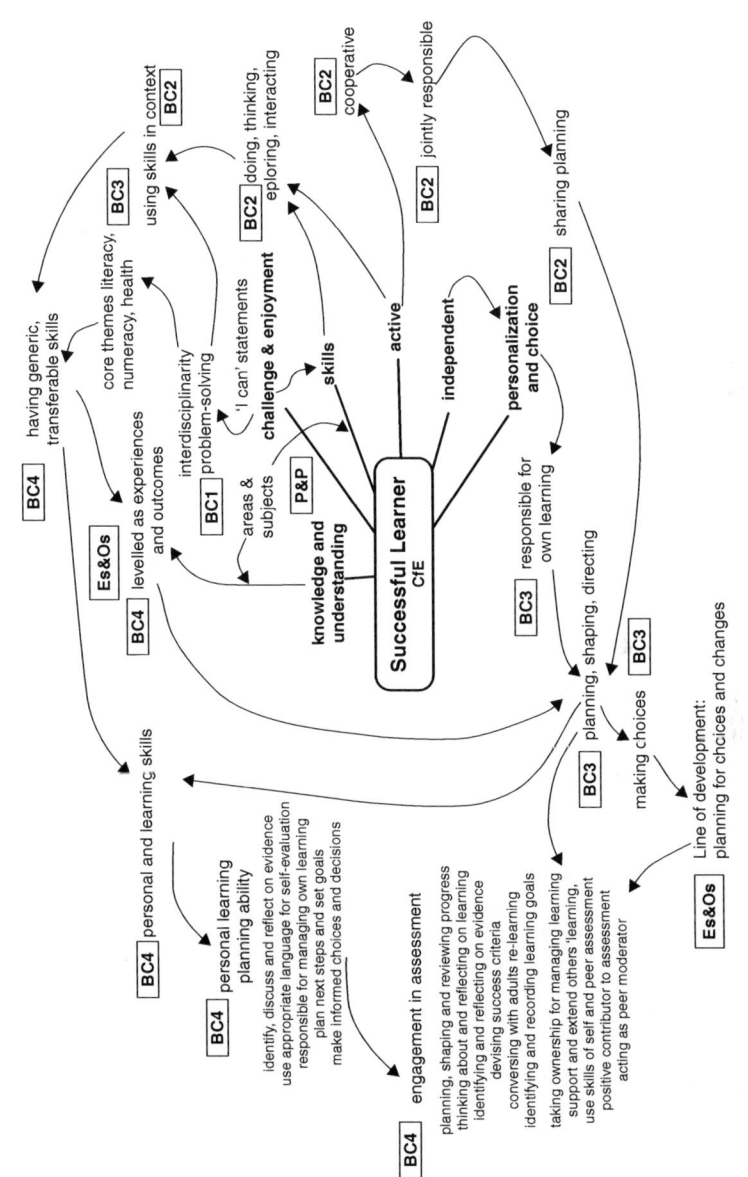

Figure 4.1 The development of 'learning how to learn' in the CfE documents, 2004–10.

- Motivation to learn which results from paying attention to developing individuals' capacity to manage their own learning described as 'self-paced and self-directed learning';
- The need to accommodate the multiple objectives of education policy as the purposes of education are both diverse and changeable. (2004, p. 2)

The document *A Curriculum for Excellence* contains the eight-page report that framed the implementation of a new curriculum for 3–18-year-olds in Scotland. In it successful learners are defined as persons with:

- enthusiasm and motivation for learning,
- determination to reach high standards of achievement,
- openness to new thinking and ideas.

They are able to:

- use literacy, communication and numeracy skills,
- use technology for learning,
- think creatively and independently,
- learn independently and as part of a group,
- make reasoned evaluations, and
- link and apply different kinds of learning in new situations. (Scottish Executive, 2004, p. 12)

This description of the learner placed an emphasis on skills and performance, although the document made several references to the need to establish 'a strong foundation of knowledge and understanding' (ibid., p. 11). The list of seven curricular principles at the end of the report fleshed out the nature of the learner a little further. Four of these were much the same as those principles that underpinned the subject-based curriculum that preceded CfE (SOEID, 1998). Three others – *Challenge and Enjoyment*, *Depth* and *Personalisation and Choice* – were significantly different and indicated the basis on which this new curriculum was construed. Under the heading *Challenge and Enjoyment*, learning was described as active and derived from experience. Children and young people would be able to make judicious choices about their learning, according to their needs and aptitudes, in a context where the purpose of their learning activities was clear to them. In other words, the underlying theoretical position was firmly constructivist. The text went on to state that the acquisition of intellectual skills occurred through the experience of interaction with the world, which provided the challenge and motivation to learn. Under the heading *Depth*, the skills of problem-solving in complex interdisciplinary contexts provided a gateway to advanced levels of understanding. This invoked Bruner's spiral, process-based curriculum in which generic intellectual skills (e.g. those of analysis) are progressively developed over the course of schooling. There was no mention of collaborative or cooperative learning other than the phrase 'as part of a group' (listed above). Under the heading *Personalisation and Choice*, the text points to the role of 'support' in maintaining the learner's motivation and engagement. This support should be provided through assessment which had to be explicitly linked to the purposes of learning. The principle of *Personalisation and Choice* meant that:

> The curriculum should respond to individual needs and support particular aptitudes and talents. It should give each young person increasing opportunities for exercising responsible personal choice as they move through their school career. Once they have achieved suitable levels of attainment across a wide range of areas of learning the choice should become as open as possible. There should be safeguards to ensure that choices are soundly based and lead to successful outcomes. (Ibid., p. 14)

Over the next six years there followed the publication of *A Curriculum for Excellence: Progress and Proposals* (Scottish Executive, 2006a) and a suite of five documents entitled *Building the Curriculum* (BC 1–5) which offered advice to teachers on the implementation of CfE. While *A Curriculum for Excellence* used the word 'pupil' sparingly, all the other documents refer exclusively to 'learners' or 'children and young people'.

Progress and Proposals (Scottish Executive, 2006a) (P&P) was the first document published after the text of *A Curriculum for Excellence* had received ministerial approval. It was largely concerned with the structures of implementation. There were four items of particular interest:

a. It expressed a desire on the part of the government's Curriculum Review Programme Board to consult with schools as to whether it would be desirable and possible for choices in relation to subjects to take place over a more extended period during the early years of secondary schooling (p. 15).
b. It endorsed *Assessment is for Learning* as critical to the implementation of the new curriculum. On page 17 it reiterated Black and Wiliam's tenet that it is the interaction between pupils and teacher and the latter's responsiveness

to what the pupils understand and can do that is crucial to ensuring learning activities are effectively directed to meet learning needs.
c. On page 13, there was a framework of experiences and outcomes to be achieved by most children and young people at 6 levels from 3–18 years of age.
d. It stated that the new curriculum was largely about 'how to teach', implying that the issue of what to teach had already been resolved.

The first document in the BC series, *The Contribution of Curriculum Areas* (BC1) laid out the content of the curriculum (ibid.). The eight areas of experience were largely the same as those for the 5–14 curriculum – with health and well-being replacing personal and social education. Literacy and numeracy were included as cross-cutting themes for which all teaching staff were responsible, and the document emphasized the importance of interdisciplinary studies and projects. The sections on each of the curricular areas listed their particular contribution to successful learning and placed an emphasis on cognition and problem-solving with a clear subordination of 'knowledge' to 'skill'. BC1 affirmed that the statements of experiences and outcomes would describe, 'the knowledge and understanding, skills, capabilities and attributes' (2006b, p. 3) that pupils should develop.

The next document in the series had the title *Active Learning in the Early Years* (BC2) (Scottish Executive, 2007). Active learning in nursery and primary school settings is described as 'learning by doing, thinking, exploring through quality interaction'. The document goes on to say that active learning involves 'intervention and relationships founded on their (childrens') interests and abilities across a variety of contexts', which result in 'an independent and cooperative learner'. There is a criticism of teaching in the 'passive' mode (Carnell and Lodge, 2003), implied by citing the use of an overly didactic approach in the early years of primary education. A new association between active learning and cooperation is created in which the former is described as 'the use and development of skills in context' and the latter as, 'Sharing, planning and contributing towards joint efforts' (ibid., p. 12). Cooperation seems to be understood more as an end in itself rather than as cognitively valuable – that is social constructivism is not clearly part of the mix. A claim that children have a natural disposition 'to wonder, to be curious, to pose questions, to experiment, to suggest, to invent and to explain' (ibid., p. 13) underpins the principle of *Challenge and Enjoyment*. However, given that active learning is identified as an essential element of the whole curriculum, it is strange that both the title and the content of this text are confined in its application to younger children. Despite the extensive documentation produced by the policymakers, there is no explicit explanation of what active learning might mean for older pupils and their teachers (Drew and Mackie, 2011). This is a strange omission, given that the new curriculum was supposedly largely concerned with changes in pedagogy. A reference to *Assessment is for Learning* provided the only specific pedagogic guidance for active learning in the secondary sector.

The third publication, *A Framework for Learning and Teaching* (BC3) (Scottish Government, 2008), described children's educational entitlement to: a broad general education followed by a senior phase with qualifications; the acquisition of skills for learning, life and work including the core skills of literacy, numeracy and health and well-being; personal support; and a move to a positive destination after school. In relation to personal support, this document stated:

> From the outset, young children are partners in the learning process, actively participating in the planning, shaping and directing of their own learning. With sensitive adult support, they will learn how to make good, informed choices and take responsibility for their own learning. (2008, p. 29)

There was a certain tension here since the personal support to which pupils were entitled was to be provided by adults other than classroom or subject teachers such as guidance or pupil support teachers or members of partnership organizations. There was a reassurance that personalization and choice 'will continue to include choices in approaches to learning within the classroom' (ibid., p. 17). This confinement of support to a mentor figure, outside the context of the classroom, could divert attention from improving the quality of interaction between teachers, pupils and the curriculum that Black and Wiliam (1998) identified as an essential element of effective teaching and learning.

BC3 included health and well-being as a cross-cutting theme for the first time. This was significant, as health and well-being became the chosen vehicle for supporting and assessing pupils' learning-to-learn skills and their commitment to self-development. It was also the site for widening the scope and range of what that self-formation would entail.

Skills for Learning, Skills for Life and Skills for Work (BC4) (Scottish Government, 2009), began with a 'Key Messages' page which emphasized that there were core, permeating cross-curricular skills which all teachers were responsible for developing. Progression in the acquisition of these skills was fixed through the specification of learning experiences and outcomes at four different levels. In this, the Scottish policymakers followed the example of Department for Education and Skills in England (DfES, 2007) who 'wilfully misinterpreted' (Gardner et al., 2008, p. 91) the research underpinning *Assessment for Learning* by converting the recommendation for formative assessment into a summative schema of dubious empirical or theoretical worth. Of particular interest was the emergence of an ever more detailed description of what was meant by a 'successful learner' under the heading of 'personal and learning skills'. These are listed as personal learning planning, leadership and thinking skills (in the form of a simplified Bloom's Taxonomy), amounting to a mixture of self-management skills and generic cognitive skills. Personal learning planning was detailed further as the ability to:

- identify, discuss and reflect on their own evidence of learning
- use appropriate language for self-evaluation
- take responsibility for managing their own learning
- help to plan their own next steps in learning and set their own learning goals
- make informed choices and decisions about their future learning. (ibid., p. 13)

This looks rather similar to the expectations placed on employees in the implementation of performance management schemes. 'Leadership', in this context, seems to equate to the administration of self-management techniques. These particular skills attract an even more detailed definition in the next document in the series: *A Framework for Assessment* (BC5) (Scottish Government, 2011).

> Learners do well when engaging fully in their learning, collaborating in planning and shaping and reviewing their progress. Approaches to assessment that enable learners to say, 'I can show that I can –' will fully involve them. At all stages, learners should understand that assessment will support them in their learning and help them develop ambition to learn in increasing breadth and depth.
>
> Children and young people can develop their confidence through thinking about and reflecting on their own learning. They should have regular time to talk about their work and to identify and reflect on the evidence of their progress and next steps, including through personal learning planning. Through frequent and regular conversations with informed adults, they are able to identify and understand the progress they are making across all aspects of their learning and achievements.
>
> For this process of reflection to be effective, learners need to be supported in developing their skills in self and peer assessment and in recognising

and evaluating evidence of their own learning. Peer assessment and other collaborative learning enables learners to support and extend each others' learning, for example by being aware of what is expected of them from looking at examples and devising and sharing success criteria. As they develop skills in self and peer assessment, learners will build confidence and take more ownership for managing their own learning. By focusing on the processes of learning as well as the achievement of outcomes, they will become reflective and positive contributors to assessment.

Using these approaches to encouraging dialogue about learning, children and young people and staff can identify next steps and learning goals based on feedback and evidence of learning. Children and young people should agree learning goals and should record them in ways that are meaningful and relevant, for example in diaries, learning logs and progress files. (Ibid., p. 19)

This marks a substantial redefinition of what it is to be a (pupil) learner in terms of work and activity. There is little indication of where choice comes into the matter as all statements of experiences and outcomes must be assessed. Additionally, their phrasing, 'I can do (make, plan etc.) x', makes it very clear who is responsible for recording and taking 'ownership' of these judgements.

The final document in the series originally had no title, it was simply referred to as 'a file', and consisted of a collection of all the statements of experiences and outcomes (Es&Os) (Education Scotland, no date) for the cross-cutting themes and the eight areas of experience. Each curricular theme or area began with a section headed *Principles and Practice*, and both these and the statements that followed, organized as lines of development, varied quite markedly in nature and focus. Overall the statements delineated the extent of the broad, general education to which pupils were entitled up to the end of their third year in secondary school. They did not to apply to the final three years of secondary education.

The three cross-cutting themes; health and well-being, literacy and numeracy were laid out, in that order, at the beginning of the document. The section for health and well-being covered nearly twice as many pages as any other area. Skills for learning were enumerated at four levels under the line of development, *Planning for Choices and Changes*, which marked the culmination of the description of this 'set of skills', which had been built up throughout the CfE documentation (see Figure 4.1). The theme of *Health and Wellbeing* also included statements of experiences and outcomes covering: self-awareness and self-worth, resilience and confidence, coping skills, managing thoughts and feelings, and managing change and risk. These statements were made under the line of development *Mental, Emotional, Social and Physical Wellbeing* and marked the blossoming of the movement towards personal micro-management, as predicted by Ranson (2008). Pupils were required to grade themselves against 18 criteria for the assessment of their emotions, personality and character.

Choice was seldom mentioned in this document except in *Languages and English* which listed *Enjoyment and Choice* as a line of development. *Assessment is for Learning* was included as a standard phrase for pedagogy in all except one of the curricular areas. There was no overall mapping of the curriculum in this document.

Conclusion

This analysis of the policymakers' attempts to make sense of 'the successful learner' reveals an increasing lack of balance in the interpretation and relations between the three characteristics of the concept that were identified earlier,

Looking at the commitment to increasing learners' autonomy, the scope for choice and decision-making by children and young people becomes progressively sidelined over the six years, only receiving serious consideration in the context of the early years (Scottish Executive, 2007). From the start 'choice' carries a caveat (Scottish Executive, 2004, p. 14) and learner autonomy ends up by reflecting current and historic practice, where the freedom to make educational choices by the young is limited on the grounds of immaturity and lack of judgement. The structural determination of educational opportunities through the way in which pupils are categorized and grouped by schools is not touched upon. The problems of transplanting practice from the non-compulsory adult education sector to schools are considerable. There is a far more uniform curricular structure based on a different set of relationships between learners, teachers and the curriculum, than is the case in adult education. Despite the commitment in *Progress and Proposals* (2006a) to consult with schools on extending choice for pupils in the early years of their secondary education, there is no return to this issue later in the CfE series. The guidance as to what is encompassed by choice, and how it may be exercised by children, is restricted to the description of interviews where an adult provides personal support by agreeing and reviewing personal learning plans with pupils. Since this activity takes place within a framework for achievement where all listed learning experiences and outcomes must be covered and assessed, conversations about choices, such as opting out of a subject and spending more time on another, or about when to learn and how to learn are unlikely to be offered.

Besides these structural considerations, the fundamental issue for learner autonomy of power and control is not dealt with. The initial statement of purpose and principles (Scottish Executive, 2004) outlines aspirations for a substantive change in relationships which is not addressed in subsequent documentation. The new curriculum requires a repositioning of the respective roles of teachers and pupils and of their relationships to curriculum, pedagogy and assessment if young people are to become actively and critically engaged in learning. This amounts to a radical alteration of the dominant regulatory discourse in schools (Bernstein, 1971). The problem is papered over by the claim, repeated in several of the documents, that all that is required to inaugurate CfE is a change in pedagogy. Furthermore, the change in pedagogy is defined as the adoption of *Assessment is for Learning* which is eventually articulated as a series of summative/formative steps (peer and self-assessment) determined by measurable (levelled) descriptions of experience and outcomes. The creativity and criticality that formative assessment of classroom and school practice might have offered are thereby 'made safe' by simply inviting children to participate within the restrictive margins provided by an elaborated treadmill of assessment activities.

For much the same reasons, children and young people's chances of becoming committed to learning through experiences of self-actualization and self-direction fare little better. If their scope for choice is severely limited then their sense of directing and controlling their own development is necessarily weakened. If reflection on experience is tied to considering the goals which have been set for them by others and is recorded by parroting phrases provided for them by others, this is unlikely to make the process motivating. 'Learner-centredness' has effectively been hollowed out by the removal of the child's agency. At the same time, under the aegis of *Health and Wellbeing*, the range and power of assessment to determine, rather than act as a support for, development is substantively increased particularly through its penetration into the affective domain.

In contrast to the lack of detail about the first two characteristics of the successful learner, the descriptions of the personal learning skills that she must master become increasingly differentiated and detailed. By the end of the CfE series 'assessment' and 'learning to learn' have become largely synonymous. The requirement that learners continuously judge and record both their own and others' progress carries the danger of becoming a burdensome form of 'assessowork' that will be driven by the need to provide evidence for quality assurance and ensuring 'all the boxes are ticked'. It has been rightly argued that the practice of peer- and self-assessment allows children to experience a greater sense of autonomy and confidence because expectations are made clearer to them. In that sense, the teaching and learning process becomes more inclusive because a number of children gain greater access to a curriculum that was previously closed to them. However, if such a practice remains in the service of an essentially dictatorial and top-down determination of what is on offer, it is merely an amelioration of the status quo, a pedagogy that lacks a transformational educational purpose.

What we appear to have in this short history of textual 'events' is an example of how one discursive form, the progressive, became increasingly invaded and modified by another, the oppressive. The resulting hybrid emerges, seemingly unnoticed and unchallenged, as something very far removed from what was hoped for. CfE was intended to mark a renewal of democratic engagement as part of Scottish devolution. The potential of 'the successful learner' to serve as an emancipatory concept seems to have been severely eroded in its on-going translation by national policymakers. Since in Scotland the policymakers include teachers, heads, local authority personnel and academics, this outcome cannot be viewed simply as the work of a malignant political cadre. How we are currently defining the 'successful learner' could be interpreted as a failure of imagination on all our parts.

References

Argyris, C. and Schon, D. (1974), *Theory in Practice: Increasing Professional Effectiveness*. San Francisco: Jossey-Bass.
Armstrong, M. and Baron, A. (1998), *Performance Management; The New Realities*. London: Chartered Institute of Personnel Development.
Berger, P. L. and Luckman, T. (1967), *The Social Construction of Reality: A Treatise on the Sociology of Knowledge*. London: Penguin Books.
Bernstein, B. (2001), 'From pedagogies to knowledges', in A. Morais, J. Neves, B. Davies and H. Daniels (eds), *Towards a Sociology of Pedagogy: The Contribution of Basil Bernstein to Research*. New York: Peter Lang, pp. 363–8.
Black, P. and Wiliam, D. (1998), *Inside the Black Box: Raising Standards Through Classroom Assessment*. London: GL Assessment King's College.

Boud, D. and Solomon, N. (eds) (2001), *Work-based Learning: A New Higher Education*. Buckingham: Open University Press.

Brandes, D. and Ginnis, P. (1986), *A Guide to Student-Centred Learning*. London: Basil Blackwell.

Bruner, J. S. (1977), *The Process of Education* (2nd edn). Cambridge, MA: Harvard University Press.

Carnell, E. and Lodge, C. (2002), *Supporting Effective Learning*. London: Paul Chapman Publishing.

Dewey, J. (1973), 'My pedagogic creed', in J. McDermott (ed.), *The Philosophy of John Dewey. Vols 1 and 2 The Structure of Experience, The Lived Experience*. Chicago: University of Chicago Press, pp. 442–54.

DfES (2007), *Making Good Progress*. London: Department for Education and Skills.

Drew, V. and Mackie, L. (2011), 'Extending the constructs of active learning: implications for teachers' pedagogy and practice'. *The Curriculum Journal*, 22, 451–67.

Education Scotland (no date), *Curriculum for Excellence: Successful Learners, Confident Individuals, Responsible Citizens, Effective Contributors*. Online at www.educationscotland.gov.uk/Images/all_experiences_outcomes_tcm4-539562.pdf (accessed 04/10/12).

European Commission (2002), *A European Area of Lifelong Learning*. Brussels: European Commission.

Freire, P. (2001), *Pedagogy of Freedom: Ethics, Democracy, and Civic Courage*. Lanham, USA: Rowman and Littlefield.

Gardner, J., Holmes, B. and Leitch, R. (2008), 'Where there is smoke, there is (the potential for) fire: soft indicators of research and policy impact'. *Cambridge Journal of Education*, 38, 89–104.

Hartley, D. (2007), 'Personalisation: the emerging, revised, code of education?' *Oxford Review of Education*, 33, 629–42.

HMSO (1988), *The Education Reform Act*. London: HMSO.

hooks, B. (1994), *Teaching to Transgress: Education as the Practice of Freedom*. New York: Routledge.

Jacques, D. (2004), *Learning in Groups: A Handbook for Improving Group Work* (3rd edn). London: RoutledgeFalmer.

Jessup, F. W. (ed.) (1967), *Lifelong Learning: A Symposium of Continuing Education*. Oxford: Pergamon Press.

Knowles, M. S. (1984), *The Adult Learner: A Neglected Species* (3rd edn). Houston: Gulf Publishing.

Kolb, D. A. (1984), *Experiential Learning: Experience as a Source of Learning and Development*. Englewood Cliffs, NJ: Prentice-Hall.

Leadbeater, C. (2004), *Personalisation through Participation*. London: Demos.

Lewin, K. (1948), 'Action research and minority problems', in G. W. Lewin (ed.), *Resolving Social Conflicts: Selected Papers on Group Dynamics by Kurt Lewin*. New York: Harper & Row, pp. 201–20.

— (1964), 'Field theory and learning', in D. Cartwright. (ed.), *Field Theory in Social Science: Selected Theoretical Papers by Kurt Lewin*. New York: Harper & Row, pp. 60–86.

Locke, E. A. and Latham, G. P. (1990), *A Theory of Goal Setting and Task Performance*. Englewood Cliffs, NJ: Prentice Hall.

Maslow, A. H. (1943), 'A theory of human motivation', reproduced in J. M. Shafritz, J. S. Ott and Y. S. Jang (eds) (2005), *Classics of Organization Theory*. Belmont, CA: Thomson Wadsworth, pp. 167–78.

McIntyre, D., Pedder, D. and Ruddock, J. (2005), 'Pupil voice: comfortable and uncomfortable learnings for teachers'. *Research Papers in Education*, 20, 149–68.

Mead, G. H. (1934), *Mind, Self and Society: From the Standpoint of a Social Behaviourist*. Chicago: University of Chicago.

Organisation for Economic Co-operation and Development (1996), *Lifelong Learning for All*. Paris: OECD.

— (2004), *Policy Brief: Lifelong Learning*. OECD Observer. Paris: OECD.

(Plowden Report) Central Advisory Council for Education (1967), *Children and Their Primary Schools*. London: HMSO

Priestley, M., Robinson, S. and Biesta, G. (2012), 'Reinventing the teacher in the Scottish Curriculum for Excellence', in B. Jeffrey and G. Troman (eds), *Performativity Across UK Education: Ethnographic Cases of its Effects, Agency and Reconstructions*. Painswick: E&E Publishing, pp. 87–108.

Ranson, S. (2008), 'The changing governance of education'. *Educational Management Administration and Leadership*, 36, 201–19.

Reeves, J. (2008), 'Between a rock and a hard place? Curriculum for Excellence and the Quality Initiative in Scottish schools'. *Scottish Educational Review*, 40, 6–16.

Rogers, C. R. (1969), *Freedom to Learn*. Columbus: Charles E. Merrill Publishing.

Rose, N. (1991), *Governing the Soul: The Shaping of the Private Self*. London: Routledge.

Scottish Executive (2004), *A Curriculum for Excellence*. Edinburgh: Scottish Executive.

— (2006a), *A Curriculum for Excellence: Progress and Proposals*. Edinburgh: Scottish Executive.

— (2006b), *A Curriculum for Excellence: Building the Curriculum 1: The Contribution of Curriculum Areas*. Edinburgh: Scottish Executive.

— (2007), *A Curriculum for Excellence: Building the Curriculum 2: Active Learning in the Early Years*. Edinburgh: Scottish Executive.

— (2008), *A Curriculum for Excellence: Building the Curriculum 3: A Framework for Learning and Teaching*. Edinburgh: Scottish Government.

— (2009), *A Curriculum for Excellence: Building the Curriculum 4: Skills for Learning, Skills for Life and Skills for Work*. Edinburgh: Scottish Government.

— (2011), *A Curriculum for Excellence: Building the Curriculum 5: A Framework for Assessment*. Edinburgh: Scottish Government.

Scottish Office Education Department (1994), *5–14: A Practical Guide*. Edinburgh: HMSO.

Senge, P. (1990), *The Fifth Discipline: The Art and Practice of the Learning Organisation*. London: Random House.

Stenhouse, L. (1968), 'The Humanities Curriculum Project'. *Journal of Curriculum Studies*, 1, 26–33.

Vygotsky, L. S. (1962), *Thought and Language* (E. Hanfmann and G. Vakar, eds and trans). Cambridge, MA: MIT Press.

— (1978), *Mind in Society: The Development of Higher Psychological Processes*. Cambridge, MA: Harvard University Press.

Wiliam, D. (2007), *Assessment for Learning: Why, What and How? An Inaugural Professorial Lecture by Dylan Wiliam*. London: Institute of Education, University of London.

Yeomans, D. (1996), *Constructing Vocational Education from TVEI to GNVQ*. Online at www.leeds.ac.uk/educol/documents/00002214.htm (accessed 01/09/12).

Confident Individuals: The Implications of an 'Emotional Subject' for Curriculum Priorities and Practices

Kathryn Ecclestone

Introduction

Calls by the English Government in 2010 to resurrect Latin and to review the content and teaching of all curriculum subjects suggested that the newly elected Conservative-led coalition intended to frame its educational priorities around traditional subject disciplines and teaching methods. A year later, it shelved its own qualifications review, which attempted to reconcile calls to bolster subject disciplines with earlier enthusiasm for a process-based curriculum that develops personal, thinking and learning skills (DfE, 2011). At the same time, the Secretary of State for Education supported another review that criticized vocational qualifications (Wolf, 2011). In September 2012, media rumours suggested government interest in challenging the long-running rise in students' grade achievements. Yet, despite its seeming ideological opposition to long-running policy goals of inclusion, higher levels of achievement and participation, and 'parity of esteem' between academic and vocational qualifications, the English Government does not offer confident or robust opposition to them. Instead, ambivalence and contradictions seem to characterize English curriculum policy.

The situation in Scotland appears to be very different. Here, political and professional enthusiasm for the dispositions-based Curriculum for Excellence (CfE) embeds long-held progressive goals, through what many see as the ideals of primary education, throughout the entire system from 3–13. As Walter Humes notes in this volume, endorsement in CfE of developing transferable capacities, reducing central prescription in content and outcomes and resurrecting professional independence in curriculum implementation continues a powerful public rhetoric about education that reflects particular democratic ideals. According to Humes, the contrast in this rhetoric with the English education system is another part of CfE's appeal. Nevertheless, despite their broad support for CfE, some commentators note tensions such as lack of a coherent theory of learning, seemingly conflicting aims, vagueness about content, the framing of educational goals around the demands of work and the global economy, a tendency for mantras about the central role of attributes such as confidence, etc., and the continuation of target-driven pressures that undermine professional independence and agency (see Humes, this volume; Priestley and Humes, 2010).

As a contribution to a critical evaluation of the implications of CfE for debates about what counts as a modern and progressive curriculum, this chapter explores the extent to which CfE reflects shifts and continuities in curriculum debates in England, Scotland and other countries. It focuses on another significant, yet overlooked tension in CfE, namely its reflection of a powerful prevailing hostility among researchers, commentators and teachers towards curricula based on traditional subject content, and corresponding enthusiasm for skills or 'capabilities' rooted in life-related and personalized knowledge rather than traditional disciplines.

In contrast to widespread enthusiasm for curricula that regard dispositions and 'skills' such as confidence, collaboration and enjoyment in learning as not merely integral to success, achievement and 'well-being', but as precursors or foundations for them, any challenge is often taken as a sign of a conservative and elitist educational and social ideology. Notwithstanding this possible response, this chapter takes a sceptical approach to such enthusiasm by disentangling the various strands of educational and political concern that shift confidence from being a by-product of achievement, enjoyment, overcoming challenges or a background factor in good teaching, to its current elevated status as a high stakes educational goal and outcome. It argues that although this shift emerges in large part from a long tradition of child-centred education, it has a new significance in the context of broader public, professional and political uncertainty about appropriate curriculum content, teaching and assessment, fuelled by deep pessimism about the well-being of children and young people. One effect is a widely supported view that educators cannot engage and motivate their students unless overt attention is paid to their emotional needs, and unless they develop various affective 'skills' and dispositions. The chapter goes onto propose that these assumptions shift confidence from being a commonsense strand in a general ethics of care for students, to an 'emotional' subject, thereby becoming a major preoccupation in teachers' interpretations of curriculum goals and purposes, and subsequent implementation. The final section asks whether an unanticipated outcome of a dispositions-based curriculum in a context of crisis and pessimism is to create new forms of inequality.

Confidence as a high-stakes educational and social goal

Slippery meanings

On the surface, the idea that teachers should build confidence seems so banally obvious that it does not deserve concerted analysis. It goes without saying that confidence is an important aspect of creating a positive classroom or institutional ethos or culture, as well as a by-product of doing something well. In a similarly obvious way, teachers might make confidence an explicit goal, perhaps for hesitant or struggling individuals who need judicious praise or careful scaffolding of tasks in ways that realize success. The same difficulties in engaging critically with commonsense obviousness also apply to other underlying principles of CfE. It therefore seems churlish and unnecessary to question whether teachers should pay direct attention to the development of capacities such as being a successful learner or a confident individual.

As Humes also notes in this volume, these notions are both slippery and mantric and therefore need critical scrutiny. An overlooked problem is the steady rise over the past 15 years or so of attributes such as confidence from a desirable by-product or incidental aspect of learning and teaching to an explicit foundation for learning, achievement and well-being. In this respect, its status in CfE mirrors the attempt by the English Qualifications and Curriculum Authority in 2006 to propose that confidence is integral to a set of 'personal, thinking and learning skills' (PLaTS) and, in turn, the foundation for schooling (QCA, 2006).

Political endorsement of confidence and other attributes or dispositions, as a set of key skills in both the QCA's proposals and CfE is seen by many supporters in all phases of the education system to underpin a progressive, modern and motivating curriculum. Typical of this view is an early years' perspective which presents confidence as integral to resilience in the face of uncertainty and to children and young people's ability to express their ideas, and adopt collaborative and thoughtful approaches to learning, reflection and self-awareness (Carr, 2001). In a similar vein, Guy Claxton, a well-known promoter of the popular idea of 'learning to learn', or what he calls 'learning power', encourages secondary school teachers, whatever their subject, to make confidence and other dispositions an explicit target through activities and materials within subject disciplines that encourage students to discuss, identify, assess and record their confidence, explore how they develop it in different situations, and evaluate factors that hinder or foster it (e.g. Claxton, 2002, 2007).

Despite the popular view that confidence is integral to a dispositions-based curriculum, and that it has discernible characteristics or manifestations that teachers and students can and should focus on directly, there is real difficulty in pinning down what confidence is. Educational researchers, curriculum designers, psychologists and teachers have long grappled with possibly intractable questions of whether dispositions such as confidence are skills, competences or 'capabilities', attitudes, personality traits, particular mind-sets, feelings or emotional responses to situations. Nor is there any agreement about whether confidence is transferable or situated and context-dependent, whether it can be taught, whether it is acquired consciously by focusing on it as a goal or target, or whether it is a by-product of learning, life experiences or doing other things that one is good at.

It is important to reiterate that these are old and unresolved debates that also apply to difficulties in deciding what collaboration, reflection, engagement, resilience and responsibility for learning really are, or how they are developed. Nevertheless, the most common argument for a curriculum and pedagogy that foster reflective, resilient and confident learners is that these linked notions are all 'dispositions', namely relatively enduring habits of mind and associated actions that encourage us to respond to experiences in particular ways. Following this argument, children and young people who are helped to develop them can apply them strategically to diverse learning situations (e.g. Claxton, 2002). Together with related dispositions such as self-awareness, self-esteem and resilience, some educators argue that confidence can be developed from the early years' curriculum onwards as integral to 'participation repertoires from which a learner resists, searches for and constructs learning opportunities' (Carr, 2001, p. 21). From this perspective, dispositions such as confidence are linked to our attitudes and feelings about ourselves and our views about the different identities or possible selves that we can be and become (ibid.). In turn, an enduring theme in policy-related texts from different standpoints is that dispositions, attitudes and feelings are 'resources' that can be transferred to diverse situations and contexts (e.g. DfE, 1998, 2005; Social Exclusion Unit, 1999; OECD, 2001, 2007; Duncan-Smith and Allan, 2009; Johnson et al., 2009; Sodha and Guglemi, 2009). In this scenario, confidence becomes part of 'personal' or 'emotional' capital.

The sources cited here reflect concerted attempts to present confidence as a disposition and to recognize the interaction of cultural capital, educational and social advantages and social collaboration in its development. Nevertheless, further difficulty comes from its complex relationship with closely associated dispositions such as resilience, optimism, self-awareness and self-esteem. In policy throughout the United Kingdom to promote interventions for emotional well-being in schools, these dispositions are psychological constructs and they join others such as emotional regulation, mindfulness, stoicism, altruism and emotional literacy as skills or capabilities or dispositions that can all be developed and transferred to diverse life and educational contexts as foundations for emotional well-being. Following this argument, they are highly amenable to interventions as a form of prevention against future problems (e.g. Layard, 2005; Sharples, 2007).

A crisis of confidence about confidence?

I observed in the introduction to this chapter that the emphasis in CfE on capacities is widely seen as educationally progressive. A strong imperative for this enthusiasm are long traditions that advocate student-centred and humanist education as a counter to test-driven, subject-based and selective systems.

Yet leaving aside important conceptual questions, an overlooked theme in contemporary debates is the growing pessimism among policymakers, curriculum designers, teachers and parents about children and young people's confidence. This is epitomized by policy texts from 1998 onwards which depict 'socially excluded' and 'vulnerable' groups and individuals as victims of learning difficulties, a lack of self-esteem, poor self-confidence and low aspirations, with a corresponding need for them to engage successfully in 'learning'. In such texts, the content of 'learning' is not specified. Instead, through raising aspirations and achievement and improving employability and civic engagement, the processes and outcomes of learning per se, no matter what the subject, become the main driver of social change. Confidence is crucial to this. For example, the introduction to the *Learning Age* states: 'Learning will be the key to a strong economy and an inclusive society. It will offer a way out of dependency and low-expectation towards self-reliance and self-confidence' (DfEE, 1998, p. 3).

The *Learning Age* is typical of a series of policy texts over the past 15 years which promote learning as a general process and the main vehicle for overcoming problems with aspirations, achievement, employability and engagement that are both cyclical and:

> The results [of social exclusion] are seen in the second and third generation of the same family being unemployed, and in the potential talent of young people wasted in a vicious circle of underachievement, self-deprecation and petty-crime. Learning can overcome this by building self-confidence and independence. (Ibid., p. 19)

Of course, the summary of these claims cannot do justice to their different motives and aspirations. Nevertheless, despite important differences in explanations for persistent educational and social inequalities, there is general agreement that emotions, attitudes and dispositions are resources or 'capital', and sometimes 'skills'. From this perspective, not only are they key to educational and life success, they precede both the ability and motivation to learn (e.g. Social Exclusion Unit, 1999; OECD, 2001, 2007; Duncan-Smith and Allan, 2009; Sodha and Gugleimi, 2009).

Arguments for a dispositions-based curriculum are reinforced by professional associations, policy 'think tanks', children's charities, parental groups and academics who argue that subject content, learning and teaching activities and assessment methods are outdated, irrelevant and elitist. Typical of such arguments is a book by the Association of Teachers and Lecturers (ATL), appropriately titled *Subject to Change: New Thinking on the Curriculum*. Starting from the proposition that 'Education is assumed to be primarily about the development of the mind', but [. . .] this is a 'misunderstanding', a new skills curriculum is needed for all children:

> The major difference from previous curriculum models is that it should consider the needs of the whole person without assuming that the academic or intellectual aspects should have a higher status than the others. The first truly comprehensive curriculum should rebalance the academic, situated in the mind, against those parts of humanity situated in the body, the heart and the soul. Curricula may well be designed by people for whom the mind predominates, but those designers should see that the twenty-first century requires a population with higher levels of social, emotional and moral performance, and a regenerated capacity for doing and making. (Johnson et al., 2007, pp. 69–71)

Although CfE is distinctive in a number of respects, not least in its span from 3–18, its ambivalence and seeming contradictions about the place of subject content resonate powerfully with a view that intellectual development should not be the main focus or goal of a modern, inclusive education system. In an English context, the ATL states:

> We need a bit of honesty in this analysis. Most people are not intellectuals. Most people do not lead their lives predominantly in the abstract. It is not clear that it is preferable to do otherwise: the world cannot survive only through thought. (Johnson et al., 2007, p. 72)

Again in an English context, other commentators go further, broadening their antipathy to the priority given to intellectual development in order to criticize the 'Victorian elitism', irrelevance and oppression of old school subjects. Typical of this perspective are arguments by philosopher John White that intellectual development through outdated subject disciplines disadvantages children and young people from disadvantaged backgrounds, either because they are simply irrelevant, alien and inauthentic, or because they restrict or prevent educational success and therefore have lasting negative effects (e.g. White, 2007).

A closely linked claim in support of a dispositions-based curriculum is that education does not equip citizens or society for changing work patterns and conditions, major social and personal roles or to deal with social upheaval. In a presentation to the All-Party Parliamentary Group on 'well-being in the classroom' in 2007, Claxton argued that dispositions associated with 'learning power' were integral to schools' essential role in fostering emotional well-being:

> classrooms need to be configured in such a way that young people spending eleven years or more of their lives in them emerge at the end, regardless of the number of qualifications that they have managed to achieve, with the capacity to be happiness generating individuals – able to feel confident and enthusiastic and capable in responding to the challenges that come their way. (Claxton in Sharples, 2007, p. 14)

In part, such arguments are the latest manifestation of a long-running but intensifying view that formal education is alienating, outdated, inauthentic or simply, as Matthew Taylor, Chief Executive of the Royal Society of Arts puts it, 'mind-numbingly boring' for most young people (2008). Yet two key changes from older variations on these themes are evident. First, the sources cited above reflect a widespread view that problems of disaffection, poor achievement and rising levels of stress and anxiety now extend beyond a minority disaffected, disengaged and unable to succeed in traditional schooling. Instead, a common underlying fear is that these problems encompass greater numbers of children and young people in state-funded schools than ever before and that these numbers can only increase. For example, the authors of a QCA-funded study of attitudes to and feelings about formal education among 14–19-year-olds in 45 case organizations show that among those deemed by teachers to be 'disaffected' or 'negative about education', 'only a half (51%) felt school had encouraged them to learn more and only a third (35%) felt that they had enough say in their own learning' arguing that 'the evidence of dysfunction is compelling' (Lumby, 2012, p. 275).

Contemporary calls for a dispositions-based curriculum are therefore highly inclusive, drawing in advocacy of specialist interventions and a more emotionally focused education for those assessed to have particular needs, or to need better behaviour management, as well as universal reforms to the curriculum in response to widespread pessimism about what most learners are capable of or willing to put up with, and about the support they need in order to achieve or even to engage at all.

Secondly, in comparison to older debates about how to deal with disaffection and lack of educational achievement and success, there appears to be more hostility than in the past to the idea that all students should have access to traditional subjects, albeit with special dispensation for those unable to cope with them (see Young, 2007; Rata, 2012). Instead there is growing view that traditional forms of knowledge are not merely irrelevant or difficult, or damaging for a minority, but that they are a key culprit in eroding the confidence of growing numbers of children and young people.

The perspectives summarized in this section suggest that confidence and related dispositions are not only essential for motivation and developing a strong learning identity to maximize good educational outcomes. In addition, policy texts shift attention from structural factors such as material conditions, the economy, class, race and gender, to confidence as an essential precursor for moving out of disadvantage. In turn, the acts and processes of learning and participation (or its more committed manifestation of 'engagement') that create confidence become ends in themselves.

Confidence as part of mental health and well-being

An important contribution to the elevated status of confidence as a cornerstone of educational and social success are informal and formal diagnoses and estimates that levels of stress, anxiety, category disorders and poor mental health are growing at an alarming rate (see Ecclestone, 2012; Myers, 2012). Despite very wide variations in these estimates, one effect in policy and practice is to reinforce an overtly psychologized interpretation of the characteristics of confidence and how schools might enhance them, influenced by ideas from positive psychology (e.g. Ecclestone, 2012; Kristjánsson, 2012). In numerous countries, this has led to a large expansion of interventions in educational settings designed to develop what advocates claim are measurable constructs of emotional well-being, summarized above (e.g. Weare, 2003; Sharples, 2007). From this particular perspective, confidence and its related constructs become essential components of the 'right' mindset or attitude and a springboard for appropriate responses and behaviours. This reinforces the shift from confidence as a by-product of doing something well, mastering a difficult subject or skill, or overcoming difficult life and educational experiences, into a fundamental resource, an essential form of 'capital' for educational, work and life success.

Redressing imbalances and social justice

There are also powerful ideological dimensions to accounts that present confidence as a political or social goal. For example, some argue that it is integral to well-being and 'voice' and therefore an essential counter to traditional assessment practices and forms of knowledge that deny children 'voice' and participation, and, through this, their right to well-being (e.g. Leitch, 2008). In a similar vein, Jacky Lumby argues that, unless educational systems respond directly to the emotional and relational aspects of schooling that young people tell us they need if they are to participate and achieve, schools will continue to perpetuate serious social injustice (2012; see also Claxton, 2002). From this perspective, confidence itself becomes a humanitarian concern.

From other standpoints, attention to confidence and other dispositions, require educators to understand how those from oppressed groups invest emotionally in education, and how oppression is lived emotionally as well as socially. Following such arguments, educators need to recognize and address the ways in which the 'psychic landscapes of class and gender' manifest themselves in the constant, embodied and felt experiences of everyday inequality, both inside and outside everyday classroom practices and curriculum content (e.g. Reay, 2005; Leathwood and Hey, 2009).

Outside sociological accounts, policy texts, such as the *Learning Age* cited above, both fuel and reinforce a tendency in everyday accounts to extrapolate the effects of a lack of confidence and related dispositions from specific examples into generalizations, both about certain educational experiences and about the responses of disadvantaged or excluded groups to those experiences. In this vein, it is commonplace to depict whole groups deemed to be working class, or 'non-traditional' adult students, or those who have experienced failure or been disaffected from, or negative about, formal schooling as lacking confidence and self-esteem and to need emotionally focused interventions (e.g. Ecclestone, 2010, chapter 5; Gillies, 2011).

Changing the subject

The arguments summarized so far raise the status of confidence, and the corresponding role of 'learning' in developing it, into a fundamental social and political concern. The implication is that pupils and students simply cannot learn unless they are confident and teachers cannot damage confidence, be cavalier about it, or leave it to chance. Instead, it becomes a preoccupation and a focus for direct attention. In the light of expectations placed on it, confidence can no longer be a by-product or an incidental consideration for classroom activities and teacher/student relationships. Instead, lack of confidence becomes an emotional or psychological need, then a disposition, skill or capability that can be taught and learned through particular pedagogies and then a formal educational goal and outcome. From all these perspectives, confidence acquires a high-stakes curriculum status. In response to such arguments, I focus in this section on two implications for types of curriculum knowledge seen to be valuable, and for the wider significance of CfE in debates about worthwhile knowledge.

Blurring personal, everyday and subject knowledge

Social and educational concerns that encourage direct attention to understanding 'needs' and identifying barriers to learning and achievement are inseparable from injunctions to change the curriculum by blurring the boundaries between formal pedagogy, subject content and everyday knowledge. This blurring is evident in growing numbers of education systems where scepticism about the relevance of traditional subject-based knowledge, and concern about inequalities are reinforced by constructivist ideas that shift attention and interest to processes, practices and meanings of identity and learning. From a constructivist perspective, teachers and learners need to consider and discuss together how processes and 'communities of practice' shape identity, how meanings are 'co-constructed' and how coming to know oneself transforms or hinders 'identity' (e.g. Lave and Wenger, 2001). Here, identity is a symbiotic process of self-awareness (or 'reflexivity') and 'becoming' where knowledge and pedagogy focus on the self and its participation within particular communities, rather than on externally given, disciplinary knowledge (see Young, 2008; Baldwin, 2010; Rata, 2012).

The popularity of constructivist ideas that regard authentic meanings and content of learning as derived from experiences outside educational settings, rather than from formal subject knowledge and associated pedagogies, contributes to the elevation of confidence and other affective dimensions as essential for learning, identity and achievement. In a critique of the ways in which constructivism and other learner-centred views of knowledge influence curriculum organization and associated pedagogy, Elizabeth Rata argues that contemporary emphasis on social and personal experience as the means, content and source of knowledge means that:

> such knowledge becomes not only a pedagogical resource but also the main resource for the curriculum. At that point curriculum and pedagogy are treated as the same process . . . the common theme in constructivism that shows this collapse of curriculum into pedagogy is [that] 'knowledge is not fixed and waiting to be acquired, and it cannot be organised into logical sequences that can be directly imparted to passive students. Instead students must be active in knowledge development. The constructivist perspective is that learning is a process of interpreting and organising information and experiences into meaningful units, transforming old conceptions and constructing new ones. (Golding quoted by Rata, 2012, p. 104)

Following this argument, developments explored so far take this collapse of curriculum into pedagogy further, through the collapse of both curriculum and pedagogy into personal experience and knowledge. This turns personal knowledge and emotional reactions to being required to learn knowledge outside oneself, to learn about an external rather than an internal world, into 'curricula' in their own right. Critics of the effects of these doubts on the organization of curriculum and pedagogy point to widespread agreement in the humanities, social sciences and science that there is no such thing as objective knowledge, that knowledge is no more than a social or cultural construction, that we are all 'learners' rather than 'teachers' and 'students', or that knowledge is an elitist, oppressive imposition of cultural forms of power (e.g. Young, 2008; Baldwin, 2010; Rata, 2012).

A curriculum such as CfE therefore creates new versions of old questions and divisions about what counts as important or useful knowledge. Some argue that without a commitment to realist forms of truth and knowledge, education is prone to prevailing political fashions and competing advocacy of particular skills and capabilities that erode boundaries between formal education and everyday life (e.g. Young, 2008; Furedi, 2011; Rata, 2012). Following this argument, schools not only become unable to provide children with a solid foundation of past and present knowledge as a basis for future knowledge, but they encourage the incursion of ideological fads, politically motivated pressures and associated vested interests. Notwithstanding these criticisms, CfE and earlier English attempts to elevate the status of 'personal and thinking skills' in the school curriculum suggest that the force of agreement is on the other side of such arguments.

Continuity or change?

The CfE and the English Government's review of the National Curriculum in 2011 therefore both respond to disagreements about process versus content, different views about 'relevant' or 'powerful' knowledge and pessimism about engagement and motivation. In some respects, the English report shelved by the Coalition government acknowledges tensions directly, arguing for a curriculum that supports personal empowerment, where individuals can develop as 'healthy, balanced and self-confident', subject knowledge, citizenship and employability:

> Some educationalists emphasise subject knowledge and discount the significance of more developmental aspects of education. There are also many who foreground the development of skills, competencies and dispositions whilst asserting that contemporary knowledge changes so fast that 'learning how to learn' should be prioritised. . . . We do not believe that these are either/or questions. Indeed, it is impossible to conceptualise 'learning to learn' independently of learning 'something'. Our position is therefore that both elements – knowledge and development – are essential and that policy instruments need to be deployed carefully to ensure that these are provided for within education. (DfE, 2011, pp. 19–20)

Of course, there have been political questions throughout the United Kingdom about purpose, content, methods and outcomes, and responsibility for defining and controlling them, for well over a hundred years. Numerous major reviews of primary and secondary subjects since 1945, and older struggles over the role of education in redressing social, economic and personal ills, have raised questions about the relevance and appropriateness of various forms of pedagogy, subject content and assessment. For some critics, the curriculum has hardly changed for decades (e.g. White, 2007; Johnson et al., 2009). Assurances in both Scotland and England that 'good' education develops competences and dispositions alongside and as part of curriculum knowledge might indicate that continuity rather than change is the hallmark of these recurring debates.

Nevertheless, I would argue that it is a mistake to regard contemporary disaffection with the curriculum and corresponding calls for a dispositions-based approach as new manifestations of old debates. Instead, I have aimed to show that such a view overlooks a profound and relatively recent crisis of pessimism about children and young people which also reflects its proponents' own lack of confidence about how to engage and motivate people in formal education, and particularly in learning through subject disciplines. In contrast to older forms of pessimism that focused on those who could not or would not achieve, their contemporary manifestation applies to a much wider range of children and young people. Arguably, this important imperative for the new educational and social status of confidence and other affective dimensions legitimizes calls for them to be taught and assessed. In CfE, the effect is to silence questions about what curriculum knowledge should be the focus for participation and engagement, and what forms of knowledge children and young people should be confident in acquiring and using (for a similar conclusion with regard to the domain of citizenship see Biesta, this volume). Arguably again, it is the hollowing out of subject content that renders attributes such as confidence, collaboration and independence into mantras, thereby allowing them to become impervious to critique.

The effects of an 'emotional' subject on curriculum priorities and practices

Confidence as a subject

My arguments so far suggest that confidence has become far more significant than an essential yet incidental by-product of curriculum organization, teaching and learning, or a seemingly obvious factor in classroom dynamics and is currently even more significant than a disposition that must be embedded and developed through a subject curriculum. Instead, the elevation of confidence symbolizes changing meanings of two types of 'subject'. First is the human subject, namely the social and individual factors believed to comprise the universal essence of humans in relation to our ability to understand and then change an internal world (a sense of self, as well as emotional and psychological responses to an external world) and an external world. I have argued elsewhere that the human subject is seen increasingly in education as emotionally and psychologically vulnerable and therefore in need of psychological intervention and emotional support (e.g. Ecclestone, 2011, 2012; see also McLaughlin, 2011). Second is the curriculum subject which generates disputes about what is or should be the foundation for particular forms of knowledge, how those forms of knowledge depict human experience, and how they offer or prevent access to what Young calls 'powerful knowledge', through concepts, ways of thinking and a common language (Young, 2008; see also Furedi, 2011; Rata, 2012).

In a context where boundaries between externally oriented knowledge and the everyday, emotional and commonplace worlds of individuals have become increasingly blurred, both meanings of the subject are simultaneously more emotive and emotional. As I observed above, confidence becomes an emotional subject because it is depicted as a psychological or emotional need. It is also emotive because it becomes a formal target with an associated set of practices, classroom climates and relationships to promote it, and a measurable outcome. One effect of pessimism about traditional forms of knowledge is to turn the knowledge and pedagogies necessary for developing dispositions such as confidence into a curriculum subject in its own right.

However, beyond everyday examples and anecdote, there is no strong empirical evidence of the effect of these shifts and changing assumptions about the human and curriculum subject on teachers' priorities and values in responding to initiatives such as CfE. Conversely, lack of convincing evidence for the good effects of a dispositions-based curriculum does not hinder professional support for these shifts and assumptions. Recognizing that my critical propositions about the potential effects of making confidence an overt goal need systematic study, I focus here on three areas: hollowing out the curriculum subject; avoiding stress, anxiety and challenge; and creating new judgements and new forms of inequality.

Hollowing out the curriculum subject

A functional shift towards an educational system that can realize a much wider range of educational and social purposes, including the development of desirable dispositions such as confidence, is epitomized in arguments made by the Universities' Council for the Education of Teachers' (UCET) in response to the English Government's *Every Child Matters* (ECM) which required schools to adopt a dispositions-based response to children's well-being. Rejecting popular caricatures of teachers only interested in examinations and 'crowding heads with facts', UCET reassured them that subject study remains integral to education but that teachers need to 'adjust' the way in which allegiance to their subject affirms their specialist expertise. While depicting 'subjects [as] educational resources of remarkable power, offering unlimited scope for realising an enormous range of educational purposes . . .' (Kirk and Broadhead, 2007, p. 13), they load this 'enormous range' of purposes into subjects before arguing that:

> . . . the educational purpose of learning will depend on how resourcefully teachers will be able to draw on their subject knowledge base, and how readily they will jettison the monocular professional vision that is associated with blinkered use of the subject . . . in order to develop an extended professionalism that removes 'old dichotomies' between . . . teaching a subject and enabling pupils to learn how to learn, or even being a learning coordinator or consultant; between the cultivation of learners' achievements and fostering their well-being; and between personalisation and the promotion of high standards. (2007, pp. 14–15)

Yet a similar espoused commitment to subject knowledge in the objectives of CfE is not enough to counter a broader context of crisis and the extent to which curriculum subjects are already vehicles for skills and dispositions associated with health, well-being, citizenship and environmental awareness. These factors combine to shift teachers' priorities towards emotional and affective concerns. For example, emotional competence programmes such as PAThS use the biographies of famous contemporary and historical figures to foster dispositions and skills of empathy, to enable children to speculate about the person's strategies for problem-solving or resilience, or their levels of confidence in particular situations and how they might develop it. Other tasks require children to help each other to identify confidence-building strategies (e.g. Curtis and Northgate, 2007). In typical programmes that aim to foster 'learning to learn', discussed earlier in the introduction (or, in some schools, the demand for teachers to embed PELTS, namely 'personal, emotional, learning and thinking skills' into their lessons), teachers are encouraged to create activities and instruments for students to reflect on, assess and design strategies for overcoming stress or adversity, becoming confident and reflective, becoming more mindful or resilient, and for problem-solving (e.g. Swanson, 2012).

Of course, CfE does not imply that specific emotional competence programmes should be used and nor does it endorse their underpinning claims and assumptions. Nevertheless, whether as programmes or more general classroom strategies, an explicit focus on dispositions such as confidence raises important questions about how teachers should interpret demands to develop confident learners. For example, do increased levels of confidence transfer between situations? Does raised confidence come from these activities and, in turn, lead to mastery of knowledge, or is mastering knowledge or craft skills a springboard to confidence, making a direct focus on it an unhelpful diversion? Despite assertions that teachers should develop subject knowledge and dispositions simultaneously, a context of crisis about confidence turns the curriculum into a vehicle for the bits of relevant knowledge and associated opportunities to practise confidence. The overwhelming effect is to make everyone more preoccupied with it.

Avoiding stress and anxiety

In the face of powerful arguments that confidence is a cornerstone of social justice, employability, civic engagement and learning, it is very hard indeed for teachers to resist claims that growing numbers of their pupils and students lack confidence. Nor is it easy for them to question whether lack of confidence is a fundamental and profound threat to well-being. Instead, anecdotal evidence from my own and colleagues' teaching in a high status university, as well as from parents and colleagues in schools and further education colleges, suggests that elevating confidence makes teachers more worried about their own role in seeming to foster or hinder it. If this proposition is true, teachers' selection of curriculum content, pedagogies and assessment methods is informed by concern not to undermine confidence, thereby changing in subtle but powerful ways how teachers approach these interrelated roles. For example, anecdotal evidence suggests that this fear changes how teachers deal with students, including the levels of challenge, difficulty or unpleasantness they are prepared to let them experience, responses to expressions about a lack of confidence, decisions about when to intervene in uncomfortable feelings or when to accept their necessary role in learning difficult things, or dealing with difficult events, and the explicit attention and time they devote to confidence. These related dilemmas are exacerbated by routine advice for confidence-building techniques such as offering more praise than criticism, always ending feedback on a positive note, devoting teaching and study time for explicit reflection on confidence, and asking students to explore feelings that they lack confidence before attending to problems they might be having with subject knowledge and skills.

All these pressures and dilemmas make it difficult for teachers, parents and students, as well as curriculum, designers, to acknowledge that, while difficult curriculum content and the associated tedium and challenge of activities necessary to master it can undermine confidence (or even lead to feelings of shame), such feelings are not only often temporary but can also be a crucial spur to rise to the challenge. Conversely, dispositions such as confidence might sometimes be misplaced or ill-advised and, linked to self-esteem, might be undeserved or misleading. Both phenomena suggest that teachers should sometimes resist paying too much attention to it for certain students in certain situations or even ignore it altogether. At other times, injunctions that teachers must address students' expressions of barriers to confidence and design curriculum content and associated strategies for developing it can divert them from pushing students to focus on the subject knowledge or skills which are the route to confidence. Again, anecdotal evidence used above, suggests that teachers are becoming increasingly nervous about presenting students with challenging, difficult or stressful tasks, or imposing subject knowledge that is depicted increasingly as difficult, tedious or irrelevant. Even skilled teachers who are enthusiastic about their subject apologize defensively to students for these characteristics of subject knowledge (e.g. Ecclestone, 2010, chapter 3). I acknowledge that this evidence needs more extensive testing, not merely to see how widespread it is but also to identify possible countervailing tendencies.

Of course, if erosion of confidence is persistent or experienced too often, lack of direct attention to it might have long-term negative effects. For example, specific lack of mastery can endure into adulthood or contribute to a precarious 'learning identity' across different domains. Yet, however undesirable this is, claims that it can be avoided by placing confidence and related dispositions to the heart of the curriculum remain unproven. Unresolved questions about whether it is acquired or taught, and claims about its damaging effects and unmitigated power to transform, combine to raise the stakes for teachers even higher.

Ultimately, as other commentators on CfE also observe, the performative, target-driven institutional cultures in which teachers must implement CfE drive their responses to its demands (Humes, this volume). In addition, despite a progressive Scottish political rhetoric, similar pressures prevail in all the education systems of the United Kingdom (Priestley and Humes, 2010). In this context, when building confidence becomes a target in its own right, it becomes prone to the sort of strategic rule-playing that teachers and students need to master in order to remove uncertainty, risk of failure or disappointment and raise achievement. For example, in a recent study of assessment in universities and its role in learning, one lecturer argued that confidence is crucial for learning the rules of the assessment game that increasingly make achievement and success appear to be transparent and straightforward:

> Confidence. *It's about normalising [them] into the structure that we've got for them.* I think the ones that tend to get it are the ones who see it as almost a game, almost playing, finding the rules.... 'Once I know the rules, then I'm OK'.... My aim would be that when they did the exam, they would come out and say 'I was fine, I did that, I did everything I needed to know, and I know I've passed'. That's what I'd love them to be able to do, rather than coming out and saying 'God, I hope I've passed'. (Matthew in Ashgar, 2012, p. 213, my emphasis)

New judgements and inequalities?

I began this chapter by reflecting on how hard it is to challenge injunctions that developing confidence must be an explicit educational goal, where doing so is seen as churlish and negative, or even hard-hearted and reactionary. In response to these possible perceptions, I would argue that challenge to the effects of a dispositions-based curriculum on curriculum content, related pedagogy and teachers' values and beliefs is crucial, because these can create new forms of inequality. I highlight some examples here, noting again the need for further exploration to test the extent to which they are widespread, and the classroom and other cultural factors that might encourage (or discourage) them.

First, in everyday discourses and practices for certain groups of young people, slippery definitions of dispositions can lead to a growth in casual assessments of students' vulnerability, emotional and behavioural problems and interpretations of the subsequent social and educational risks they face (see Ecclestone, 2010, chapter 10; Gillies, 2011). In a similar vein, formal evaluations of programmes to develop dispositions as part of social and emotional competence elide loose assessments of conduct problems, disaffection from formal or group-based teaching, poor social skills, emotional difficulties and lack of 'emotional literacy' (e.g. Hallam, 2009; Challen et al., 2009; Lendrum et al., 2009). One effect is that assumptions about lack of confidence, low self-esteem and vulnerability come to be associated simplistically and patronizingly with shyness, boredom, disaffection and lack of academic ability. More powerfully, everyday assessments and their casual labels mirror the ways in which the policy texts discussed above present subject-free processes of 'learning' as the main route to self-confidence and thereby to social and educational advantage and inclusion. Although well-meaning, assessments that whole social and educational groups lack confidence can be both dismissive and essentializing, thereby limiting what teachers and young people see as possible (see Darmainen, 2003; Lingard, 2005; Rata, 2012).

Secondly, everyday judgements that connect poor levels or lack of confidence to other emotional or behavioural 'issues' can also create new power dynamics based on normative judgements of 'emotionally dysfunctional families' whose children need 'support' (e.g. DfES, 2005). In some schools, peers are drawn in to these judgements by being deemed to have 'excellent emotional self-regulation and social skills', or merely to 'be confident and well-behaved', and then selected to act as 'role models' or peer mentors to those seen not to have them (Lendrum et al., 2009; see also Ecclestone and Hayes, 2008, chapter 3). An unanticipated effect of regarding confidence and associated dispositions as 'capital' might therefore be to reproduce existing social advantages and create new ones.

Last, dispositions-based pedagogies and assessments resonate with older tendencies for some educators to respond to assumed or actual affective needs in ways that risk denying certain students intellectual capital (e.g. Ecclestone, 2011; Rata, 2012). For example, young people deemed to have emotional needs and to be difficult to teach in challenging and resource-constrained circumstances can experience pedagogy and a curriculum that, despite espoused commitment to subject-based knowledge, is designed simply to build self-esteem and demonstrate professionals' care for them (Darmainen, 2003). In a similar vein, research in Australian schools shows that prioritizing support and care over intellectual demand can deny certain students crucial forms of cultural capital while expecting them to acquire these forms of capital. Here Lingard argues that, by demanding from them what schools do not provide, educators subject disadvantaged students to socially unjust pedagogies (Lingard, 2005; see also Rata, 2012).

Conclusions

In many respects, calls to pay more attention to affective dimensions of learning are far from new. Yet regarding these calls merely as modern manifestations of old debates belies profound changes in the arguments to reshape outdated forms of curricula in favour of a dispositions-based approach. I have aimed to show that such arguments are linked inextricably to a growing tendency to regard human subjects as emotionally, psychologically, socially and educationally vulnerable. This presents schools and teachers as crucial, even indispensable, for redressing vulnerability and is inseparable from a wider sense of uncertainty about what education is for, and about what counts as appropriate curriculum content, teaching and assessment.

At the heart of this change are claims for the central importance of confidence and related dispositions to life and educational success, and corresponding arguments that teachers must foster it explicitly. This makes it extremely difficult to avoid the reduction of confidence to a teachable and assessable trait, skill or behaviour. A psychological interpretation of confidence joins self-esteem, emotional literacy, optimism, stoicism and resilience and emotional regulation in a long list of attributes and dispositions that educational settings must develop. In the English context, this psychologically rooted list is being incorporated easily in a political revival of an old discourse about character building (Ecclestone, 2012).

Following arguments in this chapter, a psychologically and emotionally rooted, high-stakes interpretation of the essential role of confidence in learning undermines rhetoric about the importance of subject knowledge. In contrast, I have proposed that this interpretation presents learning a body of worthwhile, inspiring knowledge as a route into a world outside oneself as not merely irrelevant and boring, but oppressive and damaging. Even support for subjects seems increasingly to be predicated on their function as instruments for 'delivering' dispositions such as confidence. One implication is that when confidence becomes seen as a cornerstone of 'personal/emotional or identity capital', educational achievement, social justice and human rights, or 'character', anything that does not develop it is, at best, irrelevant and de-motivating and, at worst, elitist and socially unjust. I have argued that presenting confidence in this profoundly ideological way changes teachers' priorities in interpreting reforms such as CfE and, in turn, their relationships with students. An unanticipated outcome is to make teachers uncertain about how to approach students and to regard them as vulnerable to or at risk from a lack of confidence. In turn, the labelling and assumptions that arise may create new forms of inequality in terms of what 'curriculum' is offered to particular groups and individuals. Blurring pedagogies to develop confidence with curriculum priorities and underpinning knowledge exacerbates this danger.

None of what I have argued in this chapter should suggest that teachers should not care about their students' confidence. I also reiterate here my earlier acknowledgements that more systematic evidence would test my propositions about the effects of elevating confidence into a high-stakes educational goal on teachers' practices and underlying values and priorities. Notwithstanding these caveats, if a characteristic of confidence is the ability to ask questions, educators need to marshal their own confidence in order to challenge the implications of this elevated status for curriculum priorities, practices and outcomes.

References

Ashgar, M. (2012), 'The lived experience of formative assessment in a British university'. *Journal of Further and Higher Education*, 36, 205–12.

Baldwin, S. (2010), *Teachers' and Students' Relationships with Knowledge: An Exploration of the Organisation of Knowledge within Disciplinary and Educational Contexts.* Unpublished PhD thesis, University of Lancaster.

Carr, M. (2001), *Assessment in Early Childhood Settings: Learning Stories.* London: Sage Books.

Challen, A., Noden, P., West, A. and Machin, S. (2011), *UK Resilience Programme Evaluation: Final Report.* London: London School of Economics and Political Science, for the Department for Education. Online at www.education.gov.uk/publications/ (accessed 04/10/12).

Claxton, G. (2002), *Building Learning Power.* Bristol: TLO Ltd.

— (2007), 'Cultivating positive learning dispositions', in H. Daniels, H. Lauder and J. Porter (eds), *The Routledge Companion to Education.* Routledge: London.

Curtis, C. and Norgate, R. (2007), 'An evaluation of the Promoting Alternative Thinking Strategies Curriculum at Key Stage 1'. *Educational Psychology in Practice*, 23, 33–44.

Darmainen, M. (2003), 'When students are failed: "love" as an alternative education discourse?' *International Journal of Sociology of Education*, 13, 141–70.

Department for Education (2011), *The Framework for the National Curriculum. A Report by the Expert Panel for the National Curriculum Review.* London: Department for Education.

Department for Education and Employment (1998), *The Learning Age: A Renaissance for a New Britain.* London: The Stationery Office.

Department for Education and Skills (2005), *Excellence and Enjoyment: Social and Emotional Aspects of Learning.* Nottingham: DfES Publications.

Duncan-Smith, I. and Allan, G. (2009), *Early Intervention: Good Parents, Great Kids, Better Citizens.* London: Centre for Social Justice/John Smith Institute.

Ecclestone, K. (2010), *Transforming Formative Assessment in Lifelong Learning: Principles and Practices.* Buckingham: Open University Press.

— (2011), 'Emotionally-vulnerable subjects and new inequalities: the educational implications of an "epistemology of the emotions"'. *International Studies in Sociology of Education*, 21, 91–113.

— (2012), 'From emotional and psychological well-being to character education: challenging policy discourses of behavioural science and "vulnerability"'. *Research Papers in Education*, Special edition on 'emotional well-being in education', 27, 463–80.

Ecclestone, K. and Hayes, D. (2008), *The Dangerous Rise of Therapeutic Education*. London: Routledge.

Furedi, F. (2009), *Wasted: Why Education is not Educating*. London: Continuum.

Gillies, V. (2011), 'Social and emotional pedagogies: critiquing the new orthodoxy of emotion in classroom and behaviour management'. *British Journal of Sociology of Education*, 32, 185–202.

Hallam, S. (2009), 'An evaluation of the Social and Emotional Aspects of Learning (SEAL) programme'. *Oxford Review of Education*, 35, 313–30.

Johnson, M., Ellis, N., Gotch, A., Ryan, A., Foster, C., Gillespie, J. and Lowe, M. (2007), *Subject to Change: New Thinking on the Curriculum*. London: Association of Teachers and Lecturers.

Kirk, G. and Broadhead, P. (2007), *Every Child Matters and Teacher Education: A UCET Position Paper*. London: UCET. Online at www.ucet.ac.uk/downloads/394.pdf (accessed 04/10/12).

Kristjánnson, K. (2012), 'Positive psychology and positive education: old wine in new bottles?' *Educational Psychologist*, 47, 86–105.

Lave, J. and Wenger, E. (1991), *Situated Learning: Legitimate Peripheral Participation*. Cambridge: Cambridge University Press

Layard, R. (2005), *Happiness: Lessons from a New Science*. London: Allen Lane

Leathwood, C. and Hey, V. (2009), 'Gender/ed discourses and emotional sub-texts: theorising emotion in UK higher education'. *Teaching and Learning in Higher Education*, 14, 429–40.

Leitch, R. (2008), *Children's Rights, Children's Voice and Assessment for Learning*. Keynote presentation to European Special Interest Assessment Group Bi-Annual Conference, Potsdam, Germany, 29–31 August 2008.

Lendrum, A., Humphrey, N., Kalambouka, A. and Wigelsworth, M. (2009), 'Implementing primary SEAL group interventions: recommendations for practitioners'. *Emotional and Behavioural Difficulties*, 14, 229–38.

Lingard, B. (2005), 'Socially-just pedagogies in changing times'. *International Journal of Sociology of Education*, 15, 165–85.

Lumby, J. (2012), 'Disengaged and disaffected young people: surviving the system'. *British Educational Research Journal*, 38, 261–79.

McLaughlin, K. (2011), *Surviving Identity: The Rise of The 'Survivor' in Contemporary Society*. London: Routledge.

Myers, K. (2012), 'Marking time: some methodological and historical perspectives the "crisis of childhood"'. *Research Papers in Education*, Special edition on 'emotional well-being in education', 27, 409–22.

OECD (2001), *The Well-Being of Nations: The Role of Human and Social Capital*. Paris: CERI/OECD.

— (2007), *Understanding the Social Outcomes of Learning*. Paris: CERI/OECD.

Priestley, M. and Humes, W. (2010), 'The development of Scotland's Curriculum for Excellence: amnesia and déjà vu'. *Oxford Review of Education*, 36, 345–61.

Rata, E. (2012), 'The politics of knowledge in education'. *British Educational Research Journal*, 38, 103–24.

Reay, D. (2005), 'Beyond consciousness? The psychic landscape of social class'. *Sociology*, 39, 911–28.

Sharples, J. (2007), *Report from All-Party Parliamentary Group: 'Well-Being in the Classroom'*, 27 October 2007, Portcullis House, London. Oxford: Institute for the Future of the Mind.

Social Exclusion Unit (1999), *Bridging the Gap: New Opportunities for 16–19 Year Olds Not in Education or Training*. London: SEU.

Sodha, S. and Guglielmi, S. (2009), *A Stitch in Time: Tackling Educational Disengagement*. London: DEMOS.

Swanson, P. (2012), *Embedding Social Emotional Learning in Mathematics Education for Teachers*. Paper presented at the Annual Meeting of the American Educational Research Association, Vancouver Convention Centre, 16–19 April 2012.

Taylor, M. (2008), *The Rocky Road to Emotional Well-being*. Presentation to ESRC Seminar Series, Changing the subject? Interdisciplinary perspectives on emotional well-being and social justice, Oxford Brookes University, 7 December 2008.

Weare, K. (2004), *Developing the Emotionally Literate School*. London: Paul Chapman.

White, J. (2007), *What Schools Are For and Why*, IMPACT Pamphlet No 14 (London: Philosophy of Education Society of Great Britain).

Young, M. (2008), *Bringing Knowledge Back In: From Social Constructivism to Social Realism in the Sociology of Education*. London: Routledge.

— (2010), 'Alternative educational futures for a knowledge society'. *European Educational Research Journal*, 9, 1, 1–12.

6

Responsible Citizens: Citizenship Education between Social Inclusion and Democratic Politics

Gert Biesta

Introduction

The Scottish Curriculum for Excellence (CfE) lists 'responsible citizenship' as one of the four capacities which it envisages that all children and young people should develop. In the 2004 *A Curriculum for Excellence* document (Scottish Executive, 2004) responsible citizens are depicted as individuals who have 'respect for others', have a 'commitment to participate responsibly in political, economic, social and cultural life', and who are able to 'develop knowledge and understanding of the world and Scotland's place in it; understand different beliefs and cultures; make informed choices and decisions; evaluate environmental, scientific and technological issues; [and] develop informed, ethical views of complex issues' (ibid., p. 12). Scotland has not been unique in its attempt to put citizenship on the educational agenda (see, for example, Biesta, 2011), although compared to other countries it can actually be said to have been rather late in doing this (see Andrews and Mycock, 2007). The main aims of this chapter are to analyse and characterize the conception of citizenship education articulated in the context of CfE and to locate this conception within the wider literature on education, citizenship and democracy. This will make it possible to investigate the assumptions informing the Scottish approach and to highlight the choices made. The view on citizenship pursued in the context of CfE is, after all, not neutral or inevitable – it is not something that 'just is' (Ross and Munn, 2008,

p. 270) – but rather represents a particular position within the available spectrum of conceptions of democratic citizenship and citizenship education.

Citizenship education in Scotland: The socio-historical context

In a recent reconstruction of the history of citizenship education in Scotland, Munn and Arnott (2009, p. 437) argue that 'the distinctive policy environment in Scotland' has significantly 'shaped approaches to citizenship education'. This policy environment has itself been shaped by 'a "Scottish myth" about the purpose of education', one that sees education as being 'for the public good as much as for private advantage' (ibid., p. 438). While the 'Scottish myth' may not be entirely or straightforwardly true – there was indeed early and extensive educational provision which was in principle open for all, but there were also significant inequalities and limitations to access – it did provide and has continued to provide a strong rhetorical point of reference for highlighting the distinctiveness of the educational climate in Scotland. McCrone (quoted in Munn and Arnott, 2009, p. 439), for example, describes the rhetorical force of the 'Scottish myth' as follows: 'It lends support to the conservative seeking assurance that existing institutions are for the best; while for the nationalists it provides a vision of Scotland which is democratic and different from its southern neighbour; and for socialists it confirms the radical predispositions of Scotland'.

Munn and Arnott highlight two distinctive characteristics of the Scottish school system as it developed in the second half of the twentieth century. The first is the strong presence of comprehensive schools. The 1965 'Circular 600' suggested 'only one form of organisation: the six-year all-through fixed-catchment school for ages 12 to 18' (ibid., p. 440). This resulted in a school system that was much more uniform in its approach and less segregated in its population than schools in England. In 1965, for example, already 20 per cent of schools in Scotland were comprehensive, but only 4 per cent in England. This and subsequent reforms put an emphasis on a 'broad and balanced curriculum' to the extent to which 'attempts to introduce vocational education in various guises, or twin-tracked provision dividing the "academic" from the "non-academic" pupils, have not succeeded' (ibid., p. 441). 'Curricular distinctiveness' (ibid.) is the other defining characteristic of the Scottish system and here Nunn and Arnott particularly highlight the uniquely Scottish subject of Modern Studies (see also Ross and Munn, 2008). This subject was introduced in 1959 and blended 'social, economic and political approaches in studying Scottish, British and international issues', thus being an important location for the study of issues pertaining to citizenship and democracy.

Munn and Arnott show that citizenship 'featured prominently in debates about constitutional reform across the UK' and that, in Scotland, 'arguments for political devolution intensified following the 1987 General Election' (Munn and Arnott, 2009, p. 442). The establishment of the devolved Scottish Parliament in 1999 did indeed provide an important impetus for citizenship education. Early on, the Scottish Executive (which in 2007 started to refer to itself as the Scottish Government) announced five National Priorities for schools in Scotland. Priority number 4 focused on values and citizenship and 'echoed developments in England' but 'with a distinctively Scottish interpretation, not least the emphasis on *education for citizenship*, rather than citizenship education' (Blee and McClosky, 2003, p. 3).

In 1999 the Scottish Executive and the *Scottish Consultative Council on the Curriculum* (later to become *Learning and Teaching Scotland* and since then integrated into *Education Scotland*) set up a working group to focus on education for citizenship. The group produced a discussion and consultation paper in 2000 (LTScotland, 2000) and a more detailed paper 'for discussion and development' in 2002 (LTScotland, 2002). The then Minister for Education and Young People endorsed the latter paper 'as the basis for a national framework for education for citizenship from 3 to 18' and commended it 'for adoption and use in ways appropriate to local needs and circumstances' (ibid., p. 2). In 2003 Her Majesty's Inspectorate for Education (HMIE) published a follow-up document intended to assist schools in evaluating the quality and effectiveness of their provision for education for citizenship (HMIE, 2003).

Learning and Teaching Scotland's 2002 paper *Education for Citizenship in Scotland* is, in my view, the most central publication of this list, not only because it is the most detailed in its account of what citizenship is and how education can contribute to the development of the capacity for citizenship, but also because it became the official framework for further developments in the field. The contributions of HMIE are, however, also important, most notably because of the fact that education for citizenship in Scotland is driven by broad intentions rather than specified curricular input. As a result the Inspectorate is likely to have a much stronger influence on educational practice as it needs to judge the quality of many different operationalizations of the intentions. The *A Curriculum for Excellence* document occupies a middle position. It is less detailed on citizenship than the 2002 *Education for Citizenship* paper. Its specific interpretation of earlier documents is nonetheless significant because of its role as a framework for Scottish education from 3 to 18. What is the particular view on citizenship and education for citizenship that emerges from these documents?

Characterizing citizenship and citizenship education

The foreword to the 2002 *Education for Citizenship* document states 'that young people should be enabled to develop capability for thoughtful and responsible participation in political, economic, social and cultural life' (LTScotland, 2002, p. 3). This depends on the development of four aspects: 'knowledge and understanding, skills and competence, values and dispositions and creativity and enterprise' (ibid.). This, in turn, is related to two 'core themes'. The first is the idea that 'young people learn most about citizenship by being active citizens' (ibid.). The second is that the development of capability for citizenship 'should be fostered in ways that motivate young people to be active and responsible members of their communities – local, national and global' (ibid.).

These points already reveal in a nutshell what I see as the four defining characteristics of the Scottish approach to education for citizenship. The first is that there is a strong **individualistic tendency** in the approach, exemplified in the fact that citizenship is depicted as a capacity or capability, based upon a particular set of knowledge, skills and dispositions and understood in terms of individual responsibility and choice. The second is that the approach is based on a **broad conception of the domain of citizenship**, encompassing political, economic, social and cultural life. The third is the emphasis on **activity**, both with regard to the exercise of citizenship and with regard to the ways in which citizenship can be learned. The fourth is a strong emphasis on the (idea of) **community**.

Citizenship: individualistic more than collective

The individualistic take on citizenship and citizenship education is clearly exemplified in the 2002 Education for Citizenship document. It opens by saying that '(s)chools and other educational establishments have a central part to play in educating young people for life as active and responsible members of their communities' (LTScotland, 2002, p. 6), thus reiterating the idea that citizenship resides first and foremost in a personal responsibility. The document depicts citizenship responsibility as the corollary of citizenship rights. Citizenship involves 'enjoying rights and exercising responsibilities' and these 'are reciprocal in many respects' (ibid., p. 8). The document emphasizes that young people should be regarded 'as citizens of today rather than citizens in waiting', an idea linked to the *UN Convention on the Rights of the Child* which states that children 'are born with rights' (ibid.). The individualistic tendency is also visible in the overall goal of citizenship education which 'should aim to develop capability for thoughtful and responsible participation in political, economic, social and cultural life', a capability which is considered to be rooted in '*knowledge and understanding,* in a range of *generic skills and competences,* including "core skills," and in a variety of *personal qualities and dispositions*' (ibid., p. 11; emphasis in original).

The document seems to hint at a distinction between necessary and sufficient conditions for citizenship, arguing, for example, that 'being a capable citizen' is not just about possessing knowledge and skills but also about 'being able and willing to use knowledge and skills to make decisions and, where appropriate, take action' (ibid.). Capability for citizenship is therefore said to depend on a number of literacies: social, economic and cultural and also political (see ibid.). Along these lines the document pursues a common way of thinking about the possibilities of education for citizenship, namely one in which it is argued that education can work on (some of) the necessary conditions for citizenship, but, on its own, will never be sufficient for the development of effective and involved citizenship. This is why 'the contributions of formal education need to be seen alongside, and in interaction with, other influences' from, for example, 'parents, carers and the media and opportunities for community-based learning' (ibid., pp. 9–10).

The 2002 *Education for Citizenship* document analyses the capability for citizenship in terms of four related outcomes which are all seen as aspects or attributes of individuals.

1. *Knowledge and understanding* is concerned with 'the need to base opinions, views and decisions on relevant knowledge and on a critical evaluation and balanced interpretation of evidence' (ibid., p. 12). Knowledgeable citizens are aware 'of the complexities of the economic, ethical and social issues and dilemmas that confront people' and 'have some knowledge of political, social, economic and cultural ideas and phenomena' (ibid.).
2. Education for citizenship involves developing a range of *skills and competencies* 'that need to be developed along with various personal qualities such as self-esteem, confidence, initiative, determination and emotional maturity in order to be responsible and effective participants

in a community' (ibid., p. 13). Being skilled and competent means 'feeling empowered [and] knowing and valuing one's potential for positive action' (ibid.).
3. *Values and dispositions*: Education for citizenship also involves 'developing the ability to recognise and respond thoughtfully to values and value judgements that are part and parcel of political, economic, social and cultural life' (ibid.). Also, education can help to foster 'a number of personal qualities and dispositions rooted in values of respect and care for self, for others and for the environment' and promoting 'a sense of social responsibility' (ibid.).
4. Being an 'effective citizen' is also supposed to entail the capacity for 'thinking and acting creatively in political, economic, social and cultural life' and 'being enterprising in one's approach to participation in society' (ibid., p. 14).

Finally, the document mentions the need for the development of 'the integrative ability that is at the heart of effective and purposeful citizenship' (ibid.) so as to make sure that the four outcomes are not developed in isolation.

While all this points towards a strong emphasis on individuals and on citizenship as an individual responsibility and capacity – something which is further exemplified by the strong emphasis on the development of values such as 'respect and care for people and a sense of social and environmental responsibility' (ibid., p. 11) – there are other aspects which point in a different direction. Most significant in this regard is a passage in which it is acknowledged that '(w)hilst all individuals share the rights and responsibilities of citizenship, regardless of status, knowledge or skill, it is clear that citizenship may be exercised with different degrees of effectiveness' (ibid., p. 9). Here, the document refers, for example, to homelessness as a factor which may impede (young) people from exercising their citizenship rights, just as 'poverty and other forms of disadvantage' may impact on the capacity for effective citizenship. The document therefore concludes that it is in the interest both of individuals and of society as a whole 'that rights and responsibilities of citizenship are well understood, that young people develop the capability needed to function effectively as citizens in modern society' and 'that structures are provided to enable them to do so' (ibid.). Within the 2002 *Education for Citizenship* document this is, however, one of the few places where the possibility of a structural dimension of citizenship – and by implication a responsibility for citizenship that does *not* lie with the individual but rather with the state – is being considered. The general thrust of the document, however, is on the individual and his or her actions and responsibilities.

This line of thinking is continued in the *A Curriculum for Excellence* document where 'responsible citizenship' figures as one of the four capacities which the curriculum from 3–18 should enable all children and young people to develop (Scottish Executive, 2004, p. 12). *A Curriculum for Excellence* reminds its readers that the words 'wisdom, justice, compassion and integrity . . . are inscribed on the mace of the Scottish Parliament' and that these 'have helped to define values for our democracy' (ibid., p. 11). Hence it is seen as 'one of the prime purposes of education to make our young people aware of the values on which Scottish society is based and so help them to establish their own stances on matters of social justice and personal and collective responsibility' (ibid.). Therefore, young people 'need to learn about and develop these values' (ibid.). To achieve this, the curriculum 'should emphasise the rights and responsibilities of individuals and nations', 'should help young people to understand diverse cultures and beliefs and support them in developing concern, tolerance, care and respect for themselves and others', 'must promote a commitment to considered judgement and ethical action' and 'should give young people the confidence, attributes and capabilities to make valuable contributions to society' (ibid.). Although the *A Curriculum for Excellence* document acknowledges what we might call the situated character of citizenship, its depiction as value-based, its articulation in terms of responsibility, respect and commitment to responsible participation, plus the fact that it is embedded in capacity-based conception of education, all highlight the strong individualistic tendency in the conception of citizenship and citizenship education.

The 2006 HMIE publication *Education for Citizenship* (HMIE, 2006) provides a view of citizenship and citizenship education which is even more strongly individualistic than what can be found in the documents mentioned above. This is first of all because the HMIE document argues that the other three capacities of the CfE framework – confident individuals, effective contributors and successful learners – are a precondition, or at least an important part of the development of the capacity for responsible citizenship (see ibid., p. 1). Secondly, it is because the HMIE document gives a prominent position to the development of citizenship *skills* which, by their very nature, are 'tied' to the individual. Thirdly, the HMIE document presents education for citizenship as a form of values education (see ibid., p. 3), and in this context emphasizes the importance of the development of personal values which, in the document, encompass political, social, environmental and spiritual values (see ibid.). Finally, the document emphasizes that education for citizenship 'must enable learners to become critical and independent thinkers' (ibid.), something which it also links to the development of 'life skills' (ibid.).

The domain of citizenship: Social more than political

Whereas the conception of citizenship as an individual capacity based upon responsible action of individuals is clearly individualistic, and whereas the emphasis of the educational efforts on the development of knowledge, skills and dispositions has a strong focus on individuals and their traits and attributes as well, this is mitigated within the Scottish approach by a strong emphasis on the need for experiential learning within the domain of citizenship. All documents agree that the best way to learn citizenship is 'through experience and interaction with others' because 'learning about citizenship is best achieved by being an active citizen' (LTScotland, 2002, p. 10). This idea is one of the main reasons why the approach proposed in the document 'does not involve the creation of a new subject called "citizenship education"' (ibid., p. 16). Instead, the document takes the view 'that each young person's entitlement to education for citizenship can be secured through combinations of learning experiences set in the daily life of the school, discrete areas of the curriculum, cross-curricular experiences and activities involving links with the local community' (ibid.). The ethos of education for citizenship is therefore explicitly 'active' and 'participatory' and based on opportunities for 'active engagement' (ibid.). This view, which is further supported by the idea that young people should be regarded 'as citizens of today rather than citizens in waiting' (ibid., p. 8), does, however, raise the question about the kind of communities and activities considered to be relevant for citizenship learning. What, in other words, is considered to be the domain for citizenship and, hence, for education for citizenship and citizenship learning?

Most documents denote this domain in broad terms. The 2002 *Education for Citizenship* document speaks about 'thoughtful and responsible participation in political, economic, social and cultural life' (ibid., p. 11). A similar phrase is used in *A Curriculum for Excellence* where responsible citizens are individuals with a commitment 'to participate responsibly in political, economic, social and cultural life' (Scottish Executive, 2004, p. 12). This is echoed in the HMIE document where the purpose of education for citizenship is described as 'to prepare young people for political, social, economic, cultural and educational participation in society' (HMIE, 2006, p. 2). Whereas several of the documents include questions about the environment in their conception of the domain of citizenship, the HMIE document is the only document which makes mention of spiritual values alongside political, social and environmental values as the set of values that education for citizenship should seek to promote (see ibid., p. 3). A reference to religion is, however, remarkably absent in the documents.

The broad conception of the citizenship domain represents a clear choice on behalf of the authors of the 2002 *Education for Citizenship* document. The document starts from the assumption that everyone belongs to various types of community, 'both communities of place, from local to global, and communities of interest, rooted in common concern or purpose' (LTScotland, 2002, p. 8). Against this background citizenship is said to involve 'enjoying rights and responsibilities in these various types of community' (ibid.). The document then adds that this way of seeing citizenship 'encompasses the specific idea of political participation by members of a democratic state' but it also includes 'the more general notion that citizenship embraces a range of participatory activities, not all overtly political, that affect the welfare of communities' (ibid.). Examples of the latter type of citizenship include 'voluntary work, personal engagement in local concerns such as neighbourhood watch schemes or parent-teacher associations, or general engagement in civic society' (ibid.).

What is important here is that citizenship *encompasses* participation in political processes but is not confined to it. Thus, the Scottish approach is based on what we might call a *social* rather than an exclusively political conception of citizenship, one which understands citizenship in terms of membership of and concern for the many communities that make up people's lives. This includes the more narrowly political domain of citizenship, but extends to civil society and potentially includes any community. The question this raises is what the role of the political dimension in the Scottish conception of citizenship actually is. This not only has to do with the extent to which citizenship is related to questions about the (democratic) quality of collective decision-making, but also concerns questions about the relationships between citizens, the relationships between citizens and the state and the role of the state more generally in relation to its citizens. It is at this point that the documents begin to diverge.

The 2002 *Education for Citizenship* document is the most explicit about the political dimensions of and rationale for education for citizenship. It explicitly links the need for education for citizenship to the 'advent of the Scottish Parliament' which has encouraged a 'fresh focus' on the importance of people living in Scotland 'being able to understand and participate in democratic processes' (LTScotland, 2002, p. 6). Here citizenship is connected to the functioning of a democratic society and education for citizenship is brought in connection with concerns about 'disaffection and disengagement from society' (ibid.). It is therefore concluded that education 'has a key role to play in fostering a modern democratic society, whose members have a clear sense of identity and belonging, feel empowered to participate effectively in their communities and recognise their roles and responsibilities as global citizens' (ibid., p. 7). The need for education for citizenship is also linked to the development of 'a healthy and vibrant culture of democratic participation' (ibid., p. 9) and within this context the document emphasizes the need for understanding 'that perceptions of rights and responsibilities by individuals in different social groups are sometimes in conflict' (ibid., p. 8), so that education for citizenship must help young people 'develop strategies for dealing effectively with controversy' (ibid., p. 9). This is explicitly linked to democratic skills and dispositions such as 'negotiation, compromise, awareness of the impact of conflict on the overall wellbeing of the community and the environment, and development of well-informed respect for differences between people' (ibid.).

Awareness of the political dimensions of citizenship is also clear in the description of the 'knowledge and understanding' dimension of education for citizenship as this includes knowledge and understanding of 'the rights and responsibilities underpinning democratic societies; opportunities for individuals and voluntary groups to bring about social and environmental change, and the values on which such endeavours are based; (. . .) the causes of conflict and possible approaches to resolving it, recognising that controversy is normal in society and sometimes has beneficial effects' (ibid., p. 12). The 'values and dispositions' outcome makes mention of a disposition to 'develop informed and reasoned opinions about political, economic, social and environmental issues' and a disposition to 'understand and value social justice, recognising that what counts as social justice is itself contentious' (ibid., p. 14). When the document begins to address 'effective education for citizenship in practice' (ibid., pp. 16–31) the emphasis on the more political dimensions of citizenship begins to be replaced by a conception of citizenship as having to do with inclusive and participatory ways of social interaction in a range of communities. Here, citizenship begins to veer towards active involvement in environmental projects and community service – a form of 'good deeds' citizenship – where the political dimension and purpose seem to have become largely absent.

Although the *A Curriculum for Excellence* document is shorter and far more general than the *Education for Citizenship* paper, and although, as I have shown above, it does locate questions about citizenship within a wider, political context, its articulation of the abilities involved in responsible citizenship lacks an explicit political and democratic dimension and is predominantly at the social end of the spectrum. Responsible citizens are depicted as individuals who have 'respect for others' and a 'commitment to participate responsibly in political, economic, social and cultural life' and who are able to 'develop knowledge and understanding of the world and Scotland's place in it; understand different beliefs and cultures; make informed choices and decisions; evaluate environmental, scientific and technological issues; [and] develop informed, ethical views of complex issues' (Scottish Executive, 2004, p. 12).

The emphasis on the social dimensions of citizenship is even more prominent in the HMIE *Education for Citizenship* document. Although some reference to democratic processes, the Scottish Youth Parliament and issues 'such as social justice and human rights' is made, citizenship is depicted predominantly in relation to society at large, with a strong emphasis on the involvement of pupils in decision-making at school level and, to a lesser extent, the wider community (see HMIE, 2006). This reveals that from the perspective of HMIE the school is seen as the most relevant and prominent citizenship domain and the most important citizenship 'modus' is that of active involvement and participation. What is mostly lacking is a connection of citizenship with the political domain, both in terms of the 'scope' of citizenship and in terms of the way in which relevant learning processes are understood and depicted. The HMIE document thus represents a strong emphasis on the social dimensions of citizenship and is therefore even more strongly located at the social end of the citizenship spectrum.

Active citizenship: Where and what kind of activity?

Although the social dimension of citizenship and an emphasis on participation and active involvement are not unimportant for the development of citizenship knowledge and dispositions, and although an emphasis on the social dimensions of citizenship is definitely important for the preservation and maintenance of civil society, an almost exclusive emphasis on these aspects runs the danger that the political dimensions of citizenship, including an awareness of the limitations of personal responsibility for effective political action and change, remain invisible and become unattainable for children and young people. There is the danger, in other words, that citizenship becomes de-politicized and that, as a result, students are not sufficiently empowered to take effective political action in a way that goes beyond their immediate concerns and responsibilities.

There is a similar danger with regard to the third aspect of the Scottish approach: the strong emphasis on activity and active citizenship. On the one hand, the idea of active citizenship is important and significant, both with regard to understanding what citizenship is and entails and with regard to citizenship learning. After all, the most significant citizenship learning that takes place in the lives of young people is the learning that follows from their actual experiences and their actual 'condition' of citizenship (see Biesta, 2011). These experiences, which are part of the lives they lead inside and outside of the school, can be said to form the real citizenship curriculum for young people, which shows the crucial importance of opportunities for positive experiences with democratic action and decision-making in all aspects of young people's lives. In this regard it is indeed true that 'young people learn most about citizenship by being active citizens' (LTScotland, 2002, p. 3). But the crucial question here is what young people's active citizenship actually entails.

As I have already argued in the previous section, this depends partly on the domain in which citizenship activity is exercised. But it also depends on the nature of the activity. In this regard it is important not to lose sight of the specific history of the idea of active citizenship, which was introduced by conservative governments in the late 1980s and early 1990s as a way to let citizens take care of what used to be the responsibility of the government under welfare state conditions (see Faulks, 1998). While it is difficult to argue against active citizenship, it is important, therefore, to be precise about the nature of the activity and the domain in which the activity is exercised. Active citizenship in itself can either operate at the social or at the political end of the citizenship spectrum and can therefore either contribute to politicization and the development of political literacy, or be basically a- or non-political. Given the different views on the domain of citizenship it is, therefore, not entirely clear how political and how enabling active citizenship within the Scottish context will be, although the tendency seems to be on a form of active citizenship located towards the social end of the citizenship spectrum.

Community: A community of sameness more than a community of difference

The fourth and final characteristic of the Scottish approach to citizenship and education for citizenship is a strong emphasis on community. It is, perhaps, significant that in the 2002 *Education for Citizenship* document the word 'community' is used 76 times and the word 'communities' 31 times, while the word 'democratic' is used 9 times and the word 'democracy' only once. The 2002 *Education for Citizenship* document, as I have already mentioned, opens by saying that '[s]chools and other educational establishments have a central part to play in educating young people for life as active and responsible members of their communities' (LTScotland, 2002, p. 6). The point I wish to raise here is not about the fact that citizenship is depicted in relation to (local, and sometimes also global) communities, but concerns the particular way in which communities are conceived within the documents. In all documents 'community' is used as an unproblematic notion and generally also as a positive notion. The documents speak about young people and *their* communities, suggesting not only that it is clear what these communities are, but also suggesting that young people's membership of these communities is obvious and taken for granted. An important question, however, is what actually constitutes a community and what the difference might be between a social, a cultural and a political community.

Within the literature on communities there is a strong tendency to think of communities in terms of sameness, commonality and identity (see Biesta, 2004). This may be true for many cultural and, perhaps to a lesser extent, social communities – and it seems to be the conception of community implied in most of what the documents have to say about community. But whereas cultural and social communities may display a strong sense of commonality and sameness, this is not how we should understand *political* communities. One could argue – and many political philosophers have argued this point – that the very purpose of politics, and more specifically democratic politics, is to deal in one way or another with the fact of plurality, with the fact that individuals within society have different conceptions of the good life, different values and different ideas about what matters to them. Ultimately, political communities are therefore communities of plurality and difference, and it is precisely here that the difficulty of 'political existence' (Biesta, 2010) is located. Whereas, as I have shown in my discussion of the domain of citizenship, there is some awareness within the documents, particularly the earlier parts of the 2002 *Education for Citizenship* document, of the particular nature of political communities and political existence – most notably in the recognition of the plurality of perceptions of rights and responsibilities (see LTScotland, 2002, pp. 8–9) – the predominant conception of community in the documents is that of the community as a community of sameness (for a similar conclusion see Ross and Munn, 2008).

Is the responsible citizen a democratic citizen?

So far I have tried to characterize the particular take on citizenship and citizenship education that has been developed in Scotland over the past decade. The question

I wish to address in this section focuses on the choices made or implied in this approach, which will allow me to connect the analysis of the Scottish case with the wider literature on education, citizenship and democracy. The question is what kind of citizenship is actually represented in the proposals, frameworks and inspection documents and, in relation to this, what kind of conception of democracy is being pursued. In order to characterize the Scottish approach I will make use of a framework developed by Westheimer and Kahne which emerged from an analysis of citizenship education programmes in the United States (see Westheimer and Kahne, 2004). In their analysis Westheimer and Kahne make a distinction between three visions of citizenship to which they refer as the *personally responsible citizen*, the *participatory citizen* and the *justice-oriented citizen*. Each of these visions 'reflects a relatively distinct set of theoretical and curricular goals' (ibid., p. 241). Westheimer and Kahne emphasize that the three visions are *not* cumulative. 'Programs that promote justice-oriented citizens do not necessarily promote personal responsibility or participatory citizenship' (ibid.).

The *personally responsible citizen* 'acts responsibly in his or her community by, for example, picking up litter, giving blood, recycling, obeying laws, and staying out of debt' (ibid., p. 241). He or she 'contributes to food or clothing drives when asked and volunteers to help those less fortunate, whether in a soup kitchen or a senior centre' (ibid.). Thus, programmes that seek to develop personally responsible citizens, 'attempt to build character and personal responsibility by emphasizing honesty, integrity, self-discipline, and hard work' (ibid.).

Participatory citizens are those 'who actively participate in civic affairs and the social life of the community at the local, state, or national level' (ibid.). Proponents of this vision emphasize the importance of preparing students to engage in collective, community-based efforts. Educational programmes designed to support the development of participatory citizens 'focus on teaching students how government and community-based organizations work and training them to plan and participate in organized efforts to care for people in need or, for example, to guide school policies' (ibid., p. 242). Proponents of participatory citizenship argue 'that civic participation transcends particular community problems or opportunities [and that it] develops relationships, common understandings, trust and collective commitments [and thereby] adopts a broad notion of the political sphere' (ibid.).

Justice-oriented citizenship – 'the perspective that is least commonly pursued' (ibid.) – is based on the claim 'that effective democratic citizens need opportunities to analyze and understand the interplay of social, economic and political forces' (ibid.). Westheimer and Kahne refer to this approach as 'justice-oriented' because advocates of this approach call explicit attention 'to matters of injustice and to the importance of pursing social justice' (ibid.). They explain

> The vision of the justice-oriented citizen shares with the vision of the participatory citizen an emphasis on collective work related to the life and issues of the community. Its focus on responding to social problems and to structural critique makes it somewhat different, however [as they seek] to prepare students to improve society by critically analyzing and addressing social issues and injustices. (. . .) These programmes are less likely to emphasize the need for charity and voluntarism as ends in themselves and more likely to teach about social movements and how to effect systemic change. (Ibid.)

Westheimer and Kahne sum up the differences between the three approaches by suggesting that 'if participatory citizens are organizing the food drive and personally responsible citizens are donating food, justice-oriented citizens are asking why people are hungry and acting on what they discover' (ibid.).

When we look at the Scottish approach against this background, we can see elements of all three orientations. Yet what emerges from my reconstruction, so I wish to suggest, is that the conception of citizenship informing the Scottish approach is predominantly that of the personally responsible citizen. While there is also an emphasis on participation, I am inclined to understand this mainly as an educational 'strategy' – that is, on the assumption that it is through participation that children and young people develop the capacity for responsible citizenship – and less so as the indication of a different conception of citizenship. By mapping the Scottish approach onto the categories suggested by Westheimer and Kahne, it is possible to get a better understanding of the specific position presented in the documents analysed in this chapter. It makes it possible to see, in other words, that the Scottish approach represents a particular choice, and that other options are possible. The further question this raises is whether the choice presented in the Scottish approach is the 'best' choice. Answering this question all depends on how one wishes education for citizenship to function and, most importantly, in what way and to what extent one wishes education for citizenship to contribute to a particular – democratic – configuration of society. At this point I wish to briefly discuss some of the concerns raised by Westheimer and Kahne about the personally responsible citizen which, according to them, is actually the most popular approach (see ibid., p. 243).

Westheimer and Kahne argue that an emphasis on personal responsibility in citizenship is 'an inadequate response to the challenges of educating a democratic citizenry' (ibid.). The problem here is 'that the emphasis placed on individual character and behavior obscures the need for collective and public sector initiatives; that this emphasis distracts attention from analysis of the causes of social problems and from systematic solutions' and that 'voluntarism and kindness are put forward as ways of avoiding politics and policy' (ibid.) The main problem Westheimer and Kahne see is that while no one 'wants young people to lie, cheat, or steal', the values implied in the notion of the personally responsible citizen 'can be at odds with democratic goals' (ibid.). '(E)ven the widely accepted goals – fostering honesty, good neighborliness, and so on – are not *inherently* about democracy' (ibid., emphasis in original). While many of the values and traits enlisted in relation to the personally responsible citizen 'are desirable traits for people living in a community (...) they are not about democratic citizenship' (ibid.), so that '[t]o the extent that emphasis on these character traits detracts from other important democratic priorities, it may actually hinder rather than make possible democratic participation and change' (ibid.) To support their point, Westheimer and Kahne report on research that found that fewer than 32 per cent of eligible voters between the ages of 18 and 24 voted in the 1996 US presidential election, but that 'a whopping 94% of those aged 15–24 believed that "the most important thing I can do as a citizen is to help others"' (ibid.). In a very real sense, then, 'youth seems to be "learning" that citizenship does not require democratic governments, politics, and even collective endeavours' (ibid.).

Conclusions

In this chapter I have analysed the approach to citizenship and citizenship education that can be found in the documents informing the approach to citizenship education within the Scottish Curriculum for Excellence. I have not only tried to characterize the particular approach taken and the socio-historical context within which this approach has been developed, but have also tried to indicate what kind of citizenship – and hence what kind of citizen – can be said to be promoted through this particular approach. Although to a certain degree the documents that inform education for citizenship provide a balanced view, they articulate a view of citizenship education that focuses more on individual than on collective dimensions, more on a broad domain of social, cultural and political interaction than strictly on democratic politics, more on activity than on rights, and more on a community of sameness than on a community of difference. While in itself such choices are what they are, I have indicated that this way of articulating the challenges for education for citizenship runs the risk of making citizenship too much into a social experience – where the focus is on responsible behaviour – and too little into a democratic one. The risk, in other words, is that a too strong emphasis on personal responsibility, on individual capacities and abilities, and on personal values, dispositions and attitudes not only runs the risk of *depoliticizing* citizenship by seeing it mainly as a personal and social phenomenon, but also runs the risk of not doing enough to empower young people as *political* actors who have an understanding both of the opportunities and the limitations of individual political action, and who are aware that real change – change that affects structures rather than operations within existing structures – often requires collective action and initiatives from other bodies, including the state. As Westheimer and Kahne emphasize, the individualistic conception of personally responsible citizenship rarely raises questions about 'corporate responsibility . . . or about ways that government policies can advance or hinder solutions to social problems' and therefore tends to ignore 'important influences such as social movements and government policy on efforts to improve society' (ibid., p. 244). An exclusive emphasis on personally responsible citizenship 'apart from analysis of social, political, and economic contexts' may therefore well be 'inadequate for advancing democracy' (ibid.). The main reason for this is that there is actually 'nothing inherently *democratic* about personally responsible citizenship', so that 'undemocratic practices are sometimes associated with programs that rely exclusively on notions of personal responsibility' (ibid., p. 248; emphasis in original). The key challenge for contemporary citizenship education, therefore, is not to make citizenship into a matter of personal responsibility or a 'technology' of social inclusion, but to keep it strongly and explicitly focused on the democratic ideal of a common life informed by the values of equality, justice and freedom.

References

Andrews, R. and Mycock, A. (2007), 'Citizenship education in the UK: divergence within a multi-national state'. *Citizenship Teaching and Learning*, 3, 73–88.
Biesta, G. J. J. (2004) 'The community of those who have nothing in common. Education and the language of responsibility'. *Interchange*, 35, 307–24.
— (2010), 'How to exist politically and learn from it: Hannah Arendt and the problem of democratic education'. *Teachers College Record*, 112, 558–77.
— (2011), *Learning Democracy in School and Society: Education, Lifelong Learning and the Politics of Citizenship*. Rotterdam: Sense Publishers.

Faulks, K. (1998), *Citizenship in Modern Britain*. Edinburgh: Edinburgh University Press.

HMIE (2003), *How Good is Our School? Education for Citizenship*. Edinburgh: HMIE.

— (2006), *Education for Citizenship: A Portrait of Current Practice in Scottish Schools and Pre-School Centres*. Edinburgh: HMIE.

LTScotland (2000), *Education for Citizenship: A Paper for Discussion and Consultation*. Dundee: Learning and Teaching Scotland.

— (2002), *Education for Citizenship: A Paper for Discussion and Development*. Dundee: Learning and Teaching Scotland.

Munn, P. and Arnott, M. (2009), 'Citizenship in Scottish schools: the evolution of education for citizenship from the late twentieth century to the present'. *History of Education*, 38, 437–54.

Ross, H. and Munn, P. (2008), 'Representing self-in-society: education for citizenship and the social-subjects curriculum in Scotland'. *Journal of Curriculum Studies*, 40, 251–75.

Scottish Executive (2004) *A Curriculum for Excellence*. Edinburgh: Scottish Executive.

Westheimer, J. and Kahne, J. (2004), 'What kind of citizen? The politics of educating for democracy'. *American Educational Research Journal*, 41, 237–69.

Effective Contributors: Evaluating the Potential for Children and Young People's Participation in their Own Schooling and Learning[1]

E. Kay M. Tisdall

Effective contributors

Scotland's Curriculum for Excellence (CfE) is framed around its four capacities – successful learners, confident individuals, responsible citizens and effective contributors. This chapter focuses on the capacity of 'effective contributors', offering an analysis of the capacity in relation to the idea of children and young people's participation in their schooling and learning.

According to the documentation from Education Scotland,[2] the capacity of 'effective contributors' has three listed attributes – an enterprising attitude, resilience and self-reliance – and six capabilities:

- Communicate in different ways and in different settings
- Work in partnership and in teams
- Take the initiative and lead
- Apply critical thinking in new contexts
- Create and develop
- Solve problems.[3]

These lists of attributes and capabilities raise a number of questions. For example, what is the rationale for the capacity and for the list of attributes and capabilities? How will they be understood and developed through schools and experienced by children and young people?

The Education Scotland website,[4] and the series of policy documents for CfE, do not provide a rationale for the capacity, its attributes and its capabilities. In the early stages of curricular reform – the National Debate on Education (2002), the co-terminous inquiry by the Education, Culture and Sport Committee of the Scottish Parliament – the need for curricular reform was noted, including concerns about positive values, flexibility, choice and relevance (see Education, Culture and Sport Committee, 2002; Scottish Executive, 2002; Munn et al., 2004). The Scottish Executive then identified as its 'first priority to reduce the current overload in the 5–14 curriculum' and for the curriculum to be more flexible around a 'well-balanced core' (2003, p. 6). No mention was made of 'effective contributors'.

The first mention of 'effective contributors' in official documents came from the Curriculum Review Group (Scottish Executive, 2004), a group established by the Scottish Executive in 2003 'to identify the key principles to be applied in the curriculum redesign for ages 3–18'.[5] The Review Group published *A Curriculum for Excellence* in 2004. No rationale was given in the 2004 document for the choice of these particular capacities, in comparison to other possibilities.

The genesis of the capacity seems to lie elsewhere, in particular international discourses about education. These include the work being undertaken by the Organisation for Economic Co-operation and Development (OECD) and the European Commission (EC). The OECD, for example, is seeking to develop its highly influential international survey to assess student performance (PISA) 'to measure the competence level of young people and adults' (2005, p. 5). According to the OECD, competencies go beyond knowledge and skills, involving 'the ability to meet complex demands, by drawing on and mobilising psychosocial resources (including skills and attitudes) in a particular context' (2005, p. 4). They are needed for both society and individuals to succeed, in order to 'face the complex challenges of today's world' (p. 4) arising from globalization and modernization. The EC (2007) has a very similar discourse. Its document *Key Competences for Lifelong Learning* emphasizes the 'dual role' of education, both social and economic. Rather than content and knowledge, education should be about acquiring key competences that each citizens needs 'to adapt flexibly' to a 'rapidly changing and highly interconnected world' (p. 3). These documents thus demonstrate common themes: a concern to prepare children and young people for a fast-changing, complex future, both for them as individuals but also for the well-being of society; the challenge is both economic and social – and not described as educational; the context is not a local nor a national one, but an anxiety about keeping up with global change and presumably a competitive globalized marketplace. The Scottish 'effective contributors' capacity then begins to make sense, as it combines several of the subsequent competences mentioned by the OECD and EC: for example, the capacity combines the competency 'to act autonomously' and 'the ability to cooperate' (OECD, 2005); the 'sense of initiative and entrepreneurship' as well as 'social and civic competences' (European Commission, 2007). The capacity of 'effective contributors' would thus seem to be aligning itself to these broader OECD and EC frameworks.

Children and young people's participation

With little definition of 'effective contributors' in official documents, the question is raised about how this capacity will be understood by teachers, parents and – arguably most importantly – to the children and young people in schools. Hulme and colleagues (2009) undertook focus groups with secondary school pupils, who identified these personal characteristics of an 'effective contributor':

- having the right attitude and 'standing by [one's] convictions';
- the ability to 'voice ... opinions', and participate in and encourage discussion;
- a sense of leadership and commitment;
- the ability to defend one's thoughts and actions;
- the ability to work within a team. (p. 81)

Scotland should already be a leader in fostering such abilities, with its policy context. It was the first nation in the United Kingdom to establish the right of children to participate in their schooling within legislation. The *Standards in Scotland's Schools etc. Act 2000* places a legal obligation upon education authorities and thus state schooling to have 'due regard to the views of the child or young person in decisions that significantly affect them', in relation to the child or young person's school education (S.2(2)). Education authorities are required by law to consult children and young people on authorities' plans (S.5(1)). Headteachers have a legal duty to state how they plan to consult pupils and seek to involve the pupils, on decisions about the everyday running of their schools (S.6(3)).

According to the Advisory Council for Learning and Teaching in Scotland (2002), citizenship education in Scotland should recognize children and young people as citizens now, as well as citizens of the future. Children and young people must not only learn about participation in civic society, they need to see it modelled, and to participate in it, during their learning experiences:

> Schools and early education settings need to function as active learning communities in which participation by all members is encouraged and where there are effective links and partnerships with the wider communities in which they are located. Such learning communities can model, in very powerful ways, the qualities and dispositions associated with education for citizenship. Young people should see that all people in the school are treated with respect and their views sought and taken account of on relevant matters. (Advisory Council for Learning and Teaching in Scotland, 2002, pp. 16–17)

The citizenship education agenda thus must be both short- and long-term, fostering children's participation in schools and their wider communities now, as well as preparing them for their future as adults.

The United Nations Convention on the Rights of the Child (UNCRC) directly influenced these changes in Scottish education. The United Kingdom ratified the UNCRC in 1991, obligating the UK Government to turn the articles into reality in legislation, policy and practice. The Scottish Government, too, is required to fulfil the requirements of the UNCRC (Scotland Act 1998, Schedule 5, Part I, para 7). The Scottish Government's commitment has gained recent momentum. The current majority Government, the Scottish National Party, has made the clearest statements yet that children's rights frame its policies for children:

> The realisation of rights is essential if children are to be successful learners, confident individuals, effective contributors and responsible citizens. . . . The Scottish Government is committed to creating a modern, inclusive Scotland that respects the rights of all Scotland's people. Accordingly, we have taken forward a broad range of actions over the last four years which build on the content of the United Nations Convention on the Rights of the Child, acting to ensure that children's rights are recognised, respected and promoted throughout society. In doing so, we recognise the importance of ensuring that children and young people themselves understand, and are able to exercise, their rights. Curriculum for Excellence, now adopted in all schools across Scotland, will play a key role in making this ambition a reality. (Scottish Government, 2011, para 1.11)

Thus, the broader children's rights agenda is squarely connected to CfE, by the Scottish Government.

Despite Scotland's early legal commitment, and official policy support, research continues to suggest many children and young people do not feel respected in

Scottish schools, that their rights to participate as individuals and in collective decision-making are not realized: indeed, the majority do not feel that they are recognized as 'effective contributors'. The UN Committee on the Rights of the Child roundly criticized 'inadequate' participation of children and young people in schools and the Committee recommended that the Government, 'Strengthen children's participation in all matters of school, classroom and learning which affect them' (2008, p. 16). This suggests that there is much to be done to ensure children's rights to participate.

This chapter will explore to what extent schools are able to foster 'effective contributors' in Scottish schools, in light of these participative rights. It will begin by considering potential understandings of participation and how they can frame practice. It will explore what can be learned from recent research on children and young people's participation in schools. It will consider alternative ways of 'framing' children and young people's participation, that may be more challenging for schools and practitioners, and thus lead to meaningful, sustainable and effective participation and indeed the support for, and the realization of, children and young people as 'effective contributors'.

Understandings of participation

Like many words that become popular in policy and practice discourse (Cornwall and Brock, 2005), the term 'participation' risks being stretched beyond its original meanings, used as a normative 'feel-good' term (who is going to disagree with participation?) to cover a range of activities – not all of which actually realize children's right to participate as originally promoted by children's rights activists.

The UN Committee on the Rights of the Child has recognized the need to provide clarity. In its General Comment No. 12, the Committee describe 'participation' as follows.

> This term has evolved and is now widely used to describe ongoing processes, which include information-sharing and dialogue between children and adults based on mutual respect, and in which children can learn how their views and those of adults are taken into account and shape the outcome of such processes. (2009, p. 3)

On-going, rather than one-off, processes are emphasized by the UN Committee. There are information components (children and young people need information to participate, they can share their own expertise, they need to know what has happened as a result of their participation) and relational ones (dialogue rather than one-way communications, and values of mutual respect). This description thus addresses many of the continued problems for children and young people's participation: that is problems of tokenism, lack of impact and lack of sustainability (see Barnardo's Scotland et al., 2012; Tisdall, 2012a, 2013).

The description underlines that children and young people's participation is about being part of decisions, about shaping outcomes – but not necessarily self-determination. Children and young people's right to participate is often mistakenly equated to self-determination, for children and young people to choose and override everyone else's rights (see Tisdall, 2012a), or for children and young people's 'desires' to be met over their needs (see Priestley, 2010). The UNCRC, and indeed Scottish education legislation, is more subtly framed. It may well be that children should have more choice, particularly in their schooling, and more attention given to what and how they enjoy learning (see Stephen et al., 2008). But a child's right to have her view given 'due weight' (Article 12, UNCRC) is balanced by a child's right that her best interests be a primary consideration (Article 3, UNCRC). Not all participation is about individual choice and individual choice does not suit all decisions. Nor is children and young people's participation about fulfilment of their 'desires' as opposed to their needs, but rather informed involvement. Much of the drive for children and young people's participation is for them to be recognized as stakeholders, alongside other adults, that their views should be part of decision-making and an important influence when decisions impact on them greatly. The problem presently is that children and young people are frequently not even recognized as stakeholders in such decisions.

Particularly in the educational field, children and young people's rights to participate have been captured under the banner of 'pupil voice'. The notion of 'voice' has been powerful: in a country with the traditional proverb of 'children being seen but not heard', the idea of hearing children's voices has been a neat shorthand to promote children's rights. But it also has severe drawbacks (for fuller discussion, see Tisdall, 2012a, 2012b). From a very practical one, the emphasis on 'voice' risks excluding children who do not communicate verbally: children who use communication methods, perhaps because of a disability, that require more time and assisted communication (Komulainen, 2007). From an analytical one, adult publications and campaigns have claimed to put forward children's 'voices', when they are in fact adults' selection, analysis and distillation of children's views: a potentially worthwhile exercise in itself but not a pure presentation of the unadulterated 'voices' of children. From a policy one, it risks unduly emphasizing the processes of participation, of producing children and young people's views, but not the actual hearing of them, the active listening, nor potential impact. Indeed, the capacity of 'effective contributors' could better capture the potential of children and young people's participation, to recognize children and young people as both contributing and effective.

As an education lawyer, Lundy (2007) provides a sharp, children's rights critique of 'pupil voice'. She reminds the reader of the actual text of Article 12 within the UNCRC:

1. States Parties shall assure to the child who is capable of forming his or her own views the right to express those views freely in all matters affecting the child, the views of the child being given due weight in accordance with the age and maturity of the child.
2. For this purpose, the child shall in particular be provided the opportunity to be heard in any judicial and administrative proceedings affecting the child, the views of the child being given due weight in accordance with the age and maturity of the child.

Article 12 is not a pedagogical option but a legal right of children, Lundy underlines. The article applies widely, to 'all matters that affect the child'. Under Article 12, children's right to express a view is not dependent upon their capacity to express a mature view. Instead, children have to have the ability to form a view. Such elements, Lundy argues, are not always recognized in activities labelled as 'pupil voice'.

Lundy proposes instead four interrelated elements, to understand Article 12:

- Space: children must be given the opportunity to express views
- Voice: children must be facilitated to express their views
- Audience: the views must be listened to
- Influence: the views must be acted upon, as appropriate. (2007, p. 933)

She further defines the 'right of audience' as 'a guaranteed opportunity to communicate views to an identifiable individual or body with the responsibility to listen' (p. 237). 'Influence' goes beyond listening to having the potential for change.

Indeed, much of the advice given by Lundy corresponds closely with the later UNCRC Comment No. 12. Both publications emphasize the need to support children to participate – children may well need information to clarify their views and they may need assistance to express their views. Both emphasize that children's ability to participate should not be undermined by unhelpful and inaccurate ideas of children's capacity, and capacity's relationship to their participation rights. For example, the General Comment states that a child should be presumed to have the capacity to form a view and it is not up to the child to prove this capacity (2009, p. 6). There is no age threshold for a child's right to express his or her view, and a child need not have comprehensive knowledge to be considered capable. Both emphasize feedback to children on how their views have been taken into consideration.

These elements and clarifications will be kept in mind, in considering the research evidence below.

What do we know about children and young people's participation in Scottish schools?

There is no regular Scottish Government monitoring of children and young people's views of their own participation in Scottish schools. We do have evidence from large-scale research undertaken in the past five years.

On a promising note, the regular survey Being Young in Scotland (YouthLink Scotland, 2009) found two-thirds of 11 to 16-year-olds felt teachers take account of their views 'a great deal' or 'a fair amount', although this was less than they felt friends took account of their views (87%) and parents/carers did (90%). Similar questions were not asked in previous surveys, so no direct comparison is available. However, the 2007 survey found a slightly lower percentage (57%) of school pupils said they have been asked for their views by their school, perhaps suggesting some progress (Brand et al., 2008).

Cross and colleagues (2009) were commissioned by Learning and Teaching Scotland (LTS) to evaluate pupil participation in primary and secondary schools across Scotland. LTS was the non-departmental public body in Scotland, to develop and support the Scottish Curriculum; thus this commission was directly related to developing CfE. The research's fieldwork included an on-line questionnaire of primary and secondary school teachers, documentary analysis of materials from a selection of schools and local authorities and four case-study schools.

On the questionnaire, open questions were asked about the ways pupil participation was encouraged in their schools, with the following results:

For individual children and young people: individualized learning (58%, including mechanisms like individualized education plans, personal learning plans and target setting); buddying, mentoring or peer support schemes (49%); pupil mediation, guidance or counselling initiatives (23%); and school councils[6] or forums (18%).

At the classroom level: working cooperatively or learning in teams (42%); assessment strategies like personal learning plans (38%); and pupil involvement in planning or evaluation (19%).

At the school level: school councils, forums or involvement in school assemblies (75%); individual initiatives or awards like eco-schools and health promoting schools (53%); and/or specific responsibilities for pupils like playground monitors (41%).

At the community level: initiatives like environmental projects (78%); specific award schemes aimed towards community volunteering (25%); and/or charity or fund raising work (24%).

The range above closely mirrors many of the activities outlined under the capacity 'effective contributors'. Indeed, even though the fieldwork was undertaken at an early stage of CfE's development, several teacher respondents noted the relationship between pupil participation and the CfE. Children and young people also closely associated such activities with 'effective contributors' (p. 10).

Certain absences can be noted. At the community level, children and young people's participation was not identified in any substantial proportion as going beyond the school. Only a small percentage of respondents report pupils' involvement in curriculum development, evaluation or school planning decisions (p. 7, see below for discussion). A greater range of participation opportunities were reported at primary level. In secondary schools, pupils' participation was often in predetermined programmes, many focused on award competitions where pupils received rather than made decisions. This suggests that a wider participation agenda will be particularly challenging for secondary schools. It may explain the increasing cynicism of secondary school pupils as they progress through secondary school, as found in the survey commissioned by the Scottish Consumer Council (Tisdall, 2007). As young people progressed through secondary school, they were less and less likely to see the school councils as having sufficient power to make a difference. This deterred their willingness to become involved in the school council. But despite such disenchantment, a large minority of young people remained hopeful: 44 per cent either agreed or strongly agreed with the statement 'I think pupil councils are a good way of listening to pupils'.

A three-year study looked specifically at school councils in Scotland. Undertaken jointly by the Centre for Research on Families and Relationships, University of Edinburgh, and Children in Scotland, the research involved: surveys of local authorities' policies and advisers; a representative survey of school staff members responsible for school councils, across Scottish primary, secondary, special and independent schools, and a survey of school councils; and six intensive case studies in primary and secondary schools. Scotland certainly followed the UK-wide trend (see Alderson et al., 2000; Whitty and Wisby, 2007): school councils are becoming even more prevalent, with 90 per cent of responding staff in Scotland reporting 'whole school' school councils, and an even higher percentage additionally having year-level pupil groups or 'house groups'.

Although school councils have become increasingly common, the research underlined a lack of clarity on what school councils were *for*. The purpose was not usually clearly and officially presented. Virtually all respondents in the case studies seemed unclear on the school council's purpose beyond letting pupils 'have a say' or having 'pupil voice'. There are risks of 'tokenism' as a result, as one frustrated council member from School C described:

> The problem is with the School Council. It appears very good and it looks very good and everyone thinks it works well, but then we say things and we have ideas and they don't go anywhere.

More positively, interview data from staff suggest a deeper symbolic agenda. The interviews are replete with the importance of senior staff 'being seen' to be listening, that pupils 'know' that staff are listening (see Baginsky and Hannam, 1999, for the 'signalling' effect of school councils).

Other purposes are revealed by the fieldwork in schools. The most prevalent purpose was the 'laboratory of democracy', that pupils and particularly school council members should learn about having or being representatives and the processes of formal representative democracies (e.g. from voting to having agendas and minutes). Such a purpose can focus merely on process and not actual influence on decisions. This is neatly captured by the headteacher in School A:

> . . . I think the process in itself is worthwhile. Whereas for them [the school council] it's probably the outcomes; it's in their mind. But if we can get them some of their outcomes and allow them to take part in the process at the same time, I think that's a reasonable trade-off.

School council members, then, tended to be more concerned about outcomes (i.e. what actions they take and goals they accomplish), while adults involved tended to be more focused on processes within, and the symbolic value of, school councils.

According to staff respondents to the School Survey, school councils generally were well-connected to other school decision-makers: school staff report meetings and/ or correspondence with the headteacher (74.5%), the senior management team (39.3%) and/or the school board/parent council (27.0%). While the case-study schools reported such connections, in practice the qualitative research found a lack of formal interaction with school governance structures such as the senior management team or the parent council. There were exceptions, such as School A, where a school council member was on the Parent Council; still, the headteacher described this representative function as difficult to deliver. Another headteacher (School B) used the school council to give extra credence to her requests to the parent association (what would now be the parent council): 'I can now go to the parent association and say: "This is not from me; this is from the children."' In neither case does the interaction suggest a deep insertion of school councils into other school governance structures (see also Fielding, 2006).

Do school councils actually influence change? Two survey questions alluded to this:

- School councils felt strongly that their council had improved things at their school (54.1% strongly agreed and 39.6% agreed). Staff respondents were less enthusiastic but still positive (26.9% strongly agreed and 57.4% agreed).
- More specifically, councils were broadly seen as being good at trying to sort out problems that pupils told the councils about (over 70% of both staff and school council respondents agreed or strongly agreed), with a further 22.2% and 23.9%, respectively, thinking the school council was 'okay'.

The School Survey sought to track issues discussed at school councils, whether school councils made a decision on these, and whether changes resulted. From a long list of possible issues, school staff were more likely to say that school councils discussed, made decisions and achieved changes in relation to: school materials (e.g. playground games, books), projects (e.g. health promoting schools) and food in school (e.g. lunches, snacks, water). School councils were most likely to identify: school materials, breaktimes (e.g. activities) and money (e.g. fundraising, school council budget) as areas of discussion, decision and results. Topics related to academic matters (e.g. subjects taught, how well pupils are taught, choosing new teachers and teaching assistants) were the areas of influence and action least often selected by both school councils and school staff (as found above by Cross et al., 2009). Similarly, in case-study schools, issues were tracked from the start to the end of the school council's year, showing similar findings but also heightening their significance in relation to lunch time/food, toilets (condition/ cleanliness), bullying and school uniforms.

School councils in the United Kingdom have been criticized for focusing on 'inconsequential' issues, such as toilets, lockers and play areas and failing to address fundamental academic issues (Wyse, 2001; Maitles and Deuchar, 2006; ESTYN, 2008; Yamashita and Davies, 2009). This criticism was echoed by a council member in School D, who commented:

> I don't know whether they thought we would be dealing with making sure there was more toilet roll or trying to work out prices for lunch.... I keep saying we are running out of small things to fix. It's the big things that are the problems.

But an alternative perspective considers the amount of time children and young people spend at school and the importance of the everyday environment within schools to their well-being and satisfaction. For example, school toilets can be important spaces for children and young people's health, safety and relationships, Yet, they have been found all too frequently to be unhygienic places that children and young people want to avoid (thus causing potential health problems), spaces for bullying and contentious power struggles with staff (Children's Commissioner for Wales, 2004). Nonetheless, this and other research underlines that most school councils are not engaging with central areas of academic decision-making or whole school governance and policymaking.

Councils may well deliver on their symbolic purpose – at least to the staff and pupils involved. For example, a large majority of both staff and school councils thought that 'having a school council makes a difference to how pupils feel about the school' in Figure 7.1.

These findings of large-scale research are supported by wider commentary and smaller-scale research. There is an immense growth of 'participation' and 'pupil voice' activities in school, and numerous examples of practice that are reported as meaningful to all those involved, effective in their own terms, and meet the requirements of the UNCRC and Lundy's four-part model (for wider literature, see Ruddock and Flutter, 2004; Participation Works www.participationworks. org.uk). But there are continuing trends that are problematic. Such positive activities are too often dependent on individual staff members, who receive little training or career recognition for this intense work (Wyness, 2009). This leads to such activities not being embedded within schools and quickly vulnerable to

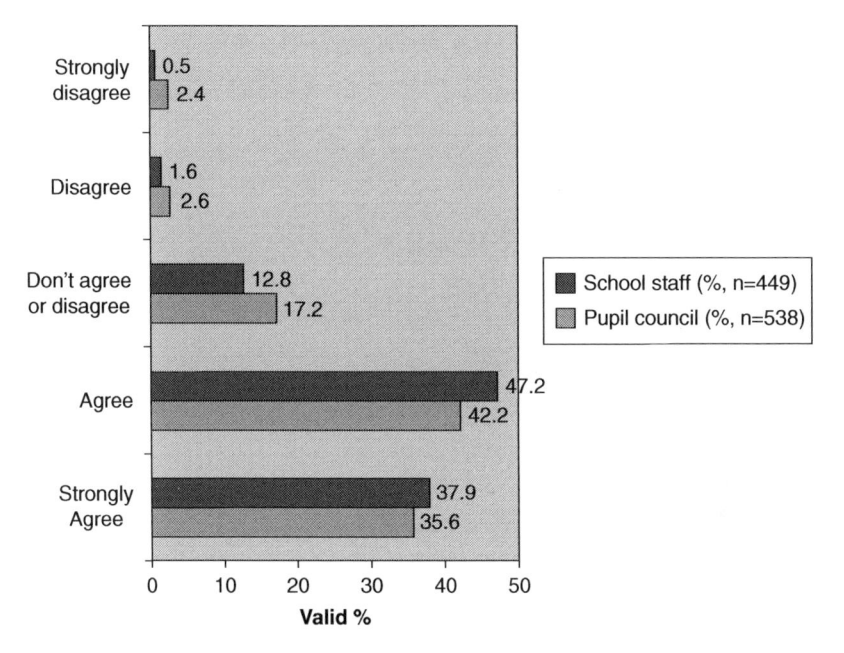

Figure 7.1 Having a school council makes a difference to how pupils feel about the school, School Survey, valid %.

staff or institutional change. Children and young people are involved in some matters that affect them – individual learning, school environmental issues, fundraising – but not 'all matters that affect them' as required by Article 12, UNCRC. Participation activities can emphasize processes, 'training up' children and young people in representative democracy or to be good citizens or to contribute to their communities – in other words a pedagogical model. While children and young people repeatedly welcome the skills they gain by such participation (e.g. Davies et al., 2006), this only addresses the space and voice of Lundy's model – and not audience nor influence. No audience need be given, in the pedagogical model, to children and young people's views, and no action is required by decision-makers. Children and young people may be recognized as effective contributors of the future – but not effective contributors now.

Moving forward?

There are numerous practical ways that schools and schooling could respond to the critique above, in the short term. For school councils, for example, they could ensure council elections are (and are perceived as) fair, they could recognize and reward the school council's adult adviser and they could tighten the connections between school councils and school governance structures. Given the different views on what a school council is for, within schools, continued dialogue between staff and pupils on what *their* school council is for would be productive – and assist in avoiding staff and/or pupils being frustrated by how their particular council functions. Other participation activities have found it helpful to allocate budgets to participation activities, even small amounts of money making symbolic and real differences to children and young people seeing their views resulting in change. CfE provides an excellent opportunity to experiment with children and young people's involvement in their own learning and curriculum, one of the areas so traditionally excluded. With such changes, children and young people can not only learn *about* these elements of being an 'effective contributor', they can develop the related abilities and capacities through lived experiences.

But CfE could encourage Scottish schooling to more fundamental change, a different way of understanding the relationships between children and young people, staff members and schooling. Peter Moss and colleagues have been challenging UK children's services for the last 20 years, on services' impoverished views of children, their failure to consider alternatives embraced by other countries, and the practice problems that result here (e.g. see Moss et al., 2000; Moss and Petrie, 2002). Children and childhood, they argue, have been perceived as dependant, weak, poor and needy. Children are seen as primarily the responsibility of their parents (despite children's institutionalization in schools and increasingly in early years services). Dominant understandings of child psychology have emphasized children as developing, incomplete adults and incompetent in comparison. Equally, children are seen as innocent, giving professionals the potential to 'save them' as children grow into adulthood – so children are not only innocent but also a redemptive vehicle. And, even more recently, we might add to Moss and colleagues' analysis a strong emphasis on children as human investment, as human capital: if we invest in them during the early years, this investment will be rewarded in substantially more contributions and less spending once they reach adulthood (Lister, 2006). This is the 'poor' child of children's services in the United Kingdom – and perhaps of the EC and OECD in their competencies' agendas.

Writing in 2002, Moss and Petrie identify the resulting trends in children's services. Services are fragmented, compartmentalized and children are atomized. The focus is on instrumentality and control, through 'what works' rather than addressing structural inequalities, addressing limited and specialized purposes, working to predetermined goals and predictable outcomes. The results are that:

> Children and their childhoods are brought ever more under the adult gaze for adult purposes. The rationale is a belief in new and effective technologies, providing buttons to push which will deliver solutions that work – interventions that this time will lead, via our children's futures, to the promised land. (2002, p. 166)

This is a familiar description to academic studies of children's services, from critiques of child protection (e.g. Parton, 2011), to youth justice and family law (e.g. James and James, 2004), to schooling (e.g. Jeffs, 2002). What Moss and colleagues particularly add is a potentially workable alternative.

Moss and colleagues encourage alternative views of children and childhood: the 'rich' child rather than the 'poor' child. They draw on early years pedagogy, particular the Reggio Emilia approach developed in northern Italy within municipal preschools. Moss and colleagues quote leading practitioners, on their alternative views of children and childhood:

> Our image of children no longer considers them as isolated and egocentric, does not see them only engaged in action with objects, does not emphasise only the cognitive aspects, does not belittle feelings or what is not logical and does not consider with ambiguity the role of the affective domain. Instead our image of the child is rich in potential, strong, powerful, competent and, most of all, connected to adults and other children. (Malaguzzi, quoted in Moss et al., 2000, p. 250)

This different view of children and childhood creates different possibilities for provision. Rather than 'children's services', suggests Moss and colleagues, there are possibilities for 'children's spaces':

> ... environments provided through the agency of public policy for collectivities of children, sometimes with adults present (the nursery) sometimes without (the playground on a housing estate); settings where young people meet each other as individuals and where they form a social group. (2002, p. 107)

The suggestion of children's spaces, and its resulting ideas of children and childhood, is provocative for this chapter. First, the ideas have arisen from a pedagogical approach and practice. CfE has itself been explicitly extended down to the age of 3, with *Pre-Birth to Three: Positive Outcomes for Scotland's Children and Families* (Learning and Teaching Scotland, 2010) showing continuity for younger children. Many of the 'different' approaches to learning promoted by CfE – active learning, cooperative learning, outdoor learning – are well-rehearsed, broadly practiced and evaluated within early years literature and practice. There are touchstones, for those interested, that are easily accessible and using some familiar ideas.

Secondly, the ideas challenge adults to realize that the capacity 'effective contributors' is not solely an objective for children and young people; school staff need to be effective contributors too (Oberski, 2009). Moss and colleagues discuss how workers with children would need to change, to work in children's spaces: 'The "worker-as-technician" will not do' (2002, p. 111). Staff would be seen as:

> . . . reflective practitioners, as thinkers, as researchers, as co-constructors of knowledge – sustaining children's relationships and culture, creating challenging environments and situations, constantly questioning their own images of the child and their understanding of children's learning and other activities, supporting the learning of each child but also learning from children. (Ibid.)

Their ideas might address the findings of Stephen and colleagues (2008), who undertook fieldwork in three secondary schools, in Scotland, and three of their associated primary schools. They found differences between children's and teachers' understandings of engagement in learning:

> For the children engagement seems to derive from activities that give pleasure, choice or a degree of 'freedom' and authenticity, and are associated with positive social and emotional outcomes. The teachers understand engagement in learning in terms of behaviour (participation in the adult agenda as evidenced by verbal and non-verbal behaviour) and cognitive activity such as purposeful writing and answering questions. (p. 26)

'Children's spaces' provides an alternative way of framing learning, and engagement with it, that could create more congruent understandings.

Thirdly, the Reggio Emilia approach has developed particular ideas about 'listening' to children and how this fits into its pedagogical approach. Moss and colleagues (2005) provide a provocative discussion of this. They first quote Rinaldi, who emphasizes listening as an approach rather than particular tasks or procedures:

> . . . listening is not only a technique and a didactic methodology, but a way of thinking and seeing ourselves in relationship with others and the world. Listening is an element that connects and that is part of human biology and is in

the concept of life itself... [It] is a right or better it is part of the essence of being human. (quoted in Moss et al., 2005, p. 6)

Listening is a way or 'ethic of relating to others' that is more than 'just about' decision-making (Moss et al., 2005, pp. 8–9).

Even with all the positive aspects of listening, Moss and colleagues identify associated risks (pp. 9–11). Power relations and their inequalities must be taken account of, for listening to fulfil its potential and to recognize that listening itself may support rather than subvert power. Listening still requires interpretation, which may be masked by the emphasis on ethics, dialogue and processes. Listening in fact can be used to better govern children, with a 'mask' of children's rights and being child-centred. Listening may create yet another conceptualization of children and childhood, 'the autonomous, calculating individual for whom self-realisation is the highest value' (p. 11). These risks are evident in the earlier discussions within this chapter, whether based on the literature, research or practice experience. They are particularly relevant when considering the capacity of 'effective contributors', which very easily could privilege the more articulate and what adults in power want to hear, advantage the already advantaged, and lead to more effective ways to manage children and young people rather than recognize and encourage active engagement.

Conclusion

The capacity of 'effective contributors', as with the other three capacities of CfE, has very positive connotations and much possibility. But it risks being repeatedly and casually produced without reflection and without much definition (Priestley, 2010; Priestley and Humes, 2010). This can gloss over that, in fact, people define it very differently. Like with school councils, if purposes are not articulated clearly and collectively agreed, there are risks of misunderstandings and frustration, and actively turning children and young people 'off' from contributing.

Of note for this chapter is that *nowhere* across the four capacities is there mention of children and young people's rights and particularly the right to participate. Yet, the recognition of children's rights in general, and children's rights to participate more particularly, has never before had such prominence in Scotland. The proposed Children and Young People Bill will have a chapter on children's rights (Scottish Government, 2012a). UNICEF's Rights Respecting Schools programme, which involves schools going through a children's rights development programme in order to achieve accreditation, has been taken up by many Scottish schools and has been positively evaluated (Sebba and Robinson, 2010). Training resources have been funded by central government to encourage participation, school councils (V3 Vote, Voice, Valued) and for children and young people's understanding of and participation in CfE more generally (BeXcellent) (reported in Scottish Government, 2012b, p. 22). All those working with children, young people and families should have a common core of skills, related to the UNCRC (ibid.). Children's rights should be framing how adults work with and support children.

For those promoting children and young people's participation at a national level, such rights developments are welcome. But these policy developments risk the continuation of a top-down approach that many children and young people never know of and never recognise as their every-day experience in schools and outwith. Moss and colleagues, and the pedagogy of listening, are particularly useful in articulating that rights are equally about relationships, they are realized through relationships, they are about values and fundamentally not about a technical form of delivery (see also Fielding, 2006). Change is required in how we conceptualize children, young people and those who work with them and with that change come real challenges for how 'spaces' are organized and public provision is provided. Moss and colleagues' work would challenge whether we can truly enhance children's capacity as 'effective contributors' without such fundamental change.

The 'effective contributors' of CfE, alongside the other capacities, provide a potential for change, a freeing of innovation, a pedagogy of 'listening' in its truest sense. But it equally could return to the worst of the assessment-dominated, hierarchical and non-participative practices that international commentators find so striking (UN Committee on the Rights of the Child, 2008, see also Woodward, 2003). Its meaning and genesis span different values – from economic to social – and it could become more about training the citizens of the future than recognizing children as citizens now. As CfE is translated by the daily practices of all those in school into a reality, there is much to observe about and learn from the potential definition and enactment of the capacity 'effective contributors'.

Acknowledgements

A number of research teams and collaborations have influenced this chapter. Such work has been supported through a programme of participation projects, funded by the Big Lottery Fund, the British Academy, the Royal Society of Edinburgh, the Economic and Social Research Council (e.g. RES-451-26-0685; RES-189-25-0174) and the Leverhulme Trust. For more information, see www.crfr.ac.uk

Notes

1. Generally, this chapter uses the phrase 'children and young people' to refer to those under the age of 18 and who are or should be in pre, primary or secondary school (and thus not squarely addressing children who are home-schooled). At times 'children' is used within this chapter, to refer to young children, to discuss children's rights under the UNCRC (which does not use the additional phrase of young people, but defines children up to the age of 18 unless majority is obtained earlier), or in quoting others' work.
2. Education Scotland is the national body, established by the Scottish Government, to support quality and improvement in Scottish education. Learning and Teaching Scotland became part of Education Scotland.
3. www.educationscotland.gov.uk/thecurriculum/whatiscurriculumforexcellence/thepurposeofthecurriculum/index.asp
4. www.educationscotland.gov.uk/thecurriculum/
5. www.educationscotland.gov.uk/thecurriculum/whatiscurriculumforexcellence/howwasthecurriculumdeveloped/processofchange/timeline.asp
6. No official and agreed definition exists of such councils across the United Kingdom. The official Welsh website on school councils provides one, fairly typical description:

    A school council is a representative group of pupils elected by their peers to discuss matters about their education and raise concerns with the senior managers and governors of their school. (www.schoolcouncilswales.org.uk/en/fe/page_at.asp?n1=30&n2=31&n3=69, accessed 16/06/09)

References

Advisory Council for Learning and Teaching in Scotland (2002), *Education for Citizenship in Scotland*. Online at www.educationscotland.gov.uk/Images/ecsp_tcm4-122094.pdf (accessed 13/09/12).

Alderson, P. (2000), 'School students' views on school councils and daily life at school'. *Children & Society*, 14, 121–34.

Baginsky, M. and Hannam, D. (1999), *School Councils: The Views of Students and Teachers (Summary)*. London: NSPCC. Online at www.nspcc.org.uk/Inform/publications/Downloads/schoolcouncils_wdf48041.pdf (accessed 06/10/10).

Barnardo's Scotland, Centre for Research on Families and Relationships, and Children in Scotland (2012), *Children and Young People's Participation in Policy-Making: Making it Meaningful, Effective and Sustainable. Briefing No. 1.* Online at www.crfr.ac.uk/reports/Participation%20briefing.pdf (accessed 18/05/12).

Brand, S., Viatte, M. and Myant, K. (2008), *Being Young in Scotland 2007: Scottish Government Findings.* Online at www.scotland.gov.uk/resource/doc/210142/0055524.pdf (accessed 31/05/12).

Children's Commissioner for Wales (2004), *Lifting the Lid.* Children's Commissioner for Wales. Online at www.childcomwales.org.uk/uploads/publications/27.pdf (accessed 31/05/12).

Cornwall, A. and Brock, K. (2005), *Beyond Buzzwords: Poverty Reduction, Participation and Empowerment in Development Policy.* United Nations Research Institute for Social Development, Online at www.unrisd.org/80256B3C005BCCF9/(httpAuxPages)/F25D3D6D27E2A1ACC12570CB002FFA9A/$file/cornwall.pdf (accessed 2/05/12).

Cross, B., Hall, J., Hall, S., Hulme, M., Lewin, J. and McKinney, S. (2009), *Pupil Participation in Scottish Schools.* University of Glasgow. Online at www.gla.ac.uk/media/media_115808_en.pdf (accessed 31/05/12).

Davies, L., Williams, C. and Yamashita, H. with Man-Hing, K. (2006), *Impact and Outcomes: Taking up the Challenge of Pupil Participation.* London: Carnegie Foundation. Online at www.participationforschools.org.uk (31/12/10).

Education, Culture and Sport Committee, Scottish Parliament (2002), *Analysis of Responses on the Purposes of Education,* Edinburgh: Scottish Parliament. Online at http://archive.scottish.parliament.uk/business/committees/historic/education/papers-02/edp02-23.pdf (accessed 24/08/12).

ESTYN (2008), *Having Your Say – Young People, Participation and School Councils.* ESTYN. Online at http://estyn.co.uk/ThematicReports/0208_Having_your_say_young_people_participation_and_school_councils.pdf (accessed 31/10/10).

European Commission (2007), *Key Competences for Life Long Learning: European Reference Framework.* Online at http://ec.europa.eu/dgs/education_culture/publ/pdf/ll-learning/keycomp_en.pdf (accessed 13/09/12).

Fielding, M. (2006), 'Leadership, radical student engagement and the necessity of person-centred education'. *International Journal Leadership in Education,* 9, 299–313.

Hart, R. (1992), *Children's Participation: The Theory and Practice of Involving Young Citizens in Community Development and Environmental Care.* London: Earthscan.

Hulme, M., Baumfield, V., Livingston, K., Menter, I. and the SCRE Centre (2009), *Curriculum for Excellence: Draft Experiences and Outcomes.* Online at www.educationscotland.gov.uk/publications/c/publication_tcm4539668.asp (accessed 1/05/12).

James, A. and James, A. (2004), *Constructing Childhood.* Basingstoke: Palgrave.

Jeffs, T. (2002), 'Schooling, education and children's rights', in B. Franklin (ed.), *The New Handbook of Children's Rights.* London: Routledge, pp. 45–59.

Komulainen, S. (2007), 'The ambiguity of the child's "voice" in social research'. *Childhood*, 14, 11–28.

Learning and Teaching Scotland (2010), *Pre Birth to Three: Positive Outcomes for Scotland's Children and Families.* Online at www.educationscotland.gov.uk/Images/PreBirthToThreeBooklet_tcm4-633448.pdf (accessed 22/05/12).

Lister, R. (2006), 'Children (but not women) first: New Labour, child welfare and gender'. *Critical Social Policy*, 26, 315–35.

Lundy, L. (2007), '"Voice" is not enough: conceptualising Article 12 of the United Nations Convention on the Rights of the Child'. *British Educational Research Journal*, 33, 927–42.

Maitles, H. and Deuchar, R. (2006), 'We don't learn democracy, we live it!: consulting the pupil voice in Scottish schools'. *Education, Citizenship and Social Justice*, 1, 249–66.

Moss, P. and Petrie, P. (2002), *From Children's Services to Children's Spaces.* London: Taylor & Francis.

Moss, P., Clark, A. and Kjørholt, A. T. (2005), 'Introduction', in A. Clark, A. T. Kjørholt and P. Moss (eds), *Beyond Listening: Children's Perspectives on Early Childhood Services.* Bristol: Policy Press, pp. 1–16.

Moss, P., Dillon, J. and Statham, J. (2000), 'The "child in need" and "the rich child": discourses, constructions and practice'. *Critical Social Policy*, 20, 233–54.

Munn, P., Stead, J., McLeod, G., Brown, J., Cowie, M., McCluskey, G., Pirrie, A. and Scott, J. (2004), 'Schools for the 21st century: the national debate on education in Scotland'. *Research Papers in Education*, 19, 433–52.

Oberski, I. (2009), 'Fostering Curriculum for Excellence teachers' freedom and creativity through developing their intuition and imagination: some insights from Steiner-Waldorf education'. *Scottish Educational Review*, 42, 20–31.

Organisation for Economic Co-operation and Development (OECD) (2005), *The Definition and Selection of Key Competencies: Executive Summary.* Online at www.oecd.org/pisa/35070367.pdf (accessed 13/09/12).

Parton, N. (2011), 'Child protection and safeguarding in England: changing and competing conceptions of risk and their implications for social work'. *British Journal of Social Work*, 41, 854–75.

Priestley, M. (2010), 'Curriculum for Excellence: transformational change or business as usual'. *Scottish Educational Review*, 42, 23–36.

Priestley, M. and Humes, W. (2010), 'The development of Scotland's Curriculum for Excellence: amnesia and déjà vu'. *Oxford Review of Education*, 36, 345–61.

Ruddock, J. and Flutter, J. (2004), *How to Improve Your School: Giving Pupils a Voice.* London: Continuum Press.

Scottish Executive (2002), *The National Debate on Education: Emerging Views.* Edinburgh: The Stationery Office.

— (2003), *Education for Excellence, Choice and Opportunity: The Executive's Response to the National Debate.* Edinburgh: The Stationery Office.

— (2004), *A Curriculum for Excellence*. Edinburgh: Scottish Executive.
Scottish Government (2011), *Consultation on Rights of Children and Young People Bill*. Online at www.scotland.gov.uk/Publications/2011/09/07110058/0 (accessed 22/05/12).
— (2012a), *Consultation on the Rights of Children and Young People Bill, Scottish Government Response*. Online at www.scotland.gov.uk/Publications/2012/05/7864 (accessed 18/05/12).
— (2012b), *Do the Right Thing: Progress Report 2012*. Online at www.scotland.gov.uk/Resource/0039/00392997.pdf (accessed 18/05/12).
Sebba, J. and Robinson, C., with Boushel, M., Carnie, F., Farlie, J., Hunt, F. and Kirby, P. (2010), *Evaluation of UNICEF UK's Rights Respecting School Award*. Online at www.unicef.org.uk/Documents/Education-Documents/RRSA_evaluation_Report.pdf (accessed 28/05/12).
Stephen, C., Cope, P., Oberski, I. and Shand, P. (2008), '"They should try to find out what the children like": exploring engagement in learning'. *Scottish Educational Review*, 40, 17–28.
Tisdall, E. K. M. (2007), *School Councils and Pupil Participation in Scottish Secondary Schools*. Glasgow: Scottish Consumer Council.
— (2012a), 'Taking forward children and young people's participation', in M. Hill, G. Head, A. Lockyer, B. Reid and R. Taylor (eds), *Children's Services: Working Together*. Harlow: Pearson, pp. 151–62.
— (2012b), 'The challenge and challenging of childhood studies? Lessons from disability studies and research with disabled children'. *Children & Society*, 26, 181–91.
— (2013, in press), 'Children should be seen and heard? Children and young people's participation in the UK', in E. K. M. Tisdall, A. Gadda and U. Butler (eds), *Children and Young People's Participation: Challenging Cross-Country Perspectives*. Basingstoke: Palgrave.
Tisdall, E. K. M. (2007), *School Councils and Pupil Participation in Scottish Secondary Schools*. Scottish Consumer Council. Online at http://scotcons.demonweb.co.uk/education/SCCFinalPupilCouncilsReport.pdf.pdf (accessed 05/04/10).
Tisdall, K. and Davis, J. (2004), 'Making a difference? Bringing children's and young people's views into policy-making'. *Children & Society*, 18, 131–42.
UN Committee on the Rights of the Child (2008), *Concluding Observations: United Kingdom of Great Britain and Northern Ireland*. CRC/C/GBR/CO/4. Online at www2.ohchr.org/english/bodies/crc/docs/AdvanceVersions/CRC.C.GBR.CO.4.pdf (accessed 18/05/12).
— (2009), *General Comment No. 12: The Right of the Child to be Heard*. CRC/C/GC/12. Online at www.childrensrights.ie/sites/default/files/information_sheets/files/CRC-GC12_RighttoBeHeard_0.pdf (accessed 18/05/12).
Welsh Assembly (no date), *School Councils*. Online at www.schoolcouncilswales.org.uk/en (accessed 18/5/12).

Whitty, G. and Wisby, E. (2007), *Real Decision Making? School Councils in Action.* Department for Education and Skills. Online at http://eprints.ioe.ac.uk/2715/1/Whitty2007Real(Report).pdf (accessed 22/05/12).

Woodward, W. (2003), 'Schools tests breach UN Convention, envoy claims', *The Guardian,* 14 July.

Wyness, M. (2009), 'Adults' involvement in children's participation: juggling children's places and spaces'. *Children & Society,* 23, 395–406.

Wyse, D. (2001), 'Felt tip pens and school councils: children's participation rights in four English schools'. *Children & Society,* 15, 209–18.

Yamashita, H. and Davies, L. (2009), 'Students as professionals', in B. Percy-Smith and N. Thomas (eds), *A Handbook of Children and Young People's Participation.* London: Routledge, pp. 230–9.

YouthLink Scotland (2009), *Being Young in Scotland 2009.* Online at www.youthlinkscotland.org/webs/245/file/Final%20BYIS%20Repor(a).pdf (accessed 31/05/12).

8

Emerging International Trends in Curriculum

Claire Sinnema and Graeme Aitken

Commonalities in national curricula

In many countries where national curricula are a feature of the educational system, there has been, in the last decade, curriculum reforms of some kind (Pepper, 2008). This chapter highlights two aspects of the commonalities in national curriculum developments – commonalities in goals driving curriculum reform, and commonalities in the emphases of those policies (see Figure 8.1). It also challenges assumptions about the extent to which those emphases might support the achievement of reform goals. We focus on the curriculum policies of English-speaking countries with curricula that came into effect between 2004 and 2012 – Scotland (Scottish Executive, 2004), Northern Ireland (Council for the Curriculum Examinations and Assessment, 2007), Wales (Welsh Assembly Government, 2008d) and New Zealand (Ministry of Education, 2007). We also draw on examples from countries that have more recently begun new rounds of national curriculum policy reforms such as England (Department for Education, 2012), Australia (Australian Curriculum Assessment and Reporting Authority, 2012) and the United States (National Governors Association, 2012). The latter two countries are unique, given the status of the curriculum in relation to federal political structures, and because the national approach to curriculum is a first for those nations. The case of Australia sees the introduction of a national curriculum for the first time, even though schooling is a residual power and major policy responsibility of the States and Territories (Lingard, 2010). Similarly, educators in the United States are for the first time working in the context of a national curriculum in the form of the Common Core Standards.

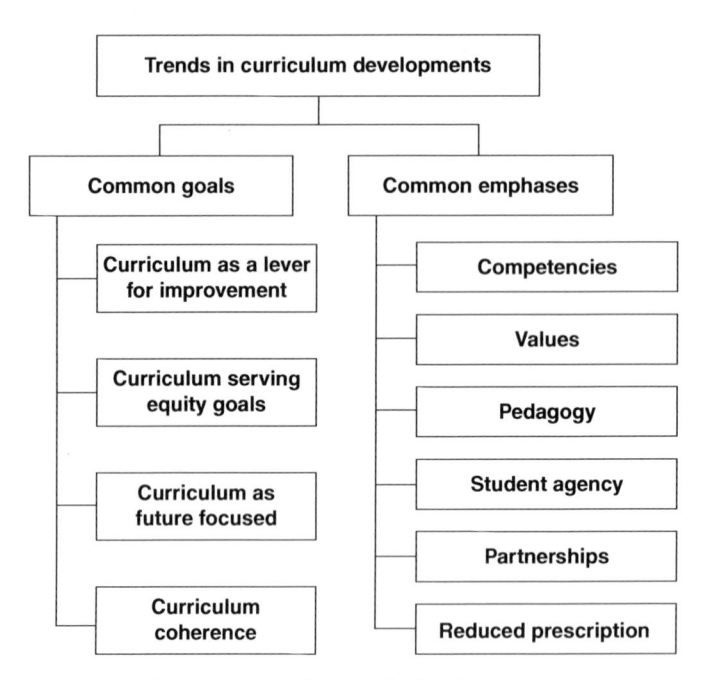

Figure 8.1 Commonalities in national curricula developments.

The goals of curriculum policy reform

There are at least four goals underpinning curriculum reform that are common across nations. Each of these goals signals recognition that curriculum is a potential key lever in educational improvement. The first goal is for curricula to have a stronger role in influencing and improving teachers' practice. The second is for curricula to serve equity goals. The third goal is for curricula to be relevant to twenty-first-century learners facing uncertain futures, and the fourth goal is for national curricula to be increasingly coherent.

Curriculum as a lever for improvement

The goal for curricula to have a stronger role in influencing and improving teachers' practice (Hopmann, 2003) arises out of growing recognition of the influence of teaching on student achievement, relative to other factors (Scheerens, Vermeulen and Pelgrum, 1989; Biddle, Good and Goodson, 1997; Kyriades, Campbell and Gagatsis, 2000). While the direct relationship between teaching and student achievement has been widely recognized, policymakers are increasingly focusing on curriculum as an influence on the influential – the teacher. The Common Core Standards in the United States, for example, 'represent considerable change from what states currently call for in their standards and in what they assess ... and they are different from what U.S. teachers report they are currently teaching' (Porter et al., 2011, p. 114). By requiring new and different approaches to teaching and assessment, curricula are increasingly positioned as a contributor to goals for educational improvement.

Curriculum serving equity goals

Increasingly, attention to education system performance focuses not only on overall educational performance, but also on the extent to which school systems are serving the needs of diverse learners, and the degree of equity in the achievement and progress of particular groups. Efforts to respond to inequities often signal the potential of curriculum reform to act as a lever for greater equity in educational outcomes for all learners. A 2007 OECD report on quality and equity of schooling in Scotland, for example, signalled that while that system is one of the highest performing and equitable of the OECD countries, challenges of inequality persist:

> Children from poorer communities and low socio-economic status homes are more likely than others to underachieve, while the gap associated with poverty and deprivation in local government areas appears to be very wide ... [there were] particular concerns over inequalities in staying-on rates, participation in different academic levels of national courses and pass rates in those courses. (OECD, 2007, p. 15)

The role of the curriculum in improving this situation is apparent in the statement about Scotland's Curriculum for Excellence aiming 'to achieve transformation in education in Scotland' (Education Scotland, no date, p. 3).

The 2007 English national curriculum was also linked to goals for improved equity in education. It was underpinned by 'The Children's Plan' (Department for Children, Schools and Families, 2007) – a plan that foregrounded goals of 'system reform to achieve world class standards' and of 'closing the gap in educational attainment for disadvantaged children' (p. 16). Equity concerns persist in the more recent curriculum review in England. The key principles set out in the review remit each explicitly refer to 'all' children and one of the principles requires attention to the needs of 'different groups, including the most able and pupils with special educational needs and disabilities' (Department for Education, 2011). Those accountabilities, however, do not apply to organizations that are exempt from the national curriculum, such as privately funded schools and academies. The Melbourne Declaration that underpins national curriculum developments in Australia also focuses on equity. The first of two educational goals for young Australians set out in the declaration is that 'Australian schooling promotes equity and excellence' (Australian Ministerial Council on Education Employment Training and Youth Affairs, 2008, p. 8). The role of the curriculum in relation to that goal is in outlining common expectations about the content and quality of learning for all students, regardless of their circumstances or the type or location of their school (Australian Curriculum Assessment and Reporting Authority, 2012).

As well as curricula serving equity goals, curricula also increasingly emphasize the value of equity as a desired curriculum outcome for students. This is the case, for example, in New Zealand where 'students will be encouraged to value equity through fairness and social justice' (Ministry of Education, 2007, p. 10) – and in Australia where the curriculum seeks 'active and informed citizens [who] are committed to the national values of equity and justice' (Australian Curriculum Assessment and Reporting Authority, 2012, p. 9).

Curriculum for uncertain futures

There is much in recent curriculum policy rhetoric that specifically emphasizes the needs of learners in the twenty-first century. In particular, curriculum policies emphasize how learners' futures are more uncertain for the present generation of students than for previous generations and that they need, therefore, to experience a curriculum that prepares them for that uncertainty. In this regard, statements in the draft Australian curriculum are typical of those in other countries. They describe the curriculum as an effort to signal important outcomes in an educational context in which learners' futures are difficult to predict, and as a response to significant changes in society requiring wider and more adaptive knowledges, understanding and skills (Australian Curriculum Assessment and Reporting Authority, 2010). This sort of future orientation is also evident in Scotland's Curriculum for Excellence, which outlines that 'it is clear that the future will require a population with the confidence and skills to meet the challenges posed by fast and far-reaching change' (HM Inspectorate of Education, 2009, p. 1). Scholars, on the other hand, have argued that a future orientation to curriculum, as a response to the inevitability of change and uncertainty, is not appropriate. Young and Muller (2010), for example assert that 'the assumptions of such "future thinking" tend to be that certain wider social changes are not only inevitable, but of positive benefit to humanity and that schooling in the future will have to follow them. This "following" is invariably viewed as unproblematic' (p. 11). Young (2008) critiques purely instrumental curricula, and argues instead for knowledge-led curricula, which look to the past, present and the future.

Curriculum coherence

Strengthening coherence is another common goal for recent curricula revisions and reform (Honig and Hatch, 2004; Oates, 2011). Efforts to strengthen coherence involve four main approaches. The first approach is one that seeks to address issues of curriculum over-crowding and fragmentation by de-cluttering and reducing content. In all of the countries examined here, there is reference to previous curricula as too all-encompassing, disconnected and unwieldy. That was certainly the case in the previous curriculum framework in New Zealand, under which students were expected, by the end of Year 10, to 'cover' more than 500 achievement objectives. Not surprisingly a review of that curriculum preceding the development of the current one recommended that concerns about the curriculum manageability be addressed (Ministry of Education, 2002).

Similarly, in England 'securing "curriculum coherence" is considered a vital objective in refining the National Curriculum' (Oates, 2010, p. 17), in Scotland the Curriculum Review Group called for the curriculum to be 'less crowded and better connected' (Scottish Executive, 2004, p. 3). Such calls to improve coherence are evident in all countries' curriculum reform processes and may arise from the consensus models of curriculum formation (Oates, 2010) whereby 'everybody finds the bit of the National Curriculum with which they agree ... [and] it becomes too baggy' (Marshall, 2011, p. 187). When this occurs curricula become all things to all people, and subsequently lack internal coherence.

Another type of coherence goal is at system-level (rather than curriculum-level). It is evident in countries where, as mentioned above, there has been a move from state-mandated curricula in federal systems to a national curriculum applied across states. This move in Australia has occurred despite ongoing debate and critique, and two previous failed attempts at a national curriculum (Briant and Doherty, 2012). It aims primarily for national coherence, but also serves efficiency purposes:

> Working nationally makes it possible to harness collective expertise and effort in the pursuit of this common goal. It also offers the potential of economies of scale and a substantial reduction in the duplication of time, effort and resources. (Australian Curriculum Assessment and Reporting Authority, 2012, p. 7)

The press for greater curriculum coherence in the United States context arises from recognition of the considerable variability among states as identified by Porter, Polikoff and Smithson (2009). Their rigorous content analysis revealed that state standards were no better aligned to national professional standards (such as the National Council of Teachers of Mathematics, 2000) than to other states' standards. The level of focus of the state standards also varied greatly across states. Hence, there has been a call for greater coherence through Common Core Standards in the United States. These standards for curriculum content are intended to have much greater focus than the current state standards (Porter et al., 2011). They are also considered by some a substantial answer to the challenge of addressing the problem of a curriculum that is 'a mile wide and an inch deep' (Common Core Standards Initiative, 2010, p. 3).

Commonalities in the emphases of recently revised national curricula

We outline in this section five common emphases evident in recently revised curricula, which reflect the priorities of policymakers. While these emphases are not necessarily reflected in all of the curriculum policies considered here, and the strength of emphasis varies across systems, their presence in most (if not all) systems makes them worthy of note.

The first is an emphasis on the kinds of learning relevant for twenty-first-century learners. The policy message is intended to shift educators' attention *beyond* content knowledge and discrete skill outcomes to encompass attention towards students' competencies for lifelong learning. The second is an emphasis in policy on values in teaching and learning. Thirdly, curriculum policies, more so than in the past, explicitly recognize that students have both the capability and the right to be deeply involved in decisions relating to their education. A fourth common emphasis is the attention given not only to content and outcomes in curriculum, but also to pedagogy. The fifth common emphasis in curricula is that of strengthening partnerships with parents in relation to teaching and learning in efforts to promote improved outcomes for students. Examples of these emphases are elaborated next.

Beyond content knowledge and skills to competencies in curriculum

Increasingly, curriculum policies are moving towards emphasizing twenty-first century key competencies for lifelong learning. Key competencies integrate knowledge, attitudes and values in ways that lead to action. They cannot be taught discretely, are context dependent, and involve practice and application in authentic real-world contexts (Rychen and Salganik, 2003). Unlike discrete skills, key competencies are described as having transformative potential (Reid, 2006); the potential to transform students' and teachers' experience of teaching and learning to be quite different from traditional approaches. An emphasis on competencies seeks to enable learners to transcend the mastery of discrete skills and acquisition of content knowledge that has traditionally been the focus of curricula. They are described by many as critical, given the complex demands and challenges of today's world. This was signalled in the OECD report on the Definition and Selection of Competencies (DeSeCo) Project:

> Globalization and modernization are creating an increasingly diverse and interconnected world. To make sense of and function well in this world, individuals need for example to master changing technologies and to make sense of large amounts of available information. They also face collective challenges as societies – such as balancing economic growth with environmental sustainability, and prosperity with social equity. In these contexts, the competencies that individuals need to meet their goals have become more complex, requiring more than the mastery of certain narrowly defined skills. (OECD, 2005, p. 4)

Key competencies also have a dispositional character, which requires attention not just to students' *ability* to use them, but their *readiness* and *willingness* to do so appropriately in a range of contexts (Carr and Claxton, 2002; Hipkins, 2007; Cowie and Hipkins, 2009). They involve a range of psychosocial resources (including skills and attitudes) that are applied in particular contexts. They promote trans-disciplinary thinking in ways that enable the development of new expertise (Australian Ministerial Council on Education, Employment, Training and Youth Affairs, 2008).

A focus on competencies, or capabilities, as they are referred to in some contexts is not without criticism. Biesta (2009), for example, describes it as a trend 'which verges on turning education into a form of therapy that is more concerned with the emotional well-being of pupils and students than with their emancipation' (p. 9). He also highlights the risk of the disappearance of attention to *what* students learn and what they learn it for.

Although expressed differently across nations (competencies, capabilities, capacities and cross-curricular skills), the call to move beyond narrowly defined skills in revisions to national curriculum policies is evident in many countries. In Australia, *general capabilities* are outlined. They are defined as 'a set of skills, behaviors and dispositions, or general capabilities that apply across subject-based content and equip [students] to be lifelong learners able to operate with confidence in a complex, information-rich, globalized world' (Australian

Curriculum Assessment and Reporting Authority, 2010, p. 18). Northern Ireland's curriculum outlines *cross-curricular skills* alongside thinking skills and personal capabilities, rather than discrete skills. Similarly, key purposes of Scotland's Curriculum for Excellence are the development of four *capacities* (to enable each child or young person to be a successful learner, a confident individual, a responsible citizen and an effective contributor) alongside promotion of interdisciplinary studies (Scottish Executive, 2004). The interdisciplinary aspect focuses on students experiencing learning in stimulating contexts, and calls for relevant, challenging and enjoyable learning. It also prioritizes students' development of deep understandings through revisiting learning and considering multiple perspectives. Interdisciplinary studies are also likely to involve students learning in contexts beyond the school site in ways that enrich their learning and emphasize competencies alongside content.

In New Zealand's national curriculum (Ministry of Education, 2007), five key competencies (thinking; using language, symbols, and texts; managing self; relating to others; participating and contributing) replace, and are significantly different to the 'essential skills' of the previous curriculum. The five competencies have a participatory, technological and dispositional orientation. They are intended to address the need for students to: participate appropriately in an increasingly diverse society; use new technologies; and to keep on learning in order to cope with rapidly changing workplaces (Brewerton, 2004). A focus on dispositions is described as important since competencies, unlike the skills outlined in the previous curriculum, focus on what people need to know *alongside* what they can do (Hipkins, 2006). Unlike skills, competencies in the revised New Zealand curriculum are promoted as requiring students to *want* to use them and to recognize how and when to do so appropriately.

The role of subjects or learning areas as prominent curriculum organizers has persisted in the face of the more recent competency-focused curricula. As Young and Muller (2010) suggest, 'It has become fashionable to proclaim the end of disciplinarity . . . but disciplines seem almost obstinately to linger on' (p. 20). That is certainly the case in the curricula examined here, as can be seen in the overview of subjects/learning areas in the most recent curriculum policy or draft policy in six countries (see Figure 8.2). However, curricula organizers that reflect disciplinary boundaries are often combined with statements of a curriculum serving instrumental rather than knowledge-focused purposes. This is seen in the developing Australian curriculum, which retains the traditional structure of scope and sequence within discrete learning areas, signals the importance of students' learning across disciplines and also of developing new kinds of expertise required in communities and workplaces of the twenty-first century.

Emerging International Trends in Curriculum

Scotland	New Zealand	Australia	Northern Ireland	Wales	England	USA (CCSS)
• Expressive arts • Health and well-being • Languages • Mathematics • Religious and moral education • Sciences • Social studies • Technologies	• English • The arts • Health and physical education • Learning languages • Mathematics and statistics • Science • Social sciences • Technology	• English • Mathematics • Science • Humanities and social science • The arts • Languages • Health and physical education • Technologies	• Language and literacy • Mathematics and numeracy • The arts • The world around us • Personal development and mutual understanding • Physical education	Foundation stage: Seven areas of learning • Personal and social development • Well-being and cultural diversity • Language, literacy and communication skills • Mathematical development • Welsh language development • Knowledge and understanding of the world • Physical development • Creative development Key stage 2/3/4: • Welsh • Music • English • Modern foreign languages • Mathematics • Science • information and communication technology • Design and technology • History • Art and design • Physical education	Core subjects (compulsory across key stages 1–4): • English • Mathematics • Science Foundation subjects for key stages 1 - 3: • Art and design • Design and technology • Geography • History • Information and communication technology • Music • Modern foreign languages (at Key Stage 3 only) • Physical education • Citizenship (at Key Stage 3) Foundation subjects for key stages 4: • Citizenship • Information and communication technology • Physical education	• English language Arts • Literacy in history • Literacy in social studies • Literacy in science • Literacy in technical subjects • Mathematics

Figure 8.2 International curriculum frameworks.

The place of values in curriculum

Increasingly, national curricula reflect a demand to emphasize values in teaching and learning, not as a stand-alone or peripheral consideration, but as a vital element of curriculum design. As Lovat and Toomey (2009) put it, 'no longer is Values Education on the periphery of a curriculum that enshrines the central roles to be played by the teacher and the school in our society. It is at the very heart of these roles' (p. 11). There is a risk, though, of values education approaches being overly simplified through practices that focus on implementing lists of agreed values without exploring the wide range of concepts and meanings across ideologies (Keown, Parker and Tiakiwai, 2005). The expression of values in recent curricular reforms typically make clear that, while values education should transform beliefs and behaviour, this does not require the imposition on students of different sets of beliefs and values than those they already held. It does, though, mean 'challenging students to see that whatever beliefs and values they brought with them are but one set, one life-world, and to consider the life-worlds of others' (Lovat and Toomey, 2009, p. 8). In many curricula, normative sets of values are emphasized alongside more open 'citizenship' approaches in which students are encouraged to develop their own values (Gillies, 2006).

While values have always had a place in the New Zealand curriculum, this aspect is much more prominent in the most recent curriculum (Ministry of Education, 2007) than in previous curriculum frameworks and goes beyond merely determining sets of desirable values to be upheld. In addition to setting out a list of values deemed to be widely supported, which students should be encouraged to hold (including for example excellence, equity, integrity, respect), the 2007 curriculum signals that students should learn about the concept of values, and how to express, explore and critically analyse values (Keown et al., 2005). Northern Ireland's curriculum, likewise, emphasizes the development of moral thinking, values and action (Council for the Curriculum Examinations and Assessment, 2007). In Australia's curriculum ethical behaviour is included as one of the general capabilities and it promotes understandings about values in relation to ethical behaviour (Australian Curriculum Assessment and Reporting Authority, 2011).

Attention to pedagogy

Increasingly, curriculum policies are presenting direction not only about the content and outcomes of learning, but also about the pedagogical approaches that should be employed to achieve those outcomes. In some cases that direction is prescriptive, it is provided as guidance but explicitly linked to outcomes-based curriculum statements.

Concern with matters pedagogical is apparent, for example, in the introduction to Scotland's Curriculum for Excellence which highlights that '[the curriculum is] concerned both with what is to be learned and how it is taught' (Scottish Executive, 2002, p. 9). The concern with *how* content is to be taught is evident in the curriculum principles, which the curriculum states are intended to be applied at a classroom level and to assist teachers in their practices. Principles such as 'personalisation and choice' have clear pedagogical implications. The 'challenge and enjoyment' principle, the curriculum explains, requires that students are active in their learning.

Pedagogical direction in curriculum is also apparent in policy statements of Northern Ireland, Wales and New Zealand. In Northern Ireland, for example, there are statements about 'sound educational practice' (Council for the Curriculum Examinations and Assessment, 2007). The foundation stage developmental curriculum of Wales sends particularly strong messages about the kind of pedagogy that students ought to experience, including calls for real-world exploration, practical activities, open-ended questions and problem-solving. The direction in the New Zealand Curriculum (Ministry of Education, 2007) is less specific in terms of strategies, but sets out a model of effective pedagogy that has a *teaching as inquiry* orientation. The inclusion of this model resulted from a curriculum development process involving collaboration between academics, practitioners and other stakeholders alongside policymakers. It requires educators to engage in three kinds of inquiry as they seek to achieve curriculum goals – focusing inquiry, teaching inquiry and learning inquiry (Aitken and Sinnema, 2008; Sinnema and Aitken, 2011). The focusing inquiry requires careful attention to prioritizing what matters most for students given the curriculum requirements, community expectations, and most importantly, the learning needs, interests and experiences of the learner. The teaching inquiry requires attention to both outcomes-linked research evidence and practitioner experience to inform decisions about what teaching strategies will be tried. It encourages teachers to view research evidence as the basis for explaining findings about the impact of their own practice on their students' learning, and as sources of better-informed conjectures about what might enhance learning for students in their classrooms. The learning inquiry requires consideration of the impact of teaching actions on student outcomes and experience, and inquiry into the relationship between the teaching and those outcomes. The New Zealand Curriculum also sets out broad statements of pedagogical approaches for which there is evidence of positive impacts on student learning. These prompt teachers to create a supportive learning environment, encourage reflective thought and action, enhance the relevance of new learning, facilitate shared learning, make connections to prior learning and experience and provide sufficient opportunities to learn. This prescription of broad approaches differs from the more specific teaching methods prescribed in other reform initiatives such as the literacy and numeracy strategy in the English system. In contrast, the United States Common Core Standards explicitly exclude attention to pedagogy; clarifications accompanying the standards make clear that they establish *what* students need to learn, but do not dictate *how* teachers should teach.

Promoting student agency in curriculum

While not as prominent as the aforementioned curricula emphases (key competencies and values for example) there is an emergence of calls by curriculum policymakers for student agency in teaching and learning. This promotes the notion of learners exerting control over their experience of teaching, learning and assessment.

Attention to student agency in Curriculum for Excellence, for example, is apparent in statements about the application of the 'personalisation and choice' principle. The focus is on changing the nature of choices for learners throughout schooling – a progression from choices about activities then topic and contexts for learning in the junior phases, through to decisions about programmes in the senior phase (Scottish Government, 2008).

In Wales, commitment to student agency is strongly evident in the 'Listening to learners' documents that accompany the curriculum. As a key response to the United Nations Convention on the Rights of the Child (United Nations General Assembly, 1989), these documents promote support of the convention by clearly outlining children's rights at school: all pupils have a right to be heard; and, all pupils should have an opportunity to have their views considered when decisions are taken that affect them. The right of consultation should extend over a wide range of issues in school including the school curriculum and assessment arrangements; and consultation should promote equality of opportunity and lead to an improved educational experience (Welsh Assembly Government, 2008b, 2008c). At the foundation stage, balance between teacher and child-initiated activity is required – 'there must be a balance between structured learning through child-initiated activities and those directed by practitioners. A well-planned curriculum gives children opportunities to be creatively involved in their own learning' (Welsh Assembly Government, 2008a, p. 6).

These calls, when considered in light of both scholarly work on student agency and the multiple accountabilities surrounding curriculum implementation are somewhat problematic. Emirbayer and Mische (1998) describe agency as the ability to exert control over, and give direction to one's life. Student agency, therefore, involves students making connections between their past learning experience, and aspirations for the future, which enable *them* to take action in the present. It affords students autonomy, control and influence on action in ways that acknowledge their competence (Tomanovic, 2003). This contrasts with a kind of participation whereby students act mainly in response to teachers' decisions and demands – a distinction between what Shier (2010) frames as participation as social control versus participation as empowerment. Embedding these notions of agency in curricula is complex however, given competing curriculum and assessment requirements that are not necessarily conducive to aspirations for student agency. That complexity, and the contested terrain of student agency, is not typically rationalized well in policy.

Strengthening partnerships with parents in curriculum

National curricula are increasingly emphasizing partnerships between schools, teachers and parents. This emphasis reflects high-profile research that signals partnership as crucial to system improvement and engagement with parents as a high impact means of improving outcomes for students (Epstein and Sheldon, 2006; Mourshed, Chijioke and Barber, 2010). While approaches to school-family partnerships vary widely in their effectiveness, and some can even be counterproductive (Robinson, Hohepa and Lloyd, 2008), curricula typically promote the general idea of partnership and engagement. Scotland's Curriculum for Excellence, for example, indicates the importance of working in partnership to support students, and of involving parents and caregivers in curriculum planning. Schools need, it says 'to provide scope for partners to plan appropriate learning and teaching to meet the challenges young people will encounter. Partnership working is an important element in curriculum planning' (Scottish Government, 2008, p. 9). This requirement reflects Scottish legislation (Scottish Schools (Parental Involvement) Act (Scottish Parliament (2006)) that aims to help parents to be involved with their child's education and learning, welcomed as active participants in school life, and encouraged to express their views on school education.

Parental involvement is also promoted in the New Zealand Curriculum, which has 'community engagement' as one of its eight principles, placing far greater emphasis on this notion than the previous curriculum. It requires schools and teachers to encourage greater involvement of parents and local communities in their children's learning. Most importantly, it signals the involvement of parents not just as recipients of communications from schools, but as meaningful partners in teaching and learning efforts for their children. The notion of parents' involvement is in itself not new, but its prominence as a key principle in the curriculum has given greater status to initiatives aimed at engaging families in curriculum decisions. In the United States, the desirability of engaging with parents is evident, but its purpose is slightly different to the examples highlighted above. Rather than seeking to involve parents in decisions, the common core standards focus on engagement as a means of developing common understandings between stakeholders.

Reducing prescription and increasing autonomy

There are also commonalities in moves to reduce the extent of statutory requirements relating to curriculum, reducing the degree of prescription and increasing school-level autonomy for curriculum decision-making. At the extreme in this regard is Scotland where the national curriculum is non-statutory, but provided by the Government as a national framework. Curriculum for Excellence combines both top-down government prescription, and bottom-up school development and in so doing positions teachers as agents of change (Priestley, 2010). In particular, a great deal of the curriculum content is presented as guidance, and is described as providing 'professional space for teachers and other staff to . . . meet the varied needs of all children and young people' (Scottish Executive, 2004, p. 3).

In New Zealand the 2007 national curriculum, which is statutory, increased autonomy at the school level significantly – broad statements about the purpose, rationale and structure of each learning area are statutory, but the specific outcomes-focused achievement objectives at each level in various strands for each curriculum area are no longer prescribed. Rather, they are provided as guidance, and schools select from them (and also develop their own) in response to the identified interests and learning needs of their students. Similarly, the national curriculum emphasizes the flexibility of the policy, and the requirement for schools to develop their own school curriculum:

> The national curriculum [. . .] gives schools the scope, flexibility, and authority they need to design and shape their curriculum so that teaching and learning

is meaningful and beneficial to their particular communities of students. In turn, the design of each school's curriculum should allow teachers the scope to make interpretations in response to the particular needs, interests, and talents of individuals and groups of students in their classes. (Ministry of Education, 2007, p. 37)

While New Zealand educators responded positively to the increased flexibility of the national curriculum, and the professional freedom it allowed them, they also reported low levels of confidence about implementation (Sinnema, 2011). Flexibility, it seems, was appealing but placed demands on schools for curriculum design that not all had the resources to meet.

In England, current proposals also support a curriculum that allows 'more scope for curricular provision determined at school or community level' (Department for Education, 2011, p. 7). Three possible strategies for slimming down statutory requirements have been identified:

> ... to remove subjects altogether from statutory curriculum requirements; to retain subjects as statutory but not specify what should be taught in these subjects; or to retain subjects as statutory, but to reduce the extent of the specification of what is to be taught. (Department for Education, 2011, p. 8)

While all three options reduce the statutory requirements, the degree of specificity in the programmes of study for core and foundation subjects signals much tighter national curriculum control than in the New Zealand and Scottish contexts described above. They prescribe the outcomes for learners and in many cases the contexts for learning in which those outcomes should be addressed.

While many countries retain statements within or alongside curriculum policies that signal pedagogical approaches (e.g. experiences and outcomes statements in Scotland) as well as their emphasis on school-level autonomy, in England, a more measured approach than other countries is taken. The outline of prescribed content described above, for example, reflects the review recommendation 'to balance structure, expectation and flexibility' (Department for Education, 2011, p. 38). It represents one approach to addressing the tension between a curriculum that is open in relation to input, but closed on the side of output. It also reduces the strength of influence of external evaluation agencies since, as Biesta (2008) notes, they become more responsible for checking implementation of pre-specified curriculum, than for judging the quality of multiple different approaches to operationalizing a curriculum.

Discussion

In the following section we challenge assumptions about the extent to which the goals described in curricula policies (improvement, equity, future relevance and coherence) might be supported through the emphases on competencies, pedagogy, values, student agency, partnerships and reduced prescription. In particular, we highlight challenges facing educators that may compromise the achievement of those curricula aspirations.

The rhetoric of educational improvement as a key goal of national curricula is difficult to criticize, but the focus on pedagogy in many curricula, in an effort to strengthen the practices associated with curriculum implementation, presents challenges for educators. The simultaneous trend towards reduced prescription means that pedagogical direction can be seen as vague and non-specific. There is the potential where that is the case for wide variation in how terms such as 'active learning' (promoted in the Scottish Curriculum) are interpreted, and the risk of narrow definitions of terms requiring broad and deep understanding (Priestley, 2010). While teachers tend to view that autonomy positively, it can also be perceived as placing the burden for improvement on those interpreting the curriculum rather than on those designing it. In addition, the degree to which they have agency varies from context to context – 'individuals who exercise considerable agency in one setting might be disempowered in another' (Priestley, 2011, p. 8). Furthermore, where greater specification is provided, there is the problem of assumptions about particular practices being relevant in all contexts. In New Zealand, an attempt to alleviate that problem lies in the inquiry-oriented pedagogical model outlined in the national curriculum (Sinnema and Aitken, 2011).

A further challenge relates to the extent to which statements of preferred pedagogies in curricula statements can actually influence shifts in teaching given the nature of teachers' conceptual change. Teachers' conceptions of teaching, learning and curriculum dimensions (such as competencies, values or partnerships) are built into their mental structures, frame their understanding of the world and are deeply resistant to change (Posner et al., 1982). While passive acceptance of all new curriculum ideas is not desirable in a profession like teaching, where change is warranted resistance is critical to consider. It has implications for teachers' practice, and ultimately, for the experience their students have of curriculum. Spillane, Reiser and Reimer's (2002) framework provides a cognitive perspective to explain why new information, such as that embedded in a new curriculum, does not simply supplant existing knowledge and practice. In particular, they draw attention to the influence (sometimes an unhelpful one) of prior knowledge; variation in interpretations between teachers of the same policy message; misunderstandings about new ideas as familiar in ways that hinder change; the salience of superficial, rather than deeper features; bias towards prior beliefs and values; and people's emotions and desire to maintain positive self-image thwarting implementation in line with policy intentions (Spillane et al., 2002). They emphasize how attending to implementing agents' sense-making about policy is critical, since even practitioners who do not intentionally seek to resist a policy are influenced in those ways.

Several of the curricula examined here promote pedagogical approaches that ensure student enjoyment, motivation and active learning – characteristics of learning that few would argue are not desirable. Attention to such matters in national curricula, however, is not without critique (Biesta, 2004, 2006). Oates (2010) suggests it is a category error to see national curricula as 'exciting and motivating'. National Curriculum specifications for subjects, he argues, should not include motivating contexts, or be anything other than a relatively dry statement of essential elements. Securing the motivation of students is, he says 'a subtle and sensitive process, requiring great skill on the part of teachers and schools . . . National Curriculum should focus on being a clear statement of content' (p. 7). Lambert (2011) makes a similar point, suggesting that 'despite the existence of a national curriculum – or possibly, because of the existence of a national curriculum – teachers have turned away from "knowledge" and . . . have been encouraged to overinvest energy into pedagogy and almost make a fetish out of "learning"' (p. 245).

The improvement of equity is another educational goal of undisputed value. There are, however, alignment issues when curricula with equity goals are competency focused, but measures of outcomes used for comparing system equity are content-focused, such as the literacy, numeracy and science assessments used in the Programme for International Student Assessment (OECD, 2010).

There are similar potential issues with curricula that set out goals of strengthening the equity of achievement and also increase flexibility and autonomy at the school and teacher level. There are compelling arguments for and against increased flexibility and reduced prescription. Flexibility acknowledges teachers' professional autonomy; it increases their sense of control and, therefore, commitment and satisfaction; and it enables responsiveness to local needs and interests. But flexibility increases workload because it diminishes the value of, and market for, published resources; it presupposes expertise in curriculum that may not be widely of evenly spread. It may, therefore, compromise entitlement and equity as schools and individual teachers make idiosyncratic choices about what to teach. In particular, the space for those choices, according to Young (2010), increases the likelihood of inequitable access to powerful knowledge. That inequity may also not be reflected in reports of improved success, which rather than reflecting actual improvement in the rates of success (in relation to powerful knowledge) may reflect easier standards being met by more students.

The goal for curricula to be future focused is common in many nations, but many curriculum policy statements signal both neo-conservative *and* instrumentalist interests in their content and organization (Young, 2008). They tend to provide little guidance on how to deal with future focused skills and competencies when curriculum policy statements both emphasize competencies, connectivity and integration, while also presenting organizational structures that signal the insulation of subject boundaries. As Priestley and Humes (2010) describe, there is a problem of the national curriculum in Scotland, for example, 'simultaneously taking a view of knowledge as being something constructed by learners on the one hand and being a pre-specified, essentialist body of knowledge to be acquired and tested on the other hand' (p. 26). Others argue that goal for curricula to prepare students for the future should not necessitate future-focused curricula, but rather knowledge-led curricula (Young, 2010). Such a curriculum, Young argues, has the intellectual development of students at its heart, provides students with the concepts to enable progress in their learning and distinguishes school knowledge from everyday knowledge.

The goal to improve coherence in curricula is also intuitively logical. But the reduced prescription typical of many recent developments leads to uncertainty for teachers and the risk of reduced coherence in student experience of curriculum. Careful attention also needs to be given to coherence in approaches that respond to the emphasis on partnerships since, while desirable for many reasons, the wider the involvement in decisions about curriculum content, concepts and design, the greater the risk of reduced coherence.

Here we have highlighted the need to consider coherence in the goals of, and emphases in, national curriculum developments. There are strong arguments for goals of educational improvement, and greater equity, future relevance and coherence in education. There are also legitimate calls for curriculum developments to address those goals in national curricula. No single national curriculum, however, can achieve any one of those goals. The emphasis in recently developed curricula on competencies, pedagogy, values, student agency, partnerships and reduced prescription has possibilities and potential. Progress on the goals underpinning those curricula will require attention to the conduciveness of other system elements such as assessment and qualifications, initial teacher education, professional standards, teacher professional learning and school leadership. It will also require attention to how practitioners responsible for implementing such curricula make sense of and respond to the curriculum as they give effect to that curriculum in their practice.

References

Aitken, G. and Sinnema, C. (2008), *Effective Pedagogy in Social Sciences/Tikanga ā Iwi: Best Evidence Synthesis Iteration*. Wellington: Ministry of Education.

Australian Curriculum Assessment and Reporting Authority (2010), *The Shape of the Australian Curriculum*. Online at www.acara.edu.au/verve/_resources/Shape_of_the_Australian_Curriculum.pdf (accessed 21/09/10).

— (2011), *The Australian Curriculum*. Online at www.australiancurriculum.edu.au/GeneralCapabilities/Ethical-behaviour (accessed 28/10/11).

— (2012), *The Shape of the Australian Curriculum: Version 3*. Online at www.acara.edu.au/verve/_resources/The_Shape_of_the_Australian_Curriculum_V3.pdf (accessed 08/10/12).

Australian Ministerial Council on Education, Employment, Training and Youth Affairs (2008), *Melbourne Declaration on Educational Goals for Young Australians*. Online at www.mceecdya.edu.au/verve/_resources/national_declaration_on_the_educational_goals_for_young_australians.pdf (accessed 08/10/12).

Biddle, B., Good, T. and Goodson, I. (eds) (1997), *International Handbook of Teachers and Teaching*, volume 2. Dordrecht: Kluwer Academic Publishers.

Biesta, G. J. J. (2004), 'Against learning. Reclaiming a language for education in an age of learning'. *Nordisk Pedagogik*, 23, 70–82.

— (2006), *Beyond Learning. Democratic Education for a Human Future*. Boulder, CO: Paradigm Publishers.

— (2008), 'What kind of citizen? What kind of democracy? Citizenship education and the Scottish Curriculum for Excellence'. *Scottish Educational Review*, 40, 38–52.

— (2009), 'Good education in an age of measurement: on the need to reconnect with the question of purpose in education'. *Educational Assessment, Evaluation and Accountability*, 21, 33–46.

Brewerton, M. (2004), *Reframing the Essential Skills: Implications of the OECD Defining and Selecting Key Competencies Project. A Background Paper for the Ministry of Education*. Wellington: Ministry of Education.

Briant, E. and Doherty, C. (2012), 'Teacher educators mediating curricular reform: anticipating the Australian curriculum'. *Teaching Education*, 23, 51–69.

Carr, M. and Claxton, G. (2002), 'Tracking the development of learning dispositions'. *Assessment in Education: Principles, Policy and Practice*, 9, 9–37.

Common Core Standards Initiative (2010), *Common Core State Standards for English Language, Arts and Literacy in History/Social Studies, Science, and Technical Subjects*. Online at www.corestandards.org/assets/CCSSI_ELA%20Standards.pdf (accessed 08/10/12).

Council for the Curriculum Examinations and Assessment (2007), *The Northern Ireland Curriculum: Primary*. Online at www.qub.ac.uk/schools/SchoolofEducation/ProspectiveStudents/InitialTeacherEducationPGCE/PrimarySchoolExperience/filestore/Filetoupload,72469,en.pdf (accessed 08/10/12).

Cowie, B. and Hipkins, R. (2009), *Curriculum Implementation Exploratory Studies: Final Report*. Online at www.educationcounts.govt.nz/publications/curriculum/57760/1 (accessed 08/10/12).

Department for Children, Schools and Families (2007), *The Children's Plan: Building Brighter Futures*. London: HMSO.

Department for Education (2011), *The Framework for the National Curriculum. A Report by the Expert Panel for the National Curriculum Review*. London: Department for Education.

— (2012), *The School Curriculum*. Online at www.education.gov.uk/schools/teachingandlearning/curriculum/ (accessed 15/06/12).

Education Scotland (no date), *Curriculum for Excellence: Successful Learners, Confident Individuals, Responsible Citizens, Effective Contributors*. Online at www.educationscotland.gov.uk/Images/all_experiences_outcomes_tcm4-539562.pdf (accessed 01/08/12).

Emirbayer, M. and Mische, A. (1998), 'What is agency?'. *American Journal of Sociology*, 103, 962–1023.

Epstein, J. L. and Sheldon, S. (2006), 'Moving forward: ideas for research on school, family, and community partnerships', in C. Conrad and R. Serlin (eds), *SAGE Handbook for Research in Education: Engaging Ideas and Enriching Inquiry*. California: SAGE Publications, pp. 117–38.

Gillies, D. J. M. (2006), 'A curriculum for excellence: a question of values'. *Scottish Educational Review*, 38, 25–36.

Hipkins, R. (2006), *Background to the Key Competencies*. Report prepared by NZCER for the Ministry of Education. Online at www.tki.org.nz/r/nzcurriculum/pdfs/nature-of-k-round-paper.pdf (accessed 01/05/09).

— (2007), 'Engaging teachers in re-imagining curriculum'. *Curriculum Matters*, 3, 123–34.

HM Inspectorate of Education (2009), *Improving Scottish Education: A Report by HMIE on Inspection and Review 2005–2008*. Glasgow: HM Inspectorate of Education.

Honig, M. I. and Hatch, T. C. (2004), 'Crafting coherence: how schools strategically manage multiple, external demands'. *Educational Researcher*, 33, 16–30.

Hopmann, S. T. (2003), 'On the evaluation of curriculum reforms'. *Journal of Curriculum Studies*, 35, 459–78.

Keown, P., Parker, L. and Tiakiwai, S. (2005), *Values in the New Zealand Curriculum: A Literature Review on Values in the Curriculum*. Wellington: Ministry of Education.

Kyriades, L., Campbell, R. J. and Gagatsis, A. (2000), 'The significance of the classroom effect in primary schools: an application of Creemers' comprehensive model of educational effectiveness'. *School Effectiveness and School Improvement*, 11, 501–29.

Lambert, D. (2011), 'Reviewing the case for geography, and the knowledge turn in the English National Curriculum'. *Curriculum Journal*, 22, 243–64.

Lingard, B. (2010), 'Policy borrowing, policy learning: testing times in Australian schooling'. *Critical Studies in Education*, 51, 129–47.

Lovat, T. and Toomey, R. (2009), *Values Education and Quality Teaching: The Double Helix Effect*. Dordrecht, Netherlands: Springer.

Marshall, B. (2011), 'English in the National Curriculum: a simple redraft or a major rewrite?'. *Curriculum Journal*, 22, 187–99.

Ministry of Education (2002), *Curriculum Stocktake Report to the Minister of Education*. Online at www.educationcounts.govt.nz/publications/curriculum/5815 (accessed 08/10/12).

— (2007), *The New Zealand Curriculum*. Wellington: Learning Media.

Moursed, M., Chijioke, C. and Barber, M. (2010), *How the World's Most Improved School Systems Keep Getting Better*. London: McKinsey and Company.

National Council of Teachers of Mathematics (2000), *Principles and Standards for School Mathematics*. Reston, VA: National Council for Teachers of Mathematics.

National Governors Association (2012), *Common Core State Standards Initiative* Online at www.corestandards.org/ (accessed 15/05/12).

Oates, T. (2010), *Could Do Better: Using International Comparisons to Refine the National Curriculum in England*. Cambridge: University of Cambridge.

— (2011), 'Could do better: using international comparisons to refine the National Curriculum in England'. *Curriculum Journal*, 22, 121–50.

OECD (2005), *The Definition and Selection of Key Competencies: Executive Summary*. Online at www.pisa.oecd.org/dataoecd/47/61/35070367.pdf (accessed 08/10/12).

— (2007), *Quality and Equity of Schooling in Scotland. Reviews of National Policies for Education*. Paris: OECD.

— (2010), *PISA 2009 Results: Overcoming Social Background – Equity in Learning Opportunities and Outcomes*, volume 2. Paris: OECD.

Pepper, D. (2008), *Primary Curriculum Change: Directions of Travel in 10 Countries*. London: Qualifications and Curriculum Authority.

Porter, A., Polikoff, M. S. and Smithson, J. (2009), 'Is there a de facto national intended curriculum? Evidence from state content standards'. *Educational Evaluation and Policy Analysis*, 31, 238–68.

Porter, A., McMaken, J., Hwang, J. and Yang, R. (2011), 'Common core standards: the new U.S. intended curriculum'. *Educational Researcher*, 40, 103–16.

Posner, G. J., Strike, K. A., Hewson, P. W. and Gertzog, W. A. (1982). 'Accomodation of a scientific conception: towards a theory of conceptual change'. *Science Education*, 66, 211–27.

Priestley, M. (2010), 'Curriculum for excellence: transformational change or business as usual?' *Scottish Educational Review*, 42, 23–36.

— (2011), 'Schools, teachers and curriculum change: a balancing act?' *Journal of Educational Change*, 12, 1–23.

Priestley, M. and Humes, W. (2010), 'The development of Scotland's Curriculum for Excellence: amnesia and déjà vu'. *Oxford Review of Education*, 36, 345–61.

Reid, A. (2006), 'Key competencies: a new way forward or more of the same?' *Curriculum Matters*, 2, 43–62.

Robinson, V., Hohepa, M. and Lloyd, C. (2008), *School Leadership and Student Outcomes: Identifying What Works and Why. Best Evidence Synthesis Iteration*. Wellington: Ministry of Education.

Rychen, D. and Salganik, L. (eds) (2003), *Key Competencies for a Successful Life and a Well Functioning Society*. Cambridge, MA: Hogrefe and Huber.

Scheerens, J., Vermeulen, C. and Pelgrum, W. J. (1989), 'Generalizability of instructional and school effectiveness indicators across nations'. *International Journal of Educational Research*, 13, 789–99.

Scottish Executive (2004), *A Curriculum for Excellence: The Curriculum Review Group*. Edinburgh: Scottish Executive.

Scottish Government (2008), *Curriculum for Excellence – Building the Curriculum 3: A Framework for Learning and Teaching*. Edinburgh: Scottish Government.

Scottish Parliament (2006), *Scottish Schools (Parental Involvement) Act,* Scottish Parliament (Scottish Parliament, 10 May 2006).

Shier, H. (2010), 'Children as public actors: navigating the tensions'. *Children and Society*, 24, 24–37.

Sinnema, C. (2011), *Monitoring and Evaluating Curriculum Implementation. Final Evaluation Report on the Implementation of the New Zealand Curriculum 2008–2009*. Wellington: The Ministry of Education.

Sinnema, C. and Aitken, G. (2011), 'Teaching as inquiry in the New Zealand curriculum: origins and implementation', in J. Parr, H. Hedges and S. May (eds), *Changing Trajectories of Teaching and Learning*. Wellington: NZCER, pp. 29–48.

Spillane, J., Reiser, B. J. and Reimer, T. (2002), 'Policy implementation and cognition: reframing and refocusing implementation research'. *Review of Educational Research*, 72, 387–431.

Tomanovic, S. (2003), 'Negotiating children's participation and autonomy within families'. *International Journal of Children's Rights*, 11, 51–71.

United Nations General Assembly (1989), *Convention on the Rights of the Child,* Treaty Series, volume 1577.

Welsh Assembly Government (2008a), *Framework for Children's Learning for 3 to 7-year-olds in Wales*. Cardiff: Welsh Assembly Government.

— (2008b), *Listening to Learners – Primary*. Online at http://wales.gov.uk/topics/educationandskills/schoolshome/curriculuminwales/listeningtolearners/listeninglearnersprimary/?lang=en (accessed 25/11/12).

— (2008c), *Listening to Learners – Secondary*. Online at http://wales.gov.uk/dcells/publications/curriculum_and_assessment/2300767/2302217/introductionpdf?lang=en (accessed 25/11/12).

— (2008d), *National Curriculum – Key Stages 2, 3 and 4*. Online at http://wales.gov.uk/topics/educationandskills/schoolshome/curriculuminwales/arevisedcurriculumforwales/nationalcurriculum/?lang=en (accessed 25/11/12).

Young, M. (2008), *Bringing Knowledge Back In: From Social Constructivism to Social Realism in the Sociology of Education*. London: Routledge.

— (2010), 'The future of education in a knowledge society: the radical case for a subject-based curriculum'. *Journal of the Pacific Circle Consortium for Education*, 22, 21–32.

Young, M. and Muller, J. (2010), 'Three educational scenarios for the future: lessons from the sociology of knowledge'. *European Journal of Education*, 45, 11–27.

Developing the Teacher – or Not?

Ian Menter and Moira Hulme

Introduction

In this chapter we review the connections between curriculum reform and the reform of teachers' work, especially over the last ten years. It is therefore an analysis of links between pedagogical and curriculum policy. Although the central focus is on Scotland, we also refer to parallel developments elsewhere in the United Kingdom and internationally. We draw on our own work in Scotland (including involvement in a major consultation with teachers and others) and the United Kingdom (including studies of teacher engagement in enquiry and responses to pay restructuring). The main theme that emerges from the chapter is the question of whether teachers are being 're-professionalized' and empowered by the reforms, or whether, on the other hand, they are actually being drawn into and subjected to new forms of management and control, thus reducing their scope for agency and autonomy.

Curricular and pedagogical reform

Since 1988 when the UK Government in London first asserted direct control of the school curriculum in England, Northern Ireland and Wales, we have seen continuing efforts towards improvement and modernization of schooling. In Scotland, there were also major curricular reforms around this time, led from the Scottish Office, but influenced by the desire of the Scottish policy community to ensure a distinctive trajectory north of the border (Priestley, 2002). Many of the debates that were carried out in the media and in public policy during this period were already very familiar to teachers and educationists within their professional circles. But the discussion of what is taught in schools assumed a much wider public significance that was unprecedented since the arrival of compulsory state education. While this was perhaps most visible in England it was also happening across the wider United Kingdom and since the moves towards formal devolution of education policy following the 1998 referendum, has continued apace in all four parts of the United Kingdom, albeit with different emphases (Jones, 2003).

But this has not only been a UK phenomenon. As we have seen the growing significance attached to 'the knowledge economy' across the world, so politicians and policymakers in developed and developing nations have seen curricular reform as a key political agenda item (Jones et al., 2008; Rizvi and Lingard, 2009). Following the worldwide efforts to modernize the school curriculum, there has been continuing concern in many countries about the danger of 'falling behind'. These anxieties have been fed by the introduction of a number of global comparisons, such as PISA (Programme for International Student Assessment) and TIMSS (Trends in International Mathematics and Science Study), which have sought to demonstrate how pupil attainment compares in different nation-states in aspects such as literacy, mathematics and science. As such concerns have accelerated there was a realization that curriculum is not the only aspect of an education system that may influence 'outcomes'. A growing body of work and of political discourse focused on the quality of teaching and indeed the quality of teachers. The debates have turned then to include the nature of teacher performance and teacher education and training. Much of this concern has been fostered by reports published by international organizations such as the Organisation for Economic Cooperation and Development (OECD) and by transnational corporations (business consultancies) such as McKinsey and Co (Ball, 2012). The titles of some of these reports alone demonstrate very succinctly how these concerns are being presented: *How the World's Best-Performing Schools Come Out on Top* (Mourshed and Barber, 2007); *Building a High Quality Teaching Profession – Lessons from Around the World* (OECD, 2011).

If we look at the curricular and pedagogical reforms in more detail we find some interesting tensions and contradictions within and between them. The debates on curriculum have focused both on 'basic skills' and on 'flexible specialization'. We have seen a continuing tension between the influences of the 'public educators' and the 'industrial trainers', to use the terms invoked by Williams in his 1960 analysis of education in England (Williams, 1960). There has been a desire to ensure that learners have the skills and knowledge required to function in and contribute to a modern democracy but also a recognition that creativity and the affective domain may be important elements in effective learning in a rapidly changing economy. So quite commonly we have seen a tension between an objectives-driven and a process-driven model of curriculum. In the Scottish case of Curriculum for Excellence (CfE), Priestley and Humes (2010) have shown how this confusion is manifested. And while selective schooling of the 'modern' form, as developed after the Second World War in England, based on now outdated notions of fixed intelligence, has largely disappeared, new and perhaps less visible forms of selection and differentiation have emerged. These are manifest not only through continuing debates about the nature and provision of vocational education, with different courses for different 'types of learner', but also in the provision of new forms of schools, most notably in England. So we have seen under New Labour and more recently under the Coalition government[1] the promotion of 'academies' and 'free schools', schools with greater independence from local government (but not necessarily from central government) (Mongon and Chapman, 2009). The increasing involvement of private sector sponsors and donors is also increasing the diversity of provision (Ball, 2007). Much of this is done in the name of providing greater choice for parents, but it remains a fact that real choice tends to be associated with wealth and privilege and thus the authenticity of the meritocracy on offer must be questioned. Certainly the continuing association between economic disadvantage and low educational attainment belies the claims for equal opportunity.

In pedagogical reform there have been similar apparently opposing tendencies. For example with the increased emphasis on pupil attainment and the introduction of national testing, there has been much concern about results. In England, schools have been judged very heavily on the basis of trends in their test and exam scores (Mansell, 2007). At the same time, teachers have been encouraged to introduce formative assessment into their routine practice ('assessment for learning'). Here the emphasis is on using evaluation and judgements to improve the focus of teaching and learning, in other words an emphasis on process rather than outcome. But yet there is little evidence that improvements in formative assessment are directly related to improvements in summative assessments ('results').

For many teachers it has been the measurement of their own performance that has been one of the biggest changes in the nature of their work over recent years. Some of these developments may be traced back to the mid-1980s when the UK Government started to make interventions into teacher education and training. However moves towards redefining teaching according to a set of standards accelerated in the late 1990s with the formal introduction of aspects of performance management including performance-related pay award systems (Mahony and Hextall, 2000; Gleeson and Husbands, 2001). The standards agenda is now firmly embedded with initial teacher education across the United Kingdom and in many other countries (Darling-Hammond and Lieberman, 2012) and is increasingly taking hold across the full career of teachers.

In England, in addition to the encroaching use of standards to measure teacher performance, there was also direct intervention into pedagogical techniques, through the introduction of 'national strategies'. Commencing with 'The Literacy Strategy', closely followed by 'The Numeracy Strategy', the Labour government that came to power in 1997 sought to address poor performance by some pupils in these areas by ensuring common 'best practice' in primary schools across England. In due course this was followed by the 'Key Stage 3 Strategy', designed to ensure that the benefits achieved in the primary schools continued to be maintained when pupils moved into the secondary phase at the age of 11 (DfEE, 2001a, 2001b).

There is no doubt that these central government interventions into teaching did achieve many of their aims, not least in raising the attainment of some of the lower performing pupils. However, they also fundamentally changed what might be called the 'governance of teaching'. The scope for teacher decision making, both about what to teach and about how to teach, had changed significantly as a result of these interventions. The dilemma posed for governments in the second decade of the twenty-first century is how to raise the professional self-esteem and standing of teachers at the same time as ensuring consistency in performance. This dilemma is captured well in some of the more recent (English) government policy papers on teaching, for example the White Paper *The Importance of Teaching*, published in 2010 (DfE, 2010). The commitment to improving standards 'for all' is matched by a commitment to emphasize the Government's support for teachers and their 'authority' in the classroom. This contrasts starkly with the vision of teachers set out in a Scottish policy document that appeared very soon afterwards, *Teaching Scotland's Future* (Donaldson, 2010; see also Hulme and Menter, 2011) which, while sharing the same commitment to improving standards, suggests teaching is a very complex and indeed intellectual occupation that must be built upon an extended form of professionalism.

In the next section we turn to Scotland as a case in point. The same tensions have been experienced there as elsewhere in the United Kingdom although some of the outcomes are quite distinctive and we can track how policy has developed and been shaped by a range of forces, drawing on a number of studies undertaken over recent years.

Linking curriculum and pedagogy: The Scottish case

Teachers' pay and conditions: The McCrone Agreement

The last decade has seen significant changes to teachers' work in Scotland. The 2001 Teachers' Agreement, *A Teaching Profession for the Twenty-First Century*, followed the report of the McCrone Inquiry which had found that, 'current conditions of service for teachers were no longer fully able to support and develop the profession' (SEED, 2001, p. 2). The Teachers' Agreement introduced improved salary scales and a new career structure including a salaried Induction year (with a maximum class contact commitment of 0.7 Full Time Equivalent) and a Chartered Teacher grade for experienced and accomplished teachers who elected to remain in the classroom. Other changes included the introduction of a 35-hour week for all teachers; a phased reduction in maximum class contact time to 22.5 hours per week across primary, secondary and special school sectors (with 7.5 hours per week for preparation and correction); and a contractual entitlement to 35 hours for continuing professional development (CPD) per annum based on an agreed annual CPD plan.

The following sections draw on three projects commissioned by the Scottish Government and allied agencies in the last decade: (1) the Teacher Working Time Research project (TWTR) (2005); (2) Research to Support Schools of Ambition (2006–10); and (3) the consultation on the draft Experiences and Outcomes of the new school curriculum (2008). Collectively these projects provide insights into the principles and processes of change experienced in Scottish schools and highlight factors that have promoted or inhibited teacher development.

Teacher Working Time

The need for curriculum development to be supported by teacher development is widely accepted and has clear implications for the use of teachers' time. The Teacher Working Time Research project was commissioned by the Scottish Negotiating Committee for Teachers (SNCT) and the Scottish Executive Education Department in August 2005 to gather evidence on whether the commitments on teachers' working week agreed following the McCrone Report had been met (Menter et al., 2006). A structured time-use diary was distributed to a nationally representative sample of 2,400 teachers registered with the General Teaching Council for Scotland. The diary was completed over one week (Monday to Sunday inclusive) in two sweeps in October 2005 (41% response rate) and January 2006 (34% response rate). The diary was accompanied by a questionnaire that provided additional information on respondents' experiences of their working work. Irrespective of status or sector most respondents reported working over 35 hours per week and indicated that their workload had increased since 2001. An average working week of 45 hours was reported, rising with seniority. Primary and secondary headteachers reported working in excess of 50 hours each week.

Teachers who participated in the TWTR project suggested that there was considerable variability in the application of the national agreement, especially in relation to local arrangements for collegiate time and off-site working (non-contact personal time for preparation and correction). While analysis of local authority policy documents revealed broad agreement on general expectations across authorities, scope for school-level discretion in giving shape to policy expectations produced perceptions of variability among teachers. This raises important issues of capacity to support collegial school-level decision-making within the new framework. Menter et al. (2006, p. 14) identified 'a need to further enhance negotiation and discussion skills of all staff in the development of school agreements on the use of time and to foster a culture in schools to enable collegiate working processes'. The TWTR project noted that while local authority documentation acknowledged the need for 'consultation and participatory decision making' (p. 16) capacity to support such deliberation was not firmly established within the profession.

The findings of the TWTR project signalled a number of tensions that were to continue to play out in local negotiations as the policy intentions of McCrone were subject to translation. Deliberation on a workload commensurate with the discharge of professional duties was juxtaposed against the dangers of promoting a 'clock watching or timesheet mentality' (p. 19). The national workload agreement was subject to processes of mediation that contributed to processes of 'individualization' and 'responsibilization' (Rose, 1996). The received message was that individual teachers as mature professionals needed to 'prioritize'; to develop skills in time management. From this perspective responsibility for changing working practices lies in no small part with the teacher and failure to manage workload within stipulated limits was a problem of over-commitment arising from poor self-management. This discourse is apparent in teachers' accounts where they positioned themselves as their own worst enemies, although there is little scope for delegation of duties in non-promoted posts. A teachers' side representative on a Local Negotiating Committee (LNCT) commented, 'there is a Calvinist streak out there of saying I will work till I drop or until the job is done' (Menter et al., 2006, p. 20).

At the same time, the priority afforded to professional development and collegial work was associated with 're-professionalization' and 'extended professionalism'. Controlled workload and specification of duties (including specification of authorized 'collegiate time' activities of over 195 hours per annum) were reconciled with claims to enhanced professional autonomy. Analysis of transcripts of interviews with LNCT joint secretaries in ten local authorities (i.e. employers' representatives and teachers' side senior elected officials) highlighted the need to allow teachers 'scope to make professional choices' and 'to achieve culture change towards full collegiate working' (Menter et al., 2006, p. 21). However time use was increasingly subject to scrutiny and close direction suggesting reduced discretion at the level of individual practitioners. Teachers were at once empowered and directed. Local deliberation resulted in the enfolding of a more performative and managerial work culture in the sense of monitoring and measuring the tasks that make up teachers' work for the purposes of regulation (Menter, Hulme and Sangster, 2012). Senior managers in the TWTR study reported that, in their view, some staff were becoming, 'less flexible, more aware of contractual obligation and less inclined to seek promotion' (p. 59). The emergence of a new prudential professional self is perhaps an unintended consequence of increased attention to working time.

The Schools of Ambition programme

The need to build work cultures capable of sustaining collegiate working and to build capacity for authentic devolved decision-making came to the fore once more in a national programme for school change. The Schools of Ambition programme (2006–10) was a collaborative partnership between 52 secondary schools, 3 universities and the Scottish Government Schools' Directorate. Devolution of responsibility and enhanced local control over the deployment of resources was a key feature of the programme. Collaboration was identified as a potentially powerful strategy to promote innovation, school improvement and teacher professional development. Other examples in the United Kingdom include the *School-Based Research Consortia Initiative* (1998–2001), the *Research Engaged Schools Programme* (2003–5) and the *Networked Learning Communities* programme (2000–6). Beyond the United Kingdom, strong models of school-university collaboration are found in the Australian *National Schools*

Network and variations on the Professional Development School model in the United States, Australia and Finland (Harradine, 1996; Teitel, 2004; Kontoniemi and Salo, 2011).

In Scotland the policy document *Ambitious, Excellent Schools* (Scottish Executive, 2004) set out a modernization agenda for Scotland's comprehensive schools. Within a framework of national guidance, schools were encouraged to explore flexible and innovative approaches to school improvement: 'to bring about a step change in ambition and achievement' (Scottish Executive, 2004, p. 12). In February 2005 local authorities were invited to nominate secondary schools to participate in the programme. Each school (or cluster of schools) submitted a 'transformational plan' outlining their priorities for change and if successful received additional funding of £100,000 per annum for three years. As the programme progressed many schools aligned their transformational plan with the impending challenge of full implementation of CfE (from August 2010). Priorities for change included the need for curriculum breadth, particularly the expansion of opportunities for more 'relevant' vocational learning to tackle issues of disaffection and disengagement and to address perceived local skills shortages. Several schools experimented with pedagogical approaches that encouraged higher levels of creativity, critical enquiry and cooperative learning (Menter et al., 2007, p. 15).

The programme offered a form of 'controlled de-control' (Du Gay, 1996) that sought to balance innovation, enquiry and accountability. A commitment to self-evaluation was a condition of the award. In June 2006 a consortium of the Universities of Glasgow, Aberdeen and Strathclyde was awarded a contract to provide support to the network of schools. There were two strands to this collaboration: (a) a mentoring strategy; and (b) an evaluation strategy to explore processes of change and lessons learned. With the support of a university mentor and an assigned professional advisor from the national support team, each school devised an evaluation strategy to map the 'distance travelled' towards locally defined goals (Menter et al., 2010a). On conclusion of the programme in 2010 each school collated a digital e-portfolio to 'tell the story' and share lessons from their experience with the wider education community.

The notion of devolved leadership and the development of strong and extensive partnership work featured prominently in school transformational plans. A range of external consultants were engaged to support the development of this work (e.g. Columba 1400, Brathay Consultancy, the Forum Consultancy, Space Unlimited and Sheppard Moscow). Project coordinators appointed from the school staff to temporary promoted posts held responsibility for managing a portfolio of SoA activities. Coordinators played an important brokerage role sharing the rationale for change, providing opportunities for cross-department and cross-hierarchy participation (Hulme et al., 2010). The emphasis on local 'ownership' was supported by reference to the new opportunities made available by curriculum reform at a national level. Local developments included participation in nationally coordinated initiatives such as the Future Learning and Teaching (FLaT) programme; local authority professional development courses on critical thinking, cooperative and collaborative learning; a range of enterprise and creativity initiatives including Arts across the Curriculum, Artists in Residence, the Scottish Arts Council Cultural Coordinators in Scottish Schools programme (CCiSS) and Scottish Screen's Moving Image Education; and Science, Technology, Engineering, and Mathematics Education (STEM-Ed) projects supported by the Small Piece Trust.

While the capacity of the schools to link curriculum development and self-evaluation was favourably noted by HMIE in their report, Lessons learned from the Schools of Ambition initiative (HMIE, 2010), the programme encountered many challenges in working towards the realization of locally specified goals. Participants suggested 'some tension' between School of Ambition goals and timelines, and local authority strategies and processes. There was a perception among some school staff that achieving the distinction and additional resource attached to School of Ambition status strained relations with other schools. Operational challenges included the need for flexibility in timetabling to support peer observation and co-teaching; as well as the considerable challenge of accommodating flexible vocational programmes (on- and off-site delivery) within the constraints of the school day. Partnership work with the Award Scheme Development and Accreditation Network (ASDAN), Skills Development Scotland, further education colleges and other training providers strengthened guidance and course choices for students aged 14 plus. However, the involvement of instructors (without teacher training) on school premises raised issues of supervision, child protection and discussion of age appropriate pedagogies and classroom climate. Enterprise initiatives that established Community Interest Companies raised new challenges for schools in working with local authorities and the Inland Revenue. At the end of the first year several headteachers reported 'we underestimated the extent to which the SoA would require all kinds of new ways of thinking about how you deliver aspects of the curriculum' (Menter et al., 2007, p. 17).

In responding creatively to new opportunities, the schools continued to work within a performative culture. Participating schools developed self-evaluation skills promoted in Scotland through established inspectorate methodologies, such as *How Good is Our School?* (HMIe, 2007) and the *Journey to Excellence* (no date); and extended their repertoire of evaluation skills through adopting an explicit research orientation to change in liaison with external partners. School leaders were most confident in demonstrating impact where they had addressed gaps in provision. Recruitment, retention and success rates on vocational programmes and the involvement of targeted groups of pupils in bespoke activities and services (e.g. outreach and counselling services) were presented as evidence of impact. Benchmarking and baseline data were generated using records of pupil attainment, attendance, referrals by staff (cause for concern, exclusion), contact with parents (on transition to secondary school, options queries, school events, parents' consultation evenings) and destinations of school leavers. External agencies such as the Centre for Confidence and Well-Being and the Hay Group worked with some of the schools to generate and analyse evaluation data.

The international literature suggests a tension between encouraging headteachers to author transformational plans that reflect complex local circumstances, and expectations of measurable success based on test and examination performance in the short-term (Thrupp and Wilmott, 2003). Participants in the SoA shared a concern that outcomes measurements should be 'more than pupil achievement in exams' and emphasized the importance of generating hard and soft indicators to establish 'value added', 'distance travelled', 'how we have enriched people's lives' (Menter et al., 2007, p. 18). Elsewhere in the United Kingdom and further afield, it has been noted that school-based curriculum development has been constrained by regulatory systems where standardization is required and sanctions imposed for failure to secure required improvements within a timescale acceptable to funders (Barker, 2005, 2008; Hargreaves and Goodson, 2006). In Scotland, the Hunter Foundation, a philanthropic organization funded by Sir Tom Hunter, withdrew support from six Glasgow secondary schools in 2009 on the reported grounds that the pace of change had not met expectations. Headteachers in the SoA programme, some of whom were contending with some of the most challenging circumstances in Scotland, approached expectations of 'transformation' within the three-year period additional funding with a degree of caution. Schools committed to large-scale year-on-year curriculum change would experience significant change as redesigned programmes were 'rolled out' and evaluated over a period of six years. Schools engaged in entrepreneurial activities would face challenges during and after the initial start-up phase. While schooled in the rhetoric of 'managed risk taking', several school leaders worked to reconcile public support for creativity with the challenge of demonstrating positive outcomes within an ambitious timescale.

The Schools of Ambition programme was a bold attempt to devolve responsibility for curriculum innovation to schools, supported by an additional resource and external support to develop capacity for research-based evaluation. As noted above, the school staff and their many partners encountered some difficulties in introducing new areas of curricular provision and new ways of working. A recurrent theme in the transcripts was the need to embed 'transformational goals' within the day-to-day work and core values of the school. Attention to teacher learning and the provision of opportunities for joint work were associated with progress. Lack of time for important development work (e.g. peer observation, mentoring, co-teaching, reflection and planning) was regarded as a major inhibitor. The 'busyness' of the school day and the multiple responsibilities of key staff restricted opportunities for collegial planning. The challenges of allocating time to 'strand leaders' while covering teaching commitments and dealing with staff absences, combined with a lack of flexibility in scheduling meetings with staff outside teaching hours (as a result of the Teachers Agreement) were noted difficulties. While it is difficult to untangle the influence of SoA from an assemblage of national and local programmes, including the reform of the curriculum, Assessment is for Learning (AifL), the strategy to address the proportion of young people not in education employment or training in Scotland (*More Choices, More Chances*, Scottish Government, 2006) and initiatives to promote enterprise and employability skills such as *Determined to Succeed* (Learning and Teaching Scotland, 2008), this experiment in local autonomy gives some indication of the will and capacity for innovation among community schools and an insight into the challenges and frustrations of devolved leadership.

Curriculum enactment and teacher development

There is an established literature that draws attention to the processes through which national education policy is mediated within local communities of practice (Ball, 1994; Spillane, 1999). This literature has drawn attention to processes of enactment and the influence of positionality and context in shaping how policy intentions play out or are 'enacted' in the field. Each of our three examples offers some insight into how policies that are positioned as offering professional advance – 'professionalizing' – are subject to mediation as they enter policy regimes where previous discourses continue to circulate. Our first example considered the national agreement on teacher duties and working time; and the association of this with enhanced professionalism and active self-management. The theme of professional agency also featured in our second example which considered the approach to innovation and whole school improvement promoted in the Schools of Ambition programme. Our final example revisits the key ideas of autonomy and accountability using the example of teachers' initial responses to the new school curriculum. The consultation on the draft guidance for a new school curriculum in Scotland identified very different support needs among the teacher workforce, which are underpinned by divergent views on professional learning and the parameters of professional responsibility.

A Curriculum for Excellence Progress and Proposals was published in March 2006. Draft experiences and outcomes for each curriculum area were released in stages from November 2007 until May 2008, accompanied by an engagement strategy to afford opportunities for feedback from teachers, parents, employers and representatives from local authorities, colleges and universities (November 2007–December 2008). Feedback was obtained via online questionnaires, an engagement 'road show' to encourage employer and parental input, regional CPD events, proforma from 256 schools engaged in six-month trials of the draft experiences and outcomes, and transcripts from 20 teacher focus groups (242 participants) convened to discuss each set of draft experiences and outcomes. In addition, telephone interviews were conducted with personnel with responsibility for curriculum support in each of the 32 local authorities. (Details of the project methodology and findings are reported in the University of Glasgow Final Report, 2009.) Final versions of the Experiences and Outcomes were published in April 2009 and full implementation of the CfE was achieved by August 2010.

For some teachers, especially those working in the later stages of primary education, CfE presented an opportunity to reclaim aspects of their professionalism. Many teachers within the focus groups welcomed what they perceived to be a move away from a 'prescriptive' approach that constrained teacher creativity. The philosophy and principles informing CfE, as expressed in the cover paper that accompanied each set of draft Experiences and Outcomes, were broadly endorsed by the profession. CfE was associated by experienced primary teachers with a partial return to more integrated or holistic ways of working. In describing the strengths of the Draft Experiences and Outcomes, the terms 'freedom' and 'flexibility' were frequently used. Senior managers suggested that the revised curriculum afforded scope for professional discretion and would allow schools to be more responsive to particular local circumstances.

> It [CfE] allows staff to use their professionalism once again, which had been removed largely from primary teachers by very prescriptive schemes of work which practically told the teacher when to breathe in and when to breathe out. (Primary depute headteacher, Numeracy)

> I thought there was a great deal of flexibility in them to allow me and my school to pursue things that we felt were relevant to our area and the kids in our school. I am quite confident that we can develop courses that suit our needs at our different stages. (Principal teacher[2] secondary, Social Studies)

> Its strength is the fact that it does not prescribe certain methodologies. In actual fact, it leaves it open for an imaginative and varied approach which could be differentiated to different groups with different background experiences. (Classteacher secondary, RE denominational)

Within the transcripts, a tension was evident between a perceived welcome (re)introduction of professional autonomy and the removal of secure and familiar frameworks to govern action. A recurring theme in the focus groups was the dilemma posed by affording a greater degree of freedom where the parameters of professional responsibility had shifted towards the management of learning resources and environments for learning (curriculum 'delivery'), rather than curriculum design (curriculum building). A reported lack of direction left many teachers unsure of how to proceed, especially in regard to assessing progression in pupil learning. The consultation generated frequent calls for elaboration and detailed exemplification, often supported by accountability concerns. The powerful influence of the schools' inspectorate, HMIe, on school-level policy and practice was noted. Despite the revised approach to inspection, with its increased emphasis on school self-evaluation, many participants questioned whether there had been a significant shift away from what was described as a 'narrow attainment agenda' (University of Glasgow, 2009, p. 26). Concern was expressed about the risks of 'getting it wrong' for pupils, teachers and the standing of the school (University of Glasgow, 2009, p. 20).

> Everything we do is measured all the time. Everything has to be measurable, so I'm wondering what the balance is between active learning, creativity and freedom and 'the measure'? (Primary headteacher, Numeracy)

> It's very refreshing going back to having some freedom, being able to have meaningful contexts for learning; but until we are really convinced that HMIe don't want 'tick box' evidence we're still going to feel quite restricted. (Primary headteacher, Literacy and English)

> We have professional autonomy, we can be creative and innovative in the best sense of all of these words, and then you are still going to be measured in a quite narrow way. I find it quite paradoxical. (Secondary principal teacher, Literacy and English)

There was some indication that teachers were reluctant to make changes that did not directly contribute to examination attainment. Teachers cited uncertainties around future arrangements for National Qualifications as contributing to their hesitance. For some teachers there was an assumption that a wider range of methodologies would require an investment in time that was not available within the constraints of the assessment calendar. The demands of 'getting through the syllabus' were seen to limit opportunities for more active, inquiry-based learning. Tension between the aspirations of CfE for new processes of learning and perceptions of an outcomes-driven system of assessment was a dominant refrain throughout consultation responses. Participants from primary and secondary schools talked of 'double vision' and 'different worlds' in describing the multiple and competing demands made of them. A primary headteacher commented that the Draft Experiences and Outcomes and the national assessments 'totally contradicted each other' (University of Glasgow, 2009, p. 28). A secondary faculty head described how teachers were caught between 'different philosophies' and expected to deliver the agenda of both (ibid.).

> There seems to be almost a double vision – one in which we are empowered and we are able to develop new things and we are professional enough to do that; and then somebody else with a slightly different agenda will come along and assess and evaluate us. There will have to be a change in how we are assessed and evaluated. (Secondary principal teacher, Literacy and English)

Prospects for teacher development are diminished when curriculum, pedagogy and assessment are only weakly or mal-aligned (Wyse et al., 2012). This lesson from previous experience is not one that successive administrations have been keen to learn (Priestley and Humes, 2010). Opportunities offered by the (re-)introduction of a less prescriptive curriculum, with the flexibility to exercise professional judgement, need to be supported by working conditions conducive to collaborative planning, critical reflection and joint work. Reflecting on assessment reform in a Scottish context, Hayward et al. (2007) reasserted the dangers of imposing reform without providing rich opportunities for teacher engagement, sustained involvement and support for teacher learning. The limited extent of trialling accomplished within the engagement year (2008) and public expressions of anxiety from teachers' associations with regard to implementation 'readiness' strengthened demands for greater 'exemplification'; an example of which is the development of an online National Assessment Resource (NAR).

Teacher education and teachers' work

Full implementation of CfE from August 2010 was quickly followed by two influential reports on teacher education and teachers' work: (1) the report of the review of teacher education in Scotland, *Teaching Scotland's Future* (Donaldson, 2011); and (2) the report of the review of teacher employment, *Advancing Teacher Professionalism* (McCormac, 2011). Both of these reports adopt 'professionalism' as a defining concept in accounts of teachers' work. Professionalism is deployed as a 'panacea' (Kennedy and Doherty, 2012) or 'condensation symbol' (Sapir, 1934) around which both employer and employee can unite. Demonstration of responsible professional behaviour is rewarded with a degree of earned autonomy. The coupling of autonomy and accountability is evident in moves to devolve greater responsibility for the delivery of national policy goals to local authorities and school leaders. The concordat signed between local government, the Convention of Scottish Local Authorities (COSLA) and the Scottish Government in November 2007 places responsibility for the delivery of national commitments relating to school education with local authorities. On the one hand this could be seen as an expression of democratic localism accompanied by an acknowledgement of the potential for a self-regulating teaching profession. A less optimistic reading might emphasize the environment needed to support strong localism and an 'activist' professional stance (Sachs, 2003). Present circumstances appear unpropitious.

Substantial reductions in public expenditure to reduce the deficit have strained the social partnership achieved between government, employers, unions and public sector workers. In the summer of 2010 teachers' unions (Educational Institute for Scotland, EIS, and the Scottish Secondary Teachers Association, SSTA) balloted members on industrial action for the first time since 1989. The introduction of new National Qualifications[3] from 2013 has faltered, with an announcement by the Curriculum for Excellence Management Board that schools 'behind the pace' could be exempt (Buie, 2011, p. 5). The involvement of universities that was stressed in the professional development strategy for CfE (LTS, 2009) has not been fully realized. The potential for sustained teacher engagement following the trials of the draft Experiences and Outcomes was largely neglected with no systematic 'scale-up' following the trialling process. Initiatives to promote school-based curriculum development and teacher learning such as the Schools of Ambition programme (2006–10) and the Chartered Teacher scheme (2003–11) have ended. At present opportunities for collaborative professional enquiry, highlighted as important by the 2009 University of Glasgow report and the 2011 Donaldson Report, appear limited. Recent research in one local authority questions the extent to which such an ambitious model for change can be realized in the absence of opportunities for teachers' active engagement in curriculum development (Priestley and Minty, 2012). Concerns remain despite the generally optimistic tone of the *Curriculum for Excellence Audit Report* (Education Scotland, 2012). Teachers continue to request targeted additional support on 'the articulation between the new National Qualifications and the Experiences and Outcomes' (ibid., p. 2); and across fundamental areas such as 'assessment, moderation and quality assurance, how best to deliver a Broad General Education S1 to S3 and how best to structure and deliver the Senior Phase' (p. 3).

Re- or de-professionalization?

In the case of Scotland it is very clear that there have been several initiatives designed to enhance teacher professionalism and that there has been general support for this direction of travel from the key stakeholders, including government, unions and employers. However even in such an apparent consensus there are tensions. Government is anxious that parents should perceive steady and continuing improvements in pupil outcomes, as that is what they feel they, as politicians, will be judged by when the next election comes. Teachers' unions are very concerned about increased workload and responsibilities and how their members will react against such developments, especially as there is no associated improvement in pay or conditions. Local authorities are concerned to be able both to balance their books, where a large proportion of education spending (including teachers' salaries) falls directly to them within tightly constrained budgets (see Menter and Hulme, 2012) and to ensure that all children are taught in well-staffed and well-equipped schools. All of these concerns are reasonable and legitimate but the tensions between them demonstrate how complex it is to reshape or redefine teacher professionalism.

In England, following several years of improved pay for successful performance (the Upper Pay Scale) there have recently been suggestions about reducing the pay of less successful teachers. This is likely to cause a considerable furore and do little to foster increased trust between teachers and government. While there is greater apparent trust within the education community in Scotland, as we have seen, that does not mean that the development of the profession is straightforward. During the 1960s and 1970s there were suggestions that the teaching profession was being 'proletarianized' (Ozga and Lawn, 1981), that is that teachers were being treated as an industrial rather than as a professional labour force. There is little overt evidence now of such a process anywhere across the United Kingdom and the terms of the debate do seem to have shifted. In a review of literature on teacher education carried out as part of the evidence gathering for the Donaldson report (Menter et al., 2010), we identified four 'models' of teacher professionalism that seemed apparent in the work we reviewed across a range of countries. These were

- The effective teacher
- The reflective teacher
- The enquiring teacher
- The transformative teacher

We might suggest that these four models are listed in order of increasing degrees of 'agency' (see Biesta and Priestley in this volume), with the effective model being that where the teacher has the least agency and in which s/he is judged largely by how successful s/he is in implementing externally set priorities and achieving them in the classroom. The transformative teacher at the other extreme is not only being generally effective as in the first model but may be reflecting on, enquiring into and indeed challenging or changing some of these priorities, seeing this as a necessary aspect of their professionalism. In other words they will be creative, critical and relatively autonomous, basing their professional actions on a clear set of values and judgements about what makes for good teaching (Biesta, 2010).

The English White Paper would seem to limit teaching largely to the first model, although there are small 'glimmers' of reflection and enquiry, for example in teaching schools or university training schools. *Teaching Scotland's Future* is premised on a commitment to at least the first three models and perhaps leaves some leeway available for the development of the transformative approach as well.

Conclusion

More than 30 years ago the historian Brian Simon asked the question 'Why no pedagogy in England?' (Simon, 1981). More recently Robin Alexander (2004) asked '*Still* no pedagogy?' In his initial expression of concern, Simon was drawing attention to the presence of a much more theorized approach to questions of teaching and learning that existed elsewhere in Europe and North America. Alexander (2008) has attempted to develop such an approach, for example in his concept of dialogic teaching. The imposition of particular approaches to literacy or numeracy teaching in England (including idiosyncratic approaches such as 'systematic synthetic phonics') does not amount to the development of a theory of pedagogy.

But in some respects the situation in England or indeed the United Kingdom is not so much a special case. It seems that increasingly around the world practices in teaching and learning are driven by a 'what works' approach, that judges the success of teaching by a limited range of measurable outcomes (Taubman, 2009; Lingard, 2010). The new managerialism across the public sector captured by the term 'performativity' is prevalent within teaching and is indicative of new forms of governance of teachers and their work that while often depicted as an enhancement of professionalism, in reality is experienced as increased control and reduced autonomy. The curriculum is there to be 'delivered' by teachers and their success will be judged by the test and exam results of the pupils that they are teaching. The scope for teacher engagement with curriculum development is limited – and it is certainly appropriate that a national education system should set parameters for curriculum – but in some jurisdictions it is much more limited now than it has been before, reducing the ability of teachers to be responsive to local circumstances and, sometimes, to individual pupil needs.

We have seen that there appears to be a greater commitment within the policy community in Scotland to create a form of teacher professionalism that does create more space for genuine teacher agency. But even there, there are continuing pressures, especially on politicians and senior policy officers to ensure that certain performance measures are achieved that will enable the country to claim that it is doing well in international comparisons. And in spite of much of the political rhetoric there can be no doubt that what happens in England is very influential on Scottish policy. The overall effect of such pressures is in part to limit the scope for autonomy and agency as an aversion to risk prevails. There tends to be a 'regression to the norm', that is to an emphasis on effective teaching narrowly defined by measurable outputs. Severe limits are placed on the scope for teachers to be transformative in their orientation towards their work.

Notes

1 Following the 2010 General Election in the United Kingdom, a coalition government formed of the Conservative and Liberal Democratic parties was established, the first time since the Second World War that there had been such a government in the United Kingdom.
2 A principal teacher is a promoted middle management position in Scottish schools.
3 CfE has been accompanied by new National Qualifications (National 4 and National 5), which replace the former Standard Grade and Intermediate qualifications at Scottish Credit and Qualifications Framework levels 4 and 5. See www.educationscotland.gov.uk/nationalqualifications/about/newqualifications/changes.asp

References

Alexander, R. (2004), 'Still no pedagogy? Principle, pragmatism and compliance in teacher education'. *Cambridge Journal of Education*, 34, 7–34.
— (2008), *Essays on Pedagogy*. London: Routledge.
Ball, S. J. (1994), *Education Reform: A Critical and Post-Structural Approach*. Buckingham: Open University Press.
— (2007), *Education plc*. London: Routledge.
— (2012), *Global Education Inc*. London: Routledge.
Barker, B. (2005), 'Transforming schools: illusion or reality?' *School Leadership and Management*, 25, 99–116.
— (2008), 'School reform policy in England since 1988: relentless pursuit of the unattainable'. *Journal of Education Policy*, 23, 669–83.
Biesta, G. (2010), *Good Education in an Age of Measurement: Ethics, Politics, Democracy*. Boulder, CO: Paradigm Publishers.
Buie, E. (2011), 'Rethink on Nationals 4 and 5'. *Times Educational Supplement Scotland*, 3 June.
Darling-Hammond, L. and Lieberman, A. (eds) (2012), *Teacher Education Around the World*. London: Routledge.
Department for Education (2010), *The Importance of Teaching* (White Paper). London: HM Government.
Department for Education and Employment (DFEE) (2001a), *Key Stage 3 National Strategy. Framework for Teaching Mathematics: Years 7, 8 and 9*. London: HMSO.
— (2001b), *Key Stage 3 National Strategy. Framework for Teaching English: Years 7, 8 and 9*. London: HMSO.

Donaldson, G. (2010), *Teaching Scotland's Future. Report of a Review of Teacher Education in Scotland*. Online at www.scotland.gov.uk/Resource/Doc/337626/0110852.pdf (accessed 09/10/12).

Du Gay, P. (1996), *Consumption and Identity at Work*. London: Sage.

Education Scotland (no date), *The Journey to Excellence*. Online at www.journeytoexcellence.org.uk/ (accessed (08/10/12).

Education Scotland (2012), *Progress in Preparing for the Implementation of Curriculum for Excellence in Secondary Schools*. Online at www.educationscotland.gov.uk/Images/CfEAuditReport23May12_tcm4-721653.pdf (accessed 23/05/12).

Gleeson, D. and Husbands, C. (eds) (2001), *The Performing School*. London: RoutledgeFalmer.

Hargreaves, A. and Goodson, I. (2006), 'Educational change over time? The sustainability and non-sustainability of three decades of secondary school change and continuity'. *Educational Administration Quarterly*, 42, 3–41.

Harradine, J. (1996), *The Role of Research in the Work of the National Schools Network*. Ryde, NSW: National Schools Network.

Hayward, L., Priestley, M. and Young, M. (2004), 'Ruffling the calm of the ocean floor: merging, practice, policy and research in assessment in Scotland'. *Oxford Review of Education*, 30, 397–416.

Her Majesty's Inspectorate of Education (HMIE) (2007), *How Good is Our School? The Journey to Excellence Part 3*. Online at www.educationscotland.gov.uk/Images/HowgoodisourschoolJtEpart3_tcm4-684258.pdf (accessed 08//10/12).

— (2010), *Lessons Learned from the Schools of Ambition Initiative*. Livingston: HMIE.

Hulme, M. and Menter, I. (2011), 'South and North – Teacher education policy in England and Scotland: a comparative textual analysis'. *Scottish Educational Review*, 43, 70–90.

Hulme, M., Menter, I., Kelly, D. and Rusby, S. (2010), 'Schools of Ambition: bridging professional and institutional boundaries', in J. Slater and R. Ravid (eds), *Collaboration in Education*. Routledge: New York, pp. 39–46.

Jones, K. (2003), *Education in Britain*. Cambridge: Polity.

Jones, K., Cunchillos, C., Hatcher, R., Hirtt, N., Innes, R., Joshua, S. and Klausenitzer, J. (2008), *Schooling in Western Europe*. London: Palgrave Macmillan.

Kennedy, A. and Doherty, R. (2012), 'Professionalism and partnership: panaceas for teacher education in Scotland?' *Journal of Education Policy*, 27, 835–48.

Kontoniemi, M. and Salo, O. (eds) (2011), *Educating Teachers in the PISA Paradise Perspectives on Teacher Education at a Finnish University*. Jyväskylä: Jyväskylän Normaalikoulu Publications No. 12.

Learning and Teaching Scotland (2008), *Determined to Succeed: Policy Expectations for Local Authority Delivery*. Online at www.ltscotland.org.uk/Images/CommunicationsLAGuidancephase2_tcm4-492583.pdf (accessed 08/10/12).

— (2009), *Towards a Professional Development Strategy for Curriculum for Excellence*, Management Board Discussion Paper. Online at www.ltscotland.org.uk/Images/ProfessionalDevStrategy_tcm4-565591.pdf (accessed 08/10/12).

Lingard, B. (2010), 'Policy borrowing, policy learning: testing times in Australian schooling'. *Critical Studies in Education*, 51, 129–47.

Mahony, P. and Hextall, I. (2000), *Reconstructing Teaching*. London: Routledge.

Mansell, W. (2007), *Education by Numbers – The Tyranny of Testing*. London: Politico's.

McCormac, G. (2011), *Advancing Professionalism in Teaching. Report of the Review of Teacher Employment in Scotland*. Online at www.scotland.gov.uk/Resource/Doc/357766/0120894.pdf (accessed 08/10/12).

Menter, I. and Hulme, M. (2012), 'Teacher education in Scotland – riding out the recession?' *Educational Research*, 54, 149–60.

Menter, I., Hulme, M. and Sangster, P. (2012), 'Performance in teacher education and research – a double whammy for teacher educators?', in B. Jeffrey and G. Troman (eds), *Performativity in Education in the UK: Effects, Consequences and Agency*. Ethnography and Education Publishing: Stroud, pp. 23–40.

Menter, I., Hulme, M., Elliott, D. and Lewin, J. (2010b), *Literature Review on Teacher Education for the Twenty First Century*. Edinburgh: Scottish Government.

Menter, I., McMahon, M., Forde, C., Hall, J., McPhee, A., Patrick, F. and Devlin, A. (2006), *Teacher Working Time Research: Final Report to the Scottish Negotiating Committee for Teachers*, Project Report. Edinburgh: Scottish Government / Scottish Joint Negotiating Committee.

Menter, I., Elliot, D., Hall, S., Hulme, M., Lowden, K., Payne, F. and Christie, D. (2007), *Research to Support Schools of Ambition*. 2007 Annual Report. Edinburgh: Scottish Government.

Menter, I., Elliot, D., Hall, S., Hulme, M., Lowden, K., Payne, F. and Christie, D. (2010a), *Research to Support Schools of Ambition*. Final Report. Edinburgh: Scottish Government.

Mongon, D. and Chapman, C. (2009), 'New provisions of schooling', in C. Chapman and H. Gunter (eds), *Radical Reforms*. London: Routledge, pp. 104–16.

Moursched, M. and Barber, M. (2007), *How The World's Top-Performing Schools Come Out on Top*. Online at www.mckinsey.com/locations/UK_Ireland/~/media/Reports/UKI/Education_report.ashx (accessed 08/10/12).

Organization for Economic Cooperation and Development (OECD) (2011), *Building a High Quality Teaching Profession*. Online at www2.ed.gov/about/inits/ed/internationaled/background.pdf (accessed 08/10/12).

Ozga, J. and Lawn, M. (1981), *Teachers, Professionalism and Class. A Study of Organized Teachers*. London: Falmer Press.

Priestley, M. (2002), 'Global discourses and national reconstruction: the impact of globalization on curriculum policy'. *Curriculum Journal*, 13, 87–104.

Priestley, M. and Humes, W. (2010), 'The development of Scotland's Curriculum for Excellence: amnesia and déjà vu'. *Oxford Review of Education*, 36, 345–61.

Priestley, M. and Minty, S. (2012), *Developing Curriculum for Excellence. Summary of Findings from Research Undertaken in a Scottish Local Authority*. Stirling: University of Stirling.

Rizvi, F. and Lingard, B. (2009), *Globalizing Education Policy*. London: Routledge.

Rose, N. (1996), 'The death of the social? Reconfiguring the territory of government'. *Economy and Society*, 25, 327–56.

Sachs, J. (2003), *The Activist Teaching Profession*. Buckingham: Open University Press.

Sapir, E. (1934), 'Symbolism', in E. R. A. Seligman (ed.), *Encyclopaedia of the Social Sciences*. New York, Macmillan, pp. 492–5.

Scottish Executive (2001), *A Teaching Profession for the 21st Century. Agreement Reached Following Recommendations Made in the McCrone Report*. Online at www.scotland.gov.uk/Resource/Doc/158413/0042924.pdf (accessed 08/10/12).

— (2004), *Ambitious Excellent Schools*. Edinburgh: Scottish Executive. Online at www.scotland.gov.uk/Resource/Doc/26800/0023694.pdf (accessed 08/10/12).

— (2006), *The NEET Strategy, More Choices, More Chances*. Online at www.scotland.gov.uk/Publications/2006/06/13100205/16 (accessed 08/10/12).

Simon, B. (1981), 'Why no pedagogy in England?', in B. Simon and W. Taylor (eds), *Education in the Eighties: The Central Issues*. London: Batsford, pp. 121–45.

Spillane, J. P. (1999), 'External reform initiatives and teachers' efforts to reconstruct their practice: the mediating role of teachers' zones of enactment'. *Journal of Curriculum Studies*, 31, 143–75.

Taubman, P. M. (2009), *Teaching by Numbers. Deconstructing the Discourse of Standards and Accountability in Education*. London: Routledge.

Teitel, L. (2004), *How Professional Development Schools Make A Difference: A Review of Research* (2nd edn). Washington, DC: National Council for Accreditation of Teacher Education.

Thrupp, M. and Willmott, R. (2003), *Education Management in Managerialist Times*. Maidenhead: Open University.

University of Glasgow (2009), *Curriculum for Excellence Draft Experiences and Outcomes: Collection, Analysis and Reporting of Data. Final Report*. Glasgow: Learning and Teaching Scotland.

Williams, R. (1960), *The Long Revolution*. Harmondsworth: Penguin.

Wyse, D., Baumfield, V., Egan, D., Hayward, L., Hulme, M., Menter, I., Gallagher, C. and Livingston, K. (2012), *Creating the Curriculum. Understanding Primary Education*. London: Routledge.

10

Teachers as Agents of Change: Teacher Agency and Emerging Models of Curriculum

Mark Priestley, Gert Biesta and Sarah Robinson

Introduction

Recent curriculum policy in the United Kingdom and elsewhere has defined teachers as 'agents of change' (Goodson, 2003; Nieveen, 2011; Priestley, 2011; Sinnema and Aitken, Menter and Hulme, this volume). This is a significant shift in emphasis following several decades of policies that worked to de-professionalize teachers, replacing teacher agency with prescriptive curricula and oppressive regimes of testing and inspection (see, for example, Gleeson and Gunter, 2001; Biesta, 2010; Keddie, Mills and Pendergast, 2011; Lingard and McGregor, this volume). The [re]turn to teacher agency, heralded in policies such as Scotland's Curriculum for Excellence (CfE), represents a change in the professional orientation of teachers. It not only gives explicit permission to teachers to exert high[er] degrees of professional agency within the contexts in which they work, but actually sees agency as an important dimension of teachers' professionalism.

The renewed emphasis on teacher agency raises a number of questions. These are partly about definition and theory, such as the question what we mean by agency and, more specifically, by teacher agency, and what it would mean for teachers to be agents of change. And they are partly empirical questions about the factors that promote or hinder teacher agency. In this chapter we address both types of question, drawing upon findings from the *Teacher Agency and Curriculum Change* project, undertaken in the context of teachers' implementation of CfE.[1] The project involved one year of ethnographic research within a single education authority in Scotland in one primary school and two secondary schools, focusing on two experienced classroom teachers in each setting. Data-collection took place in three distinct phases, where each phase was partially determined by the findings from the previous phase. Data-collection involved observation; semi-structured individual and group interviews, including, at the start of the project, a personal and professional history interview, and interviews with senior managers in each school; analysis of key policy texts; and teacher network mapping. The analysis in this chapter is drawn mainly from the interview data.[2]

In what follows we first outline a model for understanding and researching agency, focusing on the factors that contribute to the ways in which teachers might achieve agency. Secondly, we discuss empirical findings in relation to two indicative themes. The first concerns the beliefs and aspirations espoused by teachers implementing CfE; the second focuses on the professional relationships experienced by teachers in their working environments. These two themes are illustrative of the complexity of teacher agency, and should not be seen as an exhaustive view. Other themes, for example the cultures of performativity that frame teachers' work, are explored in other project publications (see Priestley, Robinson and Biesta, 2012). We conclude the chapter with some observations on the implications of our insights for the promotion of teacher agency.

Defining and theorizing teacher agency

Our interest lies in the phenomenon of agency itself and in how agency is achieved in concrete settings and under particular conditions and circumstances. Our perspective on agency is therefore not sociological but has its roots in the philosophy of action as developed by pragmatist philosophers, most notably John Dewey and George Herbert Mead (see Biesta, 2005, 2006). While agency can be defined as the way in which actors 'critically shape their responses to problematic situations' (Biesta and Tedder, 2006, p. 11), it is important not to see agency as a capacity residing in individuals, but rather to conceive of it as something that is *achieved* through engagement with very specific contextual conditions. Such an ecological approach (Biesta and Tedder, 2006) highlights that actors always act *by means* of their environment rather than simply *in* their environment. This in turn implies that 'the achievement of agency will always result from the interplay of individual efforts, available resources and contextual and structural factors as they come together in particular and, in a sense, always unique situations' (Biesta and Tedder, 2007, p. 137). Agency, in other words, is not to be understood as something that people can have; it is something that people do. It denotes a 'quality' of the engagement of actors with temporal-relational contexts-for-action, not a quality of the actors themselves. Viewing agency in such terms helps us to understand how humans are able to be reflexive and creative, acting counter to societal constraints, but also how individuals are enabled and constrained by their social and material environments.

Building on pragmatism, Emirbayer and Mische (1998) have argued for a conception of agency that aims to overcome the one-sidedness of existing theories of agency which, in their view, tend to focus either on routine, or on purpose or on judgement. They make a case for a conception of agency which encompasses the dynamic interplay between these three dimensions and which takes into consideration 'how this interplay varies within different structural contexts of action' (ibid., p. 963). For this reason they suggest that the achievement of agency should be understood as a configuration of influences from the past, orientations towards the future and engagement with the present. They refer to these three dimensions as the *iterational*, the *projective* and the *practical-evaluative* dimension respectively. In concrete actions all three dimensions play a role, but the degree to which they contribute varies. This is why Emirbayer and Mische speak of a 'chordal triad of agency within which all three dimensions resonate as separate but not always harmonious tones' (ibid., p. 972; emphasis in original). Thus they suggest that agency should be understood as a 'temporally embedded process of social engagement, informed by the past (in its habitual aspect), oriented toward the future (as a capacity to imagine alternative possibilities) and "acted out" in the present (as a capacity to contextualize past habits and future projects with the contingencies of the moment)' (ibid., p. 963).

These ideas are helpful because they illustrate that agency doesn't come from nowhere, but builds upon past achievements, understandings and patterns of action. This is expressed in the *iterational* element of agency which concerns '*the selective reactivation by actors of past patterns of thought and action, routinely incorporated in practical activity, thereby giving stability and order to social universes and helping to sustain identities, interactions, and institutions over time*' (ibid., p. 971; emphasis in original). Their approach also acknowledges that agency is in some way 'motivated', that is, that it is linked to the intention to bring about a future that is different from the present and the past. This is encapsulated in the *projective* element of agency which encompasses '*the imaginative generation by actors of possible future trajectories of action, in which received structures of thought and action may be creatively reconfigured in relation to actors' hopes, fears, and desires for the future*' (ibid.; emphasis in original). Although agency is implicated with the past and the future, it can only ever be 'acted out' in the present, which is what is expressed in the practical-evaluative dimension, which entails *'the capacity of actors to make practical and normative judgements among alternative possible trajectories of action, in response to the emerging demands, dilemmas, and ambiguities of presently evolving situations'* (ibid.; emphasis in original).

Based on the idea of agency as a situated achievement, and informed by Emirbayer's and Mische's suggestion that the achievement of agency is the outcome of the interplay of iterational, practical-evaluative and projective dimensions, we have developed the following model to guide data-collection and assist data-analysis (Figure 10.1).

The model allows us to focus on the different dimensions that contribute to the achievement of agency. Within each dimension we have identified a number of further aspects. With regard to the iterational dimension we distinguish between the influence of the more general life histories of teachers and their more specific professional histories, which includes both their own education as teachers and the accumulated experience of being a teacher. With regard to the projective dimension we distinguish between short-term and long(er)-term orientations for action. With regard to the practical-evaluative dimension (and following Archer, 1988) we make a distinction between cultural, structural and material aspects. Cultural aspects relate to ideas, values, beliefs, discourses and languages; structural aspects to relationships, roles, power and trust; and material aspects to resources and the wider physical environment in which teachers act.

In the following analysis we focus on the role of teachers' values and beliefs in the achievement of agency, and on the role of relationships. Values and

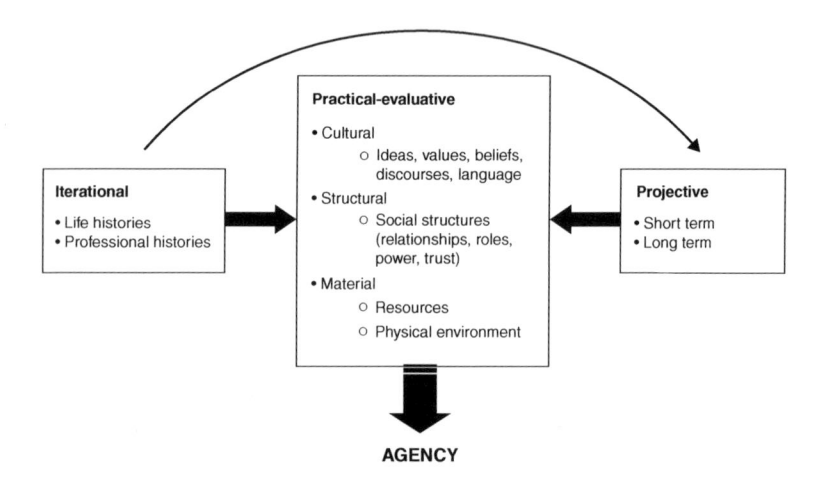

Figure 10.1 Understanding teacher agency.

beliefs partly concern the discourses through which teachers make sense of the situations in which they act (the cultural aspect of the practical-evaluative dimension), partly articulate their short-term and longer-term aspirations (the projective dimension), and partly stem from their personal and professional histories (the iterative dimension). Relationships concern the structural aspect of the practical-evaluative dimension of the achievement of agency.

Achieving agency (1): The role of values and beliefs

While we would dissent from those voices that frame teacher agency as personal capacity, we would not disagree with the notion that such capacity is an important element in the achievement of agency. Agency will be enriched if people have a broad repertoire of responses upon which they may draw. In respect of teachers, we would point to a number of iterational aspects which contribute to their agency. These include personal capacity (skills and knowledge) and what concerns us here, that is personal and professional beliefs and values. What these have in common is their rooting in past experiences.

Strongly connected to teachers' beliefs are their aspirations in respect of their work (see Meirink et al., 2009). These constitute the projective dimension of teacher agency. Aspirations may be focused on the development and welfare of students (Lasky, 2005), thus leading to agency that is protective of students' interests (Osborn et al., 1997). Such agency may either support policy intentions or it may run counter to them (Ladwig, 2010). In both cases it may be driven by sincerely held long-term aspirations, rooted strongly in teachers' values and beliefs – for example a desire to see the realization of a social justice agenda, or to inculcate the capacity in students for critical thinking. Aspirations may, however, also be more narrowly instrumental and/or short term, for example towards maintaining a 'normal desirable state' in the classroom (Brown and McIntyre, 1992) or 'playing the game' (Gleeson and Gunter, 2001). This game can take the form of fabrication of the school's image – careful impression management and discourses of excellence (Keddie, Mills and Pendergast, 2011) and the concealing of 'dirty laundry' (Cowie, Taylor and Croxford, 2007), as well as more serious corruption and cheating (Ball, 2003). The forms of agency evident in these latter cases are clearly quite different to those in the former example, and motivated by quite different aspirations. It is worth noting here that all of these forms of the projective can vary in clarity and detail and tone, and they may coexist in tension with one another. We also should not underestimate the importance of strongly held beliefs about subject identity, as these are important in shaping the form aspirations will take (Siskin, 1994; Beane, 1997).

In analysing the data, we were struck by the similarity of beliefs articulated across this small group of teachers, despite their location in different sectors of education. The teachers largely shared a professional outlook that seemed to frame many of their beliefs about students and their roles as teachers, as well as their views on the purposes of education. These views appear to be fairly narrow in scope, largely geared to short-term goals, and predominantly articulated via the language of current policy. This tends to deny teachers a critical voice as they enact policy, and reduces possibilities for the formation of alterative visions for education.

Some of the ensuing discussion may seem to portray the teachers in a negative light. This is not our intention, and we would emphasize at the outset that we were impressed throughout the project with the professionalism, competence and dedication of all of the teachers who participated in the research. Moreover, we emphasize that agency is not simply a matter of individual capacity (and belief is merely a subset of this); it is an ecological construct, also subject to structural, cultural and material influences. Teacher professional discourses are to a large extent as they are because of the teachers' positioning within their professional environments, and their agency (or lack of) is heavily influenced by factors which are often beyond their immediate control.

Views about pupils and students

The first theme concerns the views of the teachers towards students. The data present a conflicting picture of this, but some views were common to all of the teachers in the project. First, there is a strong sense of professional responsibility towards students. In general, these were teachers who wished to do their best for their students, and who frequently talked, for instance, in terms of their role in maximizing student potential. These generally positive aspects were tempered by what might be seen as a deficit view of children. This view was exhibited, tacitly at least, through use of particular language, by the majority of the teachers participating in our research. A strong common discourse lay in the repeated use of teachers of terms like 'able', 'bright', 'poor' to describe their students. Good examples of this sort of language lie in the following excerpts.

> The more able pupils still want classroom teaching from the front. They want to have things written down. (. . .) The less able pupils prefer the less structure but

they are in actual fact the ones who are less able to manage their own learning. (Teacher A)

In my opinion that is the right thing especially for people who are not the brightest. (Teacher C)

A related issue, which seems to lie in some tension to the espoused notions of ability described above, concerns teachers' views about pupils becoming more responsible for their own learning – a trend termed 'responsibilization' by Davies (2006). All of the teachers talked a great deal about personalization and choice. Such discourses underpin CfE, and this language was used regularly by our respondents, including in ways that contradicted other beliefs about children. Two teachers spoke about the shift from knowledge to skills in the new curriculum, suggesting that their role was to now develop:

... independent learners. Confident about being given a task and using the right skills in order to do it the best way they can. (Teacher C)

You are teaching a lot of the skills that we want the children to have, the independence, working on their own, choosing what they are doing, deciding which way ... (Teacher D)

These quotes are illustrative of tensions in teachers' beliefs about children and young people. They clearly see their role as a directive and active one – to fix deficits in students that have their roots in social backgrounds and general levels of ability.

And yet, at a rhetorical level at least, and in potential tension with this directive role, these teachers buy into the discourses of the new curriculum. There is a sense here that there is a grey area in the issue of whose responsibility it is to ensure that learning takes place. Thus students with 'poor' ability or students who do not take 'responsibility' for their own learning provide a justification for the teacher to abdicate some professional responsibility, blaming students as 'mad, bad or stupid' (Watzlawick, Wickland and Fisch, in Salomon, 1992, p. 45). Or conversely, such traits provide a justification for the teacher to intervene to take charge and assume responsibility, and even on occasion to protect students from what might be considered to be faults in the education system.

An example of this is found in one teacher's recourse to what has been termed 'protective mediation' (Osborn et al., 1997). She mentioned that she sometimes gave tests without telling pupils that they were being tested. Upon being questioned about this practice, she stated that she believed that excessive testing placed harmful demands upon students; thus, while she felt obliged (by the system) to administer tests, she also sought to protect students from their worst excesses. Such action suggests a high degree of agency; this teacher clearly sees alternative courses of action, and her decisions in this matter are clearly driven by her beliefs about education and young people. The direction taken in such cases is likely to be highly dependent on how teachers see their own role in the process.

Views about teaching and the teacher

There was a commonly acknowledged view that the teacher's role has changed – from that of a deliverer of knowledge to that of a facilitator of learning, and from a subject specialist to a teacher of children. Again this largely reflects policy discourses (see Biesta, 2010). All of the participants talked about this changed role – and all seemed comfortable with the perceived shift. There was some evidence that the teachers were able 'to assimilate the messages of reform institutes without changing fundamental views of . . . teaching' (Yerrick, Park, and Nugent, 1997, p. 154), and to find ways 'to view potentially contrary messages in ways that accentuate their own beliefs' (ibid.). Thus, in some cases, this role was seen in an overtly student-centred and divergent manner.

> I studied a bit of the background to philosophy and realised how that is actually teaching them social skills as well. In a good way. And teaching them not just to assume things about people, or make assumptions about life. And really quite difficult critical thinking skills as well. It was difficult to teach that. You are not teaching it actually. You are a facilitator. (Teacher E)

In others, there seemed to be a more instrumental and directive approach, one suggesting convergence and following the demands of the syllabus.

> The teacher's role is as a facilitator [laugh] to encourage and enable the learner. To have access to the stimulus you need to encourage them to make the right choices. Or to learn in a particular style. To jump through hoops and pass exams because, at the end of the day, that is how it is measured. (Teacher A)

Most of the participants expressed anxiety at the prospect of becoming agents of change. Two teachers in particular espoused views that are probably indicative of wider currents of thinking among Scottish teachers: deference to authority, a lack of willingness to take responsibility for issues seen to the remit of those further up the chain, and nervousness about being 'required' to be autonomous in their work (see Humes and Bryce, 2008). For example:

> You just do a good job. You try your best. You do not muck around. You do not do things you should not do or challenge superiors in a way unless it's obviously something genuine (Teacher B)

Interestingly, despite this apparent reluctance to rock the boat, and/or to become more actively engaged in developing the curriculum in school, all of the teachers readily criticized a range of issues that they saw as impacting negatively on their ability to do their jobs. These included the impact of accountability, particularly what they saw as the overemphasis on attainment. Many such complaints were framed by the fact that these teachers clearly took pride in their work.

Views about educational purpose

The teachers in this study demonstrated broadly similar beliefs about educational purpose. These tended to coalesce around socialization, and the development of key skills or competencies.

> Well the main thing you would come straight away is for learning. But not just academic learning. You are building them as individuals to know how to relate to others, how to socialise, interact. To get them prepared for the wider world . . . The socialisation part for me is really important . . . Schools can provide kids with things that they might not get at home, some kids obviously. (Teacher B)

> . . . it is skills for learning, skills for work, skills for life that you are focusing on more. So when you are doing a topic, you are not always thinking about the knowledge that they are going to get from it. Coz is that knowledge ever going to be used? It is nice to learn things, facts but that cannot be transferred. That is not going to help them when they leave school. Whereas the skills that help them learn those things or do a certain activity in a certain way is what will help them in the future. (Teacher C)

Such views provide a long-term element to the projective dimension of agency, albeit in a manner which is somewhat instrumental (particularly in a work-related sense). However, one is struck by what is missing. The teachers tended to articulate aims that are vague in nature: phrases such as 'reaching their potential' and 'finding themselves' are common in the data. There is talk of developing teamwork skills, and thinking skills, but no systematic evidence in the data of sense-making to further unpack what these mean, and little articulation of the fine detail. Often the aim of education is the somewhat tautological 'the aim of education is learning', but there is little clear picture of what is being learned, or why.

Surprisingly, especially in the secondary schools, there is little sense in our data of teachers seeing education as being about the acquisition of knowledge. Similarly, and perhaps equally surprising, there is also little about accreditation as a purpose of education. This was mentioned by some participants, but most often in negative terms (as a competing pressure), and rarely as an explicit purpose of education despite the high profile given to attainment data in Scottish schools. Also conspicuous by its absence is a discourse about educational values. At no point did any of our respondents talk, for example, about social justice or democratic values. Instead the discourse seemed to rest with notions of personal responsibility and participation as core goals of citizenship, for which schools should prepare students (see also Biesta, this volume).

Two further issues are worthy of mention in relation to educational purposes. The first concerns whether teacher aspirations are long or short term in nature. It is apparent that much of the professional dialogue about educational purpose was not in fact long term. Where it was, and as noted above, there tended to be a fairly strong instrumental/work-related slant to it. Our data suggest that a large proportion of teacher aspirations in respect of their teaching were relatively short term in nature, and that a good deal of day-to-day planning and activity was performed with this in mind. This concurs with earlier research (Brown and McIntyre, 1993) which strongly suggested that teacher decision-making is driven by a perceived need to maintain a 'normal desirable state' in the classroom, and especially to keep students engaged.

> I think my priority is always engaging the kids and producing lessons that they like and enjoy and can relate to. And that is always my focus. . . . I want the kids to come in and enjoy my class and enjoy what we do. And that's always my priority. It's always the question I ask at the end of every lesson at the end of every day, 'am I doing a good job, are they enjoying it, are they not enjoying it?'. (Teacher B)

> I do like going and finding different things to do just to make it more interesting for me and for the children. And just coming with the times. (Teacher C)

> For me it is the fun that they have. If they learn, you see them develop, regardless of how slow or fast it is. But they enjoy it. (Teacher D)

Discussion

This focus on process and the comparative lack of discourses around purpose and values strongly suggest a disconnection between purpose and method, and an impoverishment in teacher discourses. It is evident from our dialogues with teachers, and the above analysis, that a great proportion of the professional discourses, which framed their practices and contributed to their professional agency, had their origins in the language of policy. This is evident in the terminology used by the teachers, even where (as for example in the case described above of students taking responsibility for their learning) there were clearly large differences in how different teachers interpreted the terms used. These teachers seemed to lack a systematic set of professional discourses over and above those provided by the language of policy. This potentially reduced their agency in developing the curriculum through limiting their potential to envisage different futures, and through denying them the language with which to engage critically with policy.

Achieving agency (2): The role of relationships

Previous research (e.g. Coburn and Russell, 2008) suggests strongly that teacher agency and efficacy in enacting reform are strongly dependent upon the nature and quality of professional relationships experienced by those teachers – that is the social structures within which they are situated. Social structures form a significant part of the contexts within which teachers work. Porpora (1998, p. 339) defines these rather narrowly as the emergent properties of 'systems of human relationships among social positions'. Elder-Vass (2008) provides a more comprehensive definition, suggesting that social structures comprise the constituent parts, the relations between them, the emergent whole and the emergent properties of the whole. Social structures are thus primarily relational. The complex social structures found in schools – the myriad of relationships and roles – exert significant effects on the possibilities for teachers to achieve agency.

In this section we focus on the teachers working in the two secondary schools, to which we will refer as Hillview School and Lakeview School. What makes the comparison relevant and interesting is that there are striking similarities both between the schools and between the values and beliefs of the teachers. We have noted above the broadly similar range of beliefs and aspirations held by the teachers. The schools are extremely similar in terms of the availability of material resources: both are located within the same local authority, so are subject to the same constraints on budgets, implementing a new curriculum as a time of austerity and staffing cuts; moreover, both schools are located in very similar new buildings, with common spatial characteristics and resourcing. All of the teachers reported good relationships with facilitative and supportive senior staff.

At Hillview School, however, the teachers seemed to be more negative in their evaluations about what was made possible by CfE, and exhibited markedly lower confidence about their abilities to engage with the new curriculum than did their colleagues at Lakeside School. The sense of agency thus 'translated' into a more limited achievement of agency. The following comments provide a flavour of this.

> It will be really difficult for the things that people want to know about. Like the Curriculum for Excellence, I can't think of anybody that's feeling like they are particularly in a position to be an expert and to help people. (Teacher, Hillview School)
>
> Oh my goodness, that is a whole year and I don't know that I am any further forward with feeling confident about implementing Curriculum for Excellence. (Teacher, Hillview School)
>
> That's partly why CfE could be a really positive thing because we are constantly looking at what we are doing. And that we also share our ideas across the faculty. (Teacher, Lakeside School)
>
> That is why I am not scared about the future with Curriculum for Excellence because I made those decisions when it started three, four years ago. And I am feeling fairly secure. But I can totally understand why other people are not. (Teacher, Lakeside School)

We attribute this differing achievement of agency to differences in the relational structures and qualities of the schools.

Hillview

At Hillview strong formal connections tended to be vertical; primarily with line managers, and within faculties. Formal structures included faculty meetings and weekly meetings of faculty heads with the senior management team. Whole staff meetings were described as information giving sessions – like 'assemblies' – with little opportunity for dialogue, other than occasional breakout groups, described as 'not really an ideal forum'. There appeared to be a paucity of formal horizontal channels for communication in the school. According to one teacher, 'we do not have a lot of working across faculties'. Principal teachers (heads of departments and faculty heads) met weekly with senior management, but the outcomes of such meetings were disseminated vertically via faculties. Departmental and faculty meetings tended to focus on routine issues (e.g. student behaviour).

> It has not been something that we have discussed in faculty. And I don't know if that is just us. I don't think it is. It's everybody. We are all in the same boat. The faculty meeting ends up being taken up with things that are important but not big important things. Like little important things that we need to know about stuff going on in school. So it is giving us information rather than talking at a higher level. (Teacher, Hillview School)

> Well, we have tried to get going with some curriculum development for S2 [the second year of secondary school] and we haven't been able to get on with that because of the other things that need to be discussed at the faculty meetings. It is two or three times I have had these things on the agenda and have had to put them aside. (Teacher, Hillview School)

Such formal structures were supplemented by other formal forums for discussion, including peer observation, although increasingly these were noted to be disappearing in response to time and resourcing pressures.

Both teachers were involved in school-wide working initiatives, but it was noted that dialogue was often limited, and dissemination more often than not consisted of briefing, rather than discussion, with some evidence that this did not fully percolate down to mainstream staff. Membership of working groups was decided by senior managers. Opportunities for teachers to engage with colleagues in different faculties (at a level below middle management) were more limited. Other formal horizontal relationships did exist (e.g. guidance issues, and increasingly mechanisms for interdisciplinary working, although this was not well developed at the time of the research). However, contact was often instrumental, focused on particular issues – 'I tend not to see people unless it is for something specific' – or simply fortuitous.

In exploring this case, we were left with a sense of opportunities missed. Both respondents had well-developed educational values, and strong aspirations. Both were frustrated by the lack of opportunity to fulfil these aspirations. Our data suggest that the key factor lay in the limitations placed upon agency by the nature and scope of relationships in the school, and a corresponding lack of affordance for generative teacher dialogue – inherently a sense-making process – about the new curriculum.

> But then it's now at the point of right so can we do any of these? And it sort of reached a plateau of trying to implement some of these changes because us coming up with the idea is that doesn't mean it's going to happen. It's got to go through a whole process of the senior management team . . . and getting the okay from that. So we're at a frustrating stage where we've got lots of things we'd like to do. (Teacher, Hillview School)

These views about the nature and scope of relationships within Hillview are supported to a large extent by the transcript of the interview with a senior manager. A great deal was said about the importance of strong, supportive and visionary leadership, but there was an absence of reference – despite prompting by the interviewer – to the role of managers in developing and sustaining relationships and connections between teachers. We suggest that in this case, teachers struggled to achieve agency in their enactment of the new curriculum, and that their agency was impeded by a lack of available relational resources in the practical-evaluative domain.

Lakeside

We found a contrasting situation at Lakeside. This might be attributed to the culture of Lakeside. Interviewees talked about a culture where innovation and risk-taking are encouraged and supported, as well as a culture of sharing. The following extract from an interview with a senior manager clearly exemplifies this approach to running the school.

> And if you are encouraging staff to do things that are a wee bit different or to not always follow things in a mainstream way, there is much more chance that they will develop as teachers, as professionals and as members of staff. So when someone comes with a crazy idea and says 'I want to try and do this with the second year class', okay, have a go at that . . . If they make a mess of it and it does not work, well that is okay. 'You tried, it did not work, we will try something different next time'. (Senior manager, Lakeside School)

Such sentiments were supported by other respondents who pointed to high levels of collegiality and the approachability of managers. One teacher, talking about her line manager, said:

> There is equality because [name removed] has never been 'I am superior to you' or whatever. So it is level on that front. I know that she views herself as a teacher, and I am a teacher and we are totally level. (Teacher, Lakeside School)

In one case, a team of teachers who were extremely unhappy about an initiative they had been asked to develop, felt comfortable about complaining to their link senior manager about the allocated timescales and processes. They were listened to, and their concerns were taken on board to the extent that the timescales were altered.

Comparing relationships

It would be easy to attribute the tangible sense of teacher agency in this school to this collegial culture. However, we note that we found similar sentiments in the other school about approachable senior managers, collegial support and a desire to pull together for the sake of the students. It is in the social structures of the school that we found more substantive differences, which might explain differences in teacher agency. There appear to be a number of aspects of this. First, there were strong informal relationships at a faculty level; these were characterized by high levels of trust.

> We can all empathise with one another. In this department we can all have our sticky moments but I don't think there are any egos. There isn't anyone who thinks they are more important than anyone else or busier than anyone else. Everybody is aware of everybody else's pressures and I think we do try to have positive relationships. (Teacher interview, Lakeside School)

Secondly, there was a strong push from the senior management of the school to develop strong, reciprocal 'relationships within the school so that staff get on well with staff, staff get on well with pupils and pupils get on with other pupils'. Some of these relationships were clearly vertical; for example, while at least one senior manager was seen as patronising and unapproachable, the norm was for an open door policy. Others were horizontal. In many cases, as at Hillview, many relationships were informal in nature, growing organically out of short-term needs.

> Because again it comes down to the simple social relationships that you have. And they are all people who understand the pressures of teaching, who get frustrated by the same things we do, who have the same worries we do. Who very often have similar kids to ourselves as well. So our subjects have made us link. So sometimes the link can be because of individual people or it can be because of your subject. (Teacher interview, Lakeside School)

However, unlike the case presently at Hillview – where our data suggest that formal relationships have been progressively disappearing – at Lakeside there was a sense that they were burgeoning, as a consequence of an active policy of fostering collegial, professional relationships that work both within and across faculties.

> And we share in there what we are doing and good practice and things across these things. So we are all coming together at various points and saying how can we tackle this and what ideas have you got and how should we take this forward and how do you do this in your department. And trying to come up with a common code of skills yeah. Core skills that we can all be promoting across the whole school. (Teacher interview, Lakeside School)

We also noted the diminishing scope and frequency of peer observation of teaching at Hillview. Conversely, at Lakeside this was promoted by the senior management as a priority. We note also, that this development was not framed in a managerial or hierarchical sense; teachers appeared to be trusted to get on with it, and they appeared to welcome the opportunities it provided for sharing practice.

Another key difference between the schools in terms of relationships concerned the existence of external connections and relationships. At Lakeside both of our respondents reported the benefits of their outside links. In one case, this had involved a formal school role to develop cooperative learning. In another, the formal mechanisms were less tangible, but the benefits evident. In this case of a teacher who had been an active participant in national initiatives – with national agencies to development assessment and curriculum policy – such experience was fed back frequently into school practices, and served as a source for new ways of thinking and an interruption to habitual forms of practice.

> I think the external links are important. But if you take that I am the only one. In this faculty we are down to nine now are we? I am the only one who is doing the whole Curriculum for Excellence SQA, QDT, LTS, whatever. But what I am bringing back to them, I am not just bringing it just back for [subject removed]. I am bringing it back for the whole faculty. (Teacher, Lakeside School)

These school case studies demonstrate powerfully that there were significant differences in terms of the quality and scope of relationships experienced by the teachers (the structural dimension of the context in and through which agency in achieved). In turn this appears to explain the differences in the agency achieved by the teachers.

Discussion

We suggest here that there are a number of dimensions to the relationships at Lakeside School which make them more likely to enable teachers to achieve agency (in comparison to their colleagues at Hillview School). The first relates to the predominant *orientation* of the relationships within the school. At Hillview, these were largely hierarchical or vertical; conversely, at Lakeside, such relationships were supplemented by strong horizontal ties, which appeared to facilitate (or at least be indicative of) a collegial and collaborative culture in the school. Another difference lies in the *symmetry* of the relationships, and linked to this are issues of *reciprocity*. At Hillview, relationships tended to be slightly more asymmetric than at Lakeside, and certainly less reciprocal. Channels of communication were thus more likely to be one way, encouraging a culture of dissemination, rather than one of generative dialogue. The above factors seem to have the potential to impact on the *formality*, *strength* and *frequency* of relationships. Thus at Lakeside, the existence of relatively reciprocal, symmetric relationships seemed to generate a collaborative culture where strong, frequent, and informal teacher relationships were able to flourish. Moreover, this appears to be an autocatalytic process.

Concluding comments

One of the interesting dimensions of the new approach to curriculum that forms the focus of this book is that it repositions teachers as agents of change, thus seeming to reverse a trend of ongoing de-professionalization through regimes of testing and inspection and the establishment of wider cultures of performativity. The question this raises is what the possibilities for teachers are to regain agency in their everyday practices. In this chapter we have engaged with this question by, first, exploring how we might understand and theorize teacher agency and by, second, discussing some findings of research into teacher agency in the context of the introduction of the Scottish Curriculum for Excellence. Our theoretical model suggests that the achievement of agency is the outcome of the complex interaction of a range of different individual, social, cultural and material factors. Rather than to think of it just as a capacity – as something that relies entirely on individuals and their qualities and abilities – this thus suggests that any attempt to promote teacher agency needs to engage with this wide range of dimensions and factors, so as not to make the mistake of putting the burden entirely on individual teachers. In the empirical part of this chapter we have tried to shed light on some aspects of this complex cluster, highlighting on the one hand the importance of language, discourse, values and beliefs, and on the other hand the impact of relationships. In both cases we have tried to show how such dimensions can either promote or undermine agency. With regard to the first area, we have particularly emphasized the importance of an independent professional discourse, as our research indicates that the agency achieved by the teachers appears to be limited by the impact of policy speak on their thinking and reflection. With regard to the second area our research indicates strongly that the quality of relationships – both the relationships within schools and the relationships between schools and outside contexts and settings – can make a crucial difference with regard to teachers' achievement of agency.

Acknowledgements

We wish to extend our thanks to the participating teachers from three schools, without whose enthusiastic support this research would not have been possible.

Notes

1 The project was funded by the UK Economic and Social Research Council; project reference RES-000-22-4208.
2 Given that a great deal of what was said to us might be seen as especially sensitive, or place participants at risk, we have anonymized the data by making only generic reference to the teachers' roles (e.g. we have not made reference to teaching subjects, nor in the majority of instances whether the respondents are primary or secondary teachers). In our discussion on values and beliefs we identify individual teachers with a letter. In our discussion about relationships we compare two secondary schools, making use of fictional names for the schools. The research adheres to the guidelines for the ethical conduct of research of the British Educational Research Association.

References

Archer, M. (1988), *Culture and Agency: The Place of Culture in Social Theory*. Cambridge: Cambridge University Press.
Ball, S. J. (2003), 'The teacher's soul and the terrors of performativity'. *Journal of Education Policy*, 18, 215–28.

Beane, J. A. (1997), *Curriculum Integration: Designing the Core of a Democratic Education*. New York: Teachers College Press.

Biesta, G. J. J. (2005), 'George Herbert Mead and the theory of schooling', in D. Troehler and J. Oelkers (eds), *Pragmatism and Education*. Rotterdam: Sense Publishers, pp. 117–32.

— (2006), '"Of all affairs, communication is the most wonderful." Education as communicative praxis', in D. T. Hansen (ed.), *John Dewey and Our Educational Prospect. A Critical Engagement with Dewey's Democracy and Education*. Albany, NY: SUNY Press, pp. 23–37.

— (2010), *Good Education in an Age of Measurement: Ethics, Politics, Democracy*. London: Paradigm Publishers.

Biesta, G. J. J and Tedder, M. (2006), *How is Agency Possible? Towards an Ecological Understanding of Agency-as-achievement*. Working paper 5. Exeter: The Learning Lives project.

— (2007), 'Agency and learning in the lifecourse: towards an ecological perspective'. *Studies in the Education of Adults*, 39, 132–49.

Brown, S. and McIntyre, D. (1992), *Making Sense of Teaching*. Buckingham: Open University Press.

Coburn, C. E. and Russell, J. L. (2008), 'District policy and teachers' social networks'. *Educational Evaluation and Policy Analysis*, 30, 203–35.

Cowie, M., Taylor, D. and Croxford, L. (2007), 'Tough, intelligent accountability' in Scottish secondary schools and the role of Standard Tables and Charts (STACS): a critical appraisal. *Scottish Educational Review*, 39, 29–50.

Davies, B. (2006) 'Subjectification: the relevance of Butler's analysis for education'. *British Journal of Sociology of Education*, 27, 425–38.

Elder-Vass, D. (2008), 'Integrating institutional, relational, and embodied structure: an emergentist perspective'. *British Journal of Sociology*, 59, 281–99.

Emirbayer, M. and Mische, A. (1998), 'What is agency?' *The American Journal of Sociology*, 103, 962–1023.

Gleeson, D. and Gunter, H. (2001), 'The performing school and the modernisation of teachers', in D. Gleeson and C. Husbands (eds), *The Performing School: Managing, Teaching and Learning in a Performance Culture*. London: RoutledgeFalmer, pp. 139–58.

Goodson, I. F. (2003), *Professional Knowledge, Professional Lives*. Maidenhead: Open University Press.

Humes, W. and Bryce, T. (2008), 'The future of Scottish education', in T. G. K. Bryce and W. Humes (eds), *Scottish Education: Third Edition, Beyond Devolution*. Edinburgh: Edinburgh University Press, pp. 905–18.

Keddie, A., Mills, M. and Pendergast, D. (2011), 'Fabricating and identity in neo-liberal times: performing schooling as "number one"'. *Oxford Review of Education*, 37, 75–92.

Ladwig, J. (2010), 'Beyond academic outcomes'. *Review of Research in Education*, 34, 113–41.

Lasky, S. (2005), 'A sociocultural approach to understanding teacher identity, agency and professional vulnerability in a context of secondary school reform'. *Teaching and Teacher Education*, 21, 899–916.

Meirink, J. A., Meijer, P., Verloop, N. and Bergen, T. C. M. (2009), 'Understanding teacher learning in secondary education: the relations of teacher activities to changed beliefs and teaching and learning'. *Teaching and Teacher Education*, 25, 89–100.

Nieveen, N. (2011), *Teachers' Professional Development in Curriculum Design in the Netherlands*, Paper presented at the European Conference for Educational Research, Berlin, 14 September 2011.

Osborn, M., Croll, P., Broadfoot, P., Pollard, A., McNess, E. and Triggs, P. (1997), 'Policy into practice and practice into policy: creative mediation in the primary classroom', in G. Helsby and G. McCulloch (eds), *Teachers and the National Curriculum*. London: Cassell, pp. 52–65.

Porpora, D. V. (1998), 'Four concepts of social structure', in M. Archer, R. Bhaskar, A. Collier, T. Lawson and A. Norrie (eds), *Critical Realism: Essential Readings*. London: Routledge, pp. 339–55.

Priestley, M. (2011), 'Whatever happened to curriculum theory? Critical realism and curriculum change'. *Pedagogy, Culture and Society*, 19, 221–38.

Priestley, M., Robinson, S. and Biesta, G. J. J. (2012), 'Teacher agency, performativity and curriculum change: reinventing the teacher in the Scottish Curriculum for Excellence?', in B. Jeffrey and G. Troman (eds), *Performativity Across UK Education: Ethnographic Cases of its Effects, Agency and Reconstructions*. Painswick: E&E Publishing, pp. 87–108.

Salomon, G. (1992), 'The changing role of the teacher: from information transmitter to orchestrator of teaching', in F. K. Oser, A. Dick and J.-L. Patry (eds), *Effective and Responsible Teaching: The New Synthesis*. San Franscisco: Jossey-Bass, pp. 37–49.

Siskin, L. S. (1994), *Realms of Knowledge: Academic Departments in Secondary School*. London: Falmer Press.

Yerrick, R., Parke, H. and Nugent, J. (1997), 'Struggling to promote deeply rooted change: the "filtering effect" of teachers' beliefs on understanding transformational views of teaching science'. *Science Education*, 81, 137–57.

11

High-Stakes Assessment and New Curricula: A Queensland Case of Competing Tensions in Curriculum Development[1]

Bob Lingard and Glenda McGregor

Introduction

Despite the Australian State of Queensland having very conservative governments for a lengthy period of time (1957–89), schooling in this State has exhibited some distinctively 'progressive' features, especially with regard to senior secondary assessment. Writing in the late nineteenth and early twentieth centuries, educational pioneer, John Dewey (see Dewey, 1969) defined 'progressive education' as that which promoted active learning; democratic classrooms, 'real-world' curricula; and, the notion that education is a vital part of the 'common good' (Weiler, 2004). However, such a view of schooling is sometimes critiqued as being overly 'romantic' and at odds with the brutal social realities beyond the classroom. Dewey's early writings, for example, do not take into account the consequences of differences based upon race, class or gender. In particular, Valerie Walkerdine (1990) argues that the development of self-efficacy at the heart of progressive education further privileges middle-class children. However, we contend that during the twentieth century, various movements, such as for example, those associated with race, civil rights, gender and socio-economic forms of justice, have informed more recent progressive experiments within education and attempts to rethink curricula and pedagogy. Additionally, the contributions of educational theorists such as Basil Bernstein (1971), R. W. Connell (see for example, 1987, 1993, 1995) and Pierre Bourdieu

(1984) – and many others – have reconceptualized the notion of progressive education to include consideration of many forms of difference. Thus we use the term 'progressive education' cautiously, while being confident of its usefulness to describe forms of education that are child-centred, constructivist, democratically grounded and relevant to the world beyond the classroom. We also use the term 'progressive' to distinguish such forms of education from conservative models based upon traditional modes of hierarchical, transmission teaching requiring high levels of student passivity.

Ironically, within Queensland, conservative Ministers for Education usually left education policy production to the professional policymakers and experts, except for interventions in curriculum around ideological issues, particularly during the controversial Premiership of Joh Bjelke-Petersen (1968–87).[2] During Labor periods of government (most of the period 1989–2012) politicians took much tighter control of schooling policies. This was particularly the case with Anna Bligh as Minister and subsequently as State Premier. Unlike any other State, all public examinations at the secondary level were abolished in Queensland, following the Radford Report of 1969. From the early 1970s, senior secondary assessment in Queensland has been school-based and teacher-moderated. A 'core skills' test provides the final element of moderation, adding another dimension of equity and accountability to the system. This test assesses students' capacities in relation to higher order core curriculum goals of senior secondary school curricula.[3] Additionally, the senior school curriculum functions through school creation of work programmes and assessment strategies developed in line with broad framework syllabus documents, which offer schools considerable professional choice dependent on teacher judgement. This system is highly lauded by assessment experts across the globe (e.g. Darling-Hammond, 2010).

Schooling in Australia is the Constitutional responsibility of the States, but there has been strengthened federal government involvement, including funding, since the 1970s. In the latter stages of his Prime Ministership, conservative PM John Howard (1996–2007), was exceedingly critical of Queensland's assessment approach, desiring a return to public exams, perhaps linked to ambitions regarding a national curriculum, subsequently developed after 2007 by federal Labor governments (Rudd and Gillard). At one stage, Howard threatened federal school funding to Queensland, implying continuing federal support might be contingent on the reintroduction of public examinations. This has not happened, but the development of the Australian Curriculum[4] post 2007, particularly at the senior school level has raised issues of comparability of exit measures of school performance across States. The election of a new conservative government in Queensland in 2012 has also raised the issue of a possible return to public examinations. In this context, what is surprising is the lack of a strong professional and academic voice defending the Queensland system.[5] Research has demonstrated that upper secondary teachers in Queensland are highly assessment-literate (Lingard et al., 2006). Unfortunately, however, research also demonstrates that this assessment-literacy did not stretch to other parts of the schooling system (Lingard et al., 2001).

From the 1970s, Queensland has had a progressive system of senior secondary assessment and unique approach to tertiary selection reliant on school-based, teacher- moderated assessment. From the late 1990s, under State Labor governments, Queensland also saw a plethora of progressive changes and reforms in schooling at other levels of primary and lower secondary schooling. Research and academic thinking were central elements of this renaissance. For example, the Queensland School Reform Longitudinal Study (QSRLS) (Lingard et al., 2001), was commissioned by the State government. While this research documented supportive pedagogies, there was not enough intellectual demand, connectedness or working with difference in classroom pedagogies (Lingard, 2007). The research hypothesized that this was an effect of a stress on content coverage of curriculum and insufficient knowledge in respect to issues of difference in the classroom. One outcome was the development of the concept of the *productive pedagogies* framework, which sought to make a difference to student learning through teaching practices that were intellectually demanding, connected, supportive and worked with and valued differences (Hayes et al., 2006).

The QSRLS subsequently led to the 'New Basics' trial, which developed a new curriculum for schooling from Years 1–9 to be aligned with productive pedagogies and assessment based upon real-world, intellectually demanding activities called 'rich tasks' (Education Queensland (2004c)). Thus, the New Basics were about aligning curriculum, pedagogy and assessment and recognizing that investment in teachers and their professional knowledges and skills was central to enhancing learning outcomes for all students across primary and secondary schools and, importantly, for achieving more socially just outcomes across schools serving different socio-economic communities. The New Basics were also about what were deemed to be the central knowledge domains thought necessary to twenty-first-century futures. This was thus a curriculum reform based not on disciplines, but rather on the imagined future worker and citizen in a global context.

The New Basics exemplified the type of curriculum emerging at this time around the globe and had quite a bit in common with Scotland's Curriculum for Excellence (CfE) which aimed at producing 'successful learners, confident individuals, responsible citizens and effective contributors'. There were, however, differences: the New Basics model developed out of a specific research project; it was explicit about its theoretical framings, especially Dewey; it dealt with pedagogy and assessment in addition to curriculum; it was a trial in about 50 schools, not implemented across the system; it was trialled only in Queensland, not nationally; it was strongly supported in its implementation through critical friends in each school; and it was subject to an ongoing research gaze. Yet, as with CfE, it was a manifestation of a *process* curriculum with implicitly desired outcomes (Priestley and Humes, 2010), namely imagined future citizens and workers. In one sense, the New Basics could be seen as a re-articulation of a progressive approach in the context of rapid economic and social changes and globalization, framed to some extent by new technologies and related multiliteracies.

The evaluation of the New Basics trial was affirming, documenting its positive effects, especially on the intellectual demands made of students. The Queensland government, while supportive of the New Basics and positive about the effects of the trial, baulked at the cost of implementing this approach across the entire government school system. However, as our policy narrative will demonstrate there were other constraints on full implementation. With the election of the Rudd Labor government federally in 2007 came a national school accountability agenda with a strong mandate for introducing a more tightly controlled, discipline-based Australian Curriculum, along with national testing of literacy and numeracy via the National Assessment Plan – Literacy and Numeracy (NAPLAN). The latter is taken by all students nationally in all schools at Years 3, 5, 7 and 9.

In a sense, the national reform agenda in Australia pursued by federal Labor after 2007 is a vernacular manifestation, mediated by Australian education federalism, of what Sahlberg (2011) has called GERM, the Global Education Reform Movement. This largely, but not exclusively Anglo-American approach to school and system reform in response to globalization has the following features:[6] prescribed curriculum, focus on literacy and numeracy, test-based accountability, standardized teaching and learning, and market-oriented reforms (e.g. private sector management models, school and parental choice discourses) (p. 103). This reform agenda has seen the New Basics, and its approach to curriculum, move rapidly off the agenda in Queensland. Paradoxically, the Finnish approach that

Sahlberg juxtaposes with GERM, has much in common with the senior approach to curriculum and assessment in Queensland and with the New Basics trial. In the longer term, we think the Australian Curriculum might represent a challenge to the Queensland form of school-based, teacher-moderated assessment at the senior levels and its implicit trust of teachers and respect for their professionalism. Certainly, the national reform and accountability agendas have been influential in the demise of the New Basics experiment and its systemic impact.

On the first NAPLAN in 2008, Queensland students performed comparatively badly, especially when compared with those in New South Wales and Victoria. Additionally, Queensland's performance on the International Association for the Evaluation of Educational Achievement's (IEAs) Trends in International Maths and Science Study (TIMSS) appeared to be in decline. In response to huge media coverage of these issues and the subsequent political pressure, the Premier Anna Bligh appointed the head of the Australian Council for Educational Research (ACER), Professor Geoff Masters to report on necessary changes in Queensland schooling, as a way to enhance Queensland's comparative educational performances, especially on NAPLAN.

One specific policy outcome of the subsequent *Masters Report* was the implementation of Teaching and Learning Audits in all Queensland government schools. Much more time was also spent in schools preparing students for the tests – a major interim recommendation of the Review. The publication of NAPLAN results on the *My School* website, created by the federal government in 2010 as part of its accountability and transparency agenda, has strengthened this teaching to the test, as has extensive media coverage of school and system performance. While Queensland's 2009, 2010 and 2011 performances were better than that of 2008, all other States had improved as well, perhaps suggesting much more time spent on preparing students for NAPLAN in all Australian schools.

Our narrative then is that a progressive moment in Queensland schooling around the New Basics has been overridden by cost factors and national policy developments in respect of the national reform agenda.[7] We show the specific significance of the poor NAPLAN results in Queensland in 2008 as a central marker of the end of that progressive policy moment and the denial of any on-going impact of the New Basics. We are thinking here specifically of the new discipline-based Australian Curriculum, now being implemented for English, Maths, Science and History in P-10 across the nation, but particularly the focus on literacy and numeracy through National Partnerships on Literacy and Numeracy and Low SES School Communities and the centrality now of NAPLAN to accountability and school performance. While, as we will show, NAPLAN is not high stakes in the traditional sense of carrying great consequential significance for students, our argument is that it has become high stakes for systems, schools, teachers and through pressure deflected down the line, for students too (see Lingard and Sellar, 2013).

Our chapter is structured in the following way: we begin by contextualizing the development and aims of the New Basics in Queensland, followed by an explanation of its subsequent demise. This is followed by consideration of the national policy agenda and its impact upon policy reforms in Queensland schooling. We then reflect upon the 'conservative restoration' as part of the vernacular expression of GERM in Australia, and examine the impact of NAPLAN performance on education policy formation in Queensland and Australia. We conclude by analysing and contextualizing this curriculum change narrative. As Bernstein's (1971, p. 47) observation that 'differences within and change in the organization, transmission and evaluation of educational knowledge should be a major area of sociological interest' suggests, we argue that such changes in curriculum as documented in this chapter are signifiers of broader societal changes. Here we specifically document the ways in which schooling policy has been economized and become a central plank of national economic policy in the face of globalization and the pressing necessity of ensuring a competitive national economy within the global one (Rizvi and Lingard, 2009). We argue that the educational progressiveness of New Basics as a curriculum constructed around a desired imagined future, rather than around disciplinary knowledges, has passed.

Contextualizing the development of the New Basics in Queensland

During the 1970s and early 1980s, educational authorities throughout Australia flirted with notions of progressive curricula that fostered pedagogical models of inquiry learning and questioned the fixed nature of 'truths' (Barcan, 1993). The short-lived Whitlam federal Labor government of 1972–5 changed the social and cultural landscape of Australia. Whitlam also systematized federal involvement in schooling, aimed largely at equalizing opportunities and ensuring more socially just outcomes from schooling. Along with free tertiary education came the foregrounding of the importance of class equality, gender equity, multiculturalism and diversity, not only within mainstream society, but in Australian classrooms as well. However, by the end of the 1980s, a conservative backlash emerged in the United Kingdom, the United States as well as Australia (Cope, 1990) that championed traditional curricula and modes of teaching that were content-based and teacher-led, as opposed to the progressive approaches that were process driven and student-centred. Not everyone had been convinced by the efficacy of notions of 'progressive' education as evidenced by this opinion piece in the *Australian Financial Review*:

> [The] trendoids [say] that syllabi are now much 'richer' – that there is simply not enough time to teach the basics anymore. Would most parents rather have their 12-year old taught condom rolling or grammar and spelling? Why should priority be given to discussing lesbian lifestyles, or tree-hugging rather than much more mainstream skills? ... The trendoid argument for abolishing spelling lists and replacing them with an anything goes philosophy also constitutes a gross calumny against generations of older teachers. If the old methods were so deplorable, why aren't all Australians over 30 illiterate? ... The emphasis nowadays is on education as a 'feeling' exercise rather than a thinking one. Will this help us take on the world economically? The export market for encounter group leaders, primal scream therapists and iris readers is not very big! (27 July 1987, cited in Cope, 1990, p. 20)

The vitriol of this traditionalist backlash is striking and, within the context of the global economic recession of the late 1980s and early 1990s (Allen, 1999), such views rapidly gained support. Economic austerity encouraged the rhetoric of getting 'back to basics' in the classroom. The notion that there was a special set of skills and knowledge that underpinned all other educational achievements maintained its hold on the public and policy imaginations. Although ill-defined, 'the basics' were generally understood and validated as equating with traditional areas of factual knowledge, arithmetic, grammar, spelling and punctuation. However, by the end of the 1990s, the influence of educational research from home and abroad began to influence debates and subsequent policies in respect to schooling.

In 1998, the Conservative Queensland Borbidge government's (1996–8)[8] *Leading Schools* initiative had been launched. While this was largely an experiment in school-based management, it also sought to improve student outcomes through the adoption of educational concepts developed in the United States by Newmann and Associates (1996) from the University of Wisconsin-Madison's Centre on Organization and Restructuring of Schools. Because of their focus upon student engagement and higher-order thinking, Newmann and Associates' 'authentic' pedagogies and 'authentic' assessment promised better student outcomes in both learning and equity. This research became the construct, albeit reconceptualized and re-contextualized, upon which the QSRLS began to evaluate Queensland's *Leading Schools*' initiative.[9]

The QSRLS (1998–2000) was, at that time, the most comprehensive study of pedagogy, curriculum and assessment practices that had been commissioned in Australia. This research extended upon the work of Newmann and Associates' conceptual framework with the QSRLS models of 'productive' pedagogies and 'productive' assessment providing the lenses needed to evaluate the intellectual and social health of Queensland's classrooms. The QSRLS mapped the pedagogies and assessment practices of approximately 250 teachers in 4 lessons, across 24 primary and secondary schools over 3 years. Classroom observations and samples of student work were scaled via 20 pedagogic items and 18 assessment items in order to code the work of teachers and the outcomes of their students. Subsequently, these items were grouped into four domains of productive pedagogies: Intellectual quality; Connectedness; Supportive classroom environment; and, Working with and valuing difference. The emphasis upon elements of inclusivity, active citizenship and group identities differentiated the Queensland study from that of Newmann and Associates, as did its focus on both social as well as academic outcomes from schooling.

While rating Queensland classrooms highly within the dimension of care and supportiveness, the findings showed low levels of intellectual demand, connectedness and recognition of difference in pedagogies. Assessment tasks also rated poorly, with teachers seemingly not recognizing the need to align assessment and pedagogy. There was also a pressing need to invest in teachers' professional development and assessment literacy (Lingard et al., 2001). Such findings provided timely responses to educational challenges that became evident during concurrent community consultations undertaken by the then Premier of Queensland, Peter Beattie (elected 1998). At the same time as the QSRLS research was in progress, Beattie launched his 'Smart State' strategy in which he identified knowledge, creativity and innovation as drivers of economic growth (Adie, 2008). This was followed by extensive community consultation for developing long-term goals for schooling that would underpin the *Queensland State Education – 2010* (QSE–2010) initiative. The QSE–2010 consultations sought to investigate the major challenges facing the Queensland Department of Education, such as student retention rates, the drift of students to private schools and the implications for education of broader economic and social changes related to globalization.

During consultations, many stakeholders questioned the extent to which Queensland education was preparing young people for a globalized, technologically driven future. The subsequent 'Framework Project', led by university academic, Professor Allan Luke was the first step towards formulating a planned response (Education Queensland, 2004b) to the challenge of producing a futures-oriented curriculum for Queensland in the New Millennium. It was this initiative that subsequently delivered the New Basics Project. Drawing upon the QSRLS Report, the four domains of productive pedagogies and productive assessment that were derived from the research – Intellectual quality, Connectedness, Supportive classroom environment and Working with and valuing of difference – became *The Productive Pedagogies*, a pedagogical framework for effecting an intellectual shift in Queensland teacher classroom practices, a key contributor to the *Smart State* initiative and a fundamental element of the New Basics reform.

However, a parallel *national* curriculum reform had also been in progress across Australian States and Territories during the 1990s, led by federal Labor governments (1983–96). This was the organization of school curricula into eight 'Key learning Areas' (KLAs) based upon related fields of knowledge. For example, Studies of Society and the Environment (SOSE) comprised knowledges and skills from the disciplinary fields of history, geography and economics. SOSE also included related elements of culture, values and citizenship. In contrast, *Queensland's* New Basics Project sought to integrate across disparate subject areas, so as to enable students to complete 'real world tasks'. Teachers had to 'backward map' to determine what skills and knowledge ('repertoires of practices') would be required by students. According to the project team, the New Basics curriculum would be based upon 'envisioning the kinds of life worlds and human subjects that the education system want[ed] to contribute to and build' (Education Queensland, 2004b, p. 3). Here we see a new rationale for school curriculum; one based neither in behavioural objectives nor disciplines, but rather framed through a visioning of future workers, citizens and a desired future world. However, before implementation could be broached with teachers, a comprehensive trial of the New Basics was required and this occurred between 2000 and 2003, involving 38 state government primary and secondary schools across Queensland.

The New Basics: Producing new workers and new citizens

The QSRLS had identified significant problems in the existing structures and practices of Queensland education and this provided the political leverage needed to ensure the implementation of the New Basics trial. A renewed interest in progressive modes of education was signified by the appointment of a university educator, Professor Allan Luke, as the Deputy Director-General of Education Queensland. Appropriating the political rhetoric of the Right, 'the basics' soon became 'the *New* Basics' as he began redefining the fundamental knowledges, skills and attributes needed for the new economies, new workplaces, new technologies, diverse communities, complex cultures and new citizenship of 'New Times' (Hall, 1996). We note that the name New Basics flowed from market research that showed this nomenclature appealed to both conservatives and progressives in the broader community.

During the early 1990s, cultural theorist, Stuart Hall, had mapped a number of significant global and local shifts in economic, cultural and national manifestations that gave rise to the definition of 'New Times', the metaphor he coined to embrace a transformative process that featured the following: new ethnicities, new subjectivities, globalization, hydrid identities, informational technologies and a resurgent neo-liberal capitalism. This was the context within which Queensland's New Basics project was launched. The citizen of the New Millennium required an education that provided more than the *old* 'basics' of 'reading, writing and arithmetic'. The *New* 'basics' would facilitate knowledges and skills that would respond to the conditions of Hall's 'New Times', as noted by Queensland's Department of Education:

> The 'new basics' themselves are the basics of the schooling that our students need for a future that is already upon us: new economies, new workplaces, new technologies, new student identities, diverse communities, and complex cultures. (Education Queensland, 2004b, p. 2)

Also fundamental to the New Basics Project was the explicit attempt to improve student outcomes and close the disadvantage gaps among diverse groups of students by aligning Bernstein's (1971) 'three message systems' of curriculum, pedagogy and assessment.

At the heart of the New Basics was the premise that educational reform would not eventuate if changes were made to curriculum or pedagogy or assessment practices in isolation from each other. A triad of reforms in respect to curriculum, pedagogy and assessment underpinned the New Basics framework (Education Queensland, 2004a). First it was necessary to 'unclutter' the curriculum via four curriculum 'organizers': Life Pathways and Social Futures (Who am I and where am I going?); Multiliteracies and Communication Media (How do I make sense of and communicate with the world?); Active Citizenship (What are my rights and responsibilities in communities, cultures and economies?); and, Environments and technologies (How do I describe, analyse and shape the world around me?). Students would engage with 'core tasks' (rich tasks) – real world problems that, in their 'unpacking' would facilitate acquisition of the knowledges and skills needed for New Times. However, for Luke and his team, such reshaping of the curriculum was just the beginning:

> We can fiddle with curriculum – with goals, with materials, with texts, with skill outcomes, with 'knowledge' – endlessly, but ultimately curriculum is reshaped, remade, reborn, recorded in what we do with kids in classrooms. . . . It won't make a difference if our pedagogy isn't up to scratch. (Luke, 1999, p. 4)

Indeed, the QSRLS (2000) had found Queensland classrooms lacking in effective teaching strategies, thus necessitating a revolution in pedagogy premised upon notions of 'educational productivity' via a suite of 20 pedagogical practices grouped into the 4 dimensions of 'Productive Pedagogies'. Underpinning this framework was the need for dialogue among teachers. De-privatization of teacher practices, the creation of teacher professional learning communities and productive leadership were also necessary complements to pedagogical reform and alignment of the message systems (Lingard et al., 2003).

The third element of the New Basics triad (complementing its curriculum and pedagogy), was an approach to assessment that drew upon the work of Vygotsky's (1978) constructivism, Newman and Associates' (1996) authentic assessment, Freire's conscientization and Dewey's (2001) project learning, to propose student-centred, constructivist, complex assessment tasks – 'Rich Tasks' – for demonstrating learning outcomes that would then be collaboratively graded and moderated by teachers. This would see the migration of teacher moderation practices, central to senior schooling in Queensland, to primary and lower secondary levels.

These rich tasks were divided into three suites: Years 1–3, 4–6 and 7–9. They included such activities as multimedia presentations, creation of student web pages, artistic performances, and designing structures for the built environment, to name but three examples (Education Queensland, 2004a). However, in the spirit of modern modes of progressive education, the New Basics initiative also carried an explicit commitment to achieving social justice for those young people who were most disadvantaged and likely to be failed by the system. According to Allan Luke, the New Basics 'package' aimed to address the needs of the most 'at risk' students in the classroom, emphasizing the need to respond to 'the new poverty, the pressing need for educational strategies for a bottom quartile, for education for an emergent, heterogeneous underclass, not the working class that many of us were trained to teach' (Hunter, 2001, p. 135).

These were hopeful and ambitious goals. Unfortunately in 2012, Australian federal educational authorities are still struggling to address much the same issues, including the intransigent social class/ performance nexus. Nationally, school retention rates to Year 12 sit at around 78 per cent (ABS, 2011), despite federal government aspirations for 90 per cent retention. School refusal, student disengagement and perceptions of falling academic standards continue to preoccupy educational bureaucrats and politicians, as well as remaining key foci in the research interests of education academics. While noting a number of positive outcomes, the subsequent evaluation of the New Basics trial revealed the significant challenges of attempting such far-reaching educational transformations and the funding levels necessary for their effective implementation.

Changing contexts: From New Basics to Queensland Curriculum, Assessment and Reporting (QCAR) Framework

The evaluation of the New Basics trial revealed mixed results with most positives relating to improvement in some schools in respect to the quality of student work, the levels of intellectual demand of teachers' pedagogy and the development of assessment cultures among groups of teachers. However, there were also negatives in respect to staffing and resourcing issues and teachers' threshold knowledge' (linked to pedagogical content knowledge) and willingness to embrace change. While the New Basics experiment indicated that its tenets had the potential to deliver the kind of educational revolution anticipated by Luke and the QSRLS team, it struggled to surmount the systemic obstacles that inhibited widespread changes within state education beyond the parameters of the trial years. Thus, instead of extending the New Basics framework to the rest of Queensland, its 'core values' were claimed as informing subsequent educational policies. Such core values are described in the final report in 2004 as:

- curriculum values – a futures orientation, an uncluttered curriculum requiring a principled selection of learnings from various operational fields of knowledge and from the repertoire of social and cultural, cognitive and linguistic skills;

- teaching values – upping the ante intellectually, connecting students to the wider world, generating a supportive classroom environment, and recognizing difference;
- assessment system values – rigour, validity, comparability, accountability; and,
- action values – developing school-community links, 'closing the loop' with monitoring, feedback and support, and using program values to drive planning and organisation. (Education Queensland, 2004b, p. 10)

As the New Basics trial was drawing to a close in 2003, Education Queensland established a pilot study to investigate assessment and reporting strategies from Prep to Year 10 (the ARF Pilot Study) in schools that had continued to implement the KLA syllabuses. Its findings, when coupled with the 'core values' of the New Basics trial, subsequently shaped the development of the Queensland Curriculum, Assessment and Reporting (QCAR) Framework (QSA, 2012), which began implementation in 2008. This initiative set out to identify 'Essential Learnings' (ELs) (Education Queensland (d)) from each KLA. Although the QCAR structure reverted to the KLAs as its fundamental curriculum organizers, its conceptual framework was clearly influenced by its more ambitious predecessor, the New Basics:

> The curriculum must promote the key skills and abilities which will allow students to apply their knowledge in increasingly diverse, fluid and changing contexts. The various elements of the curriculum need to be more clearly linked to deal with this diversity and fluidity. (Education Queensland, 2007, p. 6)

Along with a 'futures' orientation, QCAR also sought to continue to consolidate teacher dialogues around school-based assessment from Prep to Year 9. This was about enhancing teacher assessment literacy in primary and lower secondary schooling.

As noted earlier, Queensland has a history of school-based moderated assessment in the senior phase of schooling that stretches back to the early 1970s. The QCAR Framework was designed to extend this collaborative assessment culture to all levels of schooling in Queensland. This initiative resonates with similar attempts within the New Basics trial to engender professional conversations among teachers in respect of curriculum, pedagogy and assessment and their alignment. However, it was being implemented during a period of significant pressure from governments demanding hard 'data' on student achievement, particularly in respect to literacy and numeracy, as part of the rise of 'policy as numbers' (Lingard, 2011). The increasing influence of international assessment regimes such as the OECD's (Organisation for Economic Co-operation and Development) Program for International Student Assessment (PISA) has had considerable influence on national governments, encouraging the development of national curricula and national testing regimes. The IEA's TIMSS and International Program of Reading Literacy Study (PIRLS) have had similar effects.

The election of the Labor Party federally in 2007 saw the fulfilment of new Prime Minister Kevin Rudd's promise to develop an Australian national curriculum by establishing a National Curriculum Board in early 2008, now known as the Australian Curriculum, Assessment and Reporting Authority (ACARA). As well as developing national Australian curricula in English, Maths, Science and History (along with plans for other subject areas), ACARA is also responsible for the administration of nationally mandated tests in literacy and numeracy. Every year, all students in Years 3, 5, 7 and 9 are assessed on the same days using national tests in Reading, Writing, Language Conventions (Spelling, Grammar and Punctuation) and Numeracy. Such external testing sits uncomfortably alongside the legacy of New Basics and subsequent QCAR attempts to unclutter the curriculum; educate for the twenty-first century; align the 'message systems' of curriculum, pedagogy and assessment; and, create contexts for teacher collaboration and moderation of student work. QCAR, like the New Basics before it, is coming under pressure from nationally and internationally driven accountability agendas that may also undermine its attempts at real curriculum reform. The newly elected conservative state government has strongly committed to the national accountability agenda and to the uptake of the Australian Curriculum, thus largely eradicating the possible effects of the New Basics and associated developments.

The National Schooling Agenda: National Curriculum and NAPLAN

Regardless of education policy being the responsibility of the States, the election of the Rudd federal Labor government in late 2007 witnessed the strengthening of the national presence in schooling in Australia. The current national approach includes new national accountabilities and testing, a national curriculum, and a range of National Partnerships between the federal government and the States and Territories. The latter include the National Partnership for Low Socio-Economic

Status School Communities, the centrepiece of the government's redistributive and social justice in schooling agenda. In the early stages of Rudd's Prime Ministership, these developments were facilitated by a new cooperative federalism in respect of schooling, facilitated by the reality of Labor governments in all the States and Territories. This political situation has now changed with non-Labor governments in Western Australia, Victoria, New South Wales, Queensland and the Northern Territory; however, this has not weakened the national agenda in schooling. The Council of Australian Governments (COAG), consisting of the Prime Minister, Deputy Prime Minister and State and Territory leaders, has been central to the establishment of the national agenda. COAG's involvement is indicative of the perceived links between the national education reform agenda, national economic competitiveness and improving workplace productivity – the economization of school policy.

Another significant national development has been the creation of ACARA's *My School* website, which lists a school's results on NAPLAN against national averages and also the school's performance measured against 60 'statistically similar schools' across the nation on a socio-economic scale (Index of Community Socio-Educational Advantage – ICSEA) developed by ACARA. The *My School* website was created by the federal Labor government as part of their accountability and transparency agenda and also the 'school choice' discourse. The website went online on 28 January 2010 with opposition from the teacher unions and educators, while being strongly supported by the Murdoch press, which has been fulsome in its praise of this policy initiative and of the Minister for Education, then Deputy Prime Minister (now PM), Julia Gillard, for pushing it through.[10] This opposition referred to the validity of the data and its likely negative effects on curricula and pedagogy, the likelihood of league tables of performance, and the related potential for the 'naming' and 'shaming' of poorly performing schools, often situated within lower SES communities.

As noted already, the annual national testing of Years 3, 5, 7 and 9 for literacy and numeracy under NAPLAN is an important manifestation of the strengthened federal presence in schooling, and new national educational accountabilities. Because results are published on the *My School,* website, the outcomes of these tests gain a great deal of media coverage in terms of cross-State and cross-school comparisons; they quickly become high-stakes for systems and schools (Lingard and Sellar, 2013), with all the potentially negative effects on pedagogies and curricula as evidenced in other national systems (Hursh, 2008; Stobart, 2008; Darling-Hammond, 2010). The Queensland government's commissioned Master's review of the State's apparently 'poor performance' on NAPLAN in

2008, demonstrates that the tests have indeed become high-stakes – a matter attended to in the next section.

NAPLAN 2008, the Masters Review and the conservative restoration in Queensland schooling

Queensland's poor performance in the 2008 NAPLAN data caused a media furore in the State, with huge media coverage by the *Courier-Mail* (Queensland's daily Murdoch-owned newspaper), and also by radio and television. There was also extensive national media coverage, which documented State system performances and Queensland's comparatively poor performance. The immediate response was for the then Labor Premier, Anna Bligh, to appoint Professor Geoff Masters, CEO of ACER, in December 2008 to review the literacy, numeracy and science performance of Queensland primary school students. Science performance was included because of the apparently poor performance of Queensland students on the IEA's 2007 TIMSS. Premier Bligh's central role can be seen as an attempt to protect the reputational capital of Queensland, which has branded itself as the 'Smart State' (Adie, 2008), a signifier of a move away from the old 'Deep North' anti-intellectual construction of the State developed across the long period of conservative political hegemony in Queensland (1957–89). The Premier's close involvement ensured that NAPLAN became high stakes for the system, senior policymakers, schools, school principals and teachers. Masters provided 'Preliminary Advice' to the Premier on 25 January 2009 and the final report in April, 2009, *A Shared Challenge Improving Literacy, Numeracy and Science Learning in Queensland Primary Schools* (hereafter the *Masters Report*) (Masters, 2009a, 2009b).

Recommendation 4 of the Interim Report stated: 'That last year's NAPLAN assessment materials – including test booklets, administration manual, marking guides, and details of the performances of last year's cohort on each test question – be made available for all Year 3, 5 and 7 teachers at the start of the 2009 school year for use in establishing students' current levels of literacy and numeracy development and to assist in identifying learning needs' (Masters, 2009a, p. 5). This is the use of previous NAPLAN materials as a 'classroom resource'; the text suggested that, 'These materials also may provide students with some useful test taking experience' (Masters, 2009a, p. 6). Preliminary Advice also recommended that the State government set a target so that

'Queensland primary school students were performing at the level of students in the highest performing states in literacy, numeracy and science within the next three years'.

The political improvement imperative driven by the Premier stressed the necessity of *rapid,* improvement on NAPLAN. This imperative, ensuring NAPLAN would become high stakes, was very evident at the Premier's release of the *Masters Report*, when she stressed the need for immediate action. Structural reforms would also follow from the State's poor NAPLAN performance in 2008. From 2015 Year 7 will be moved into secondary schooling in Queensland, bringing schooling structures into line with those in both Victoria and New South Wales, while the introduction of a new Preparatory year also will help align the ages of Queensland students with those in other States. The new conservative State government elected in May 2012 has committed to these changes as well.

In this narrative we can see a rapid evacuation by State leaders of the progressive New Basics agenda and its replacement with the Federal government's focus on accountability measures via NAPLAN and the drive towards a national curriculum. Federal reward monies in respect of the National Partnership Literacy and Numeracy are made available to the States on the basis of the extent to which they achieve targets for improvement on NAPLAN, which they set in negotiation with the federal government, through ACARA. This added further political pressure for improving NAPLAN performance in Queensland manifested in the government creating State-wide improvement targets. These targets are indicative that the moment of New Basics has faded into educational history in Queensland.

Another significant policy development that resulted from the implementation of the *Masters Report* was the creation of the Queensland Education Department's Teaching and Learning Audit instrument developed by ACER. Teaching and Learning Audits were conducted in each Queensland school in 2010 and will continue to be conducted every four years, notwithstanding Teacher Union opposition. The Teaching and Learning Audit consists of eight elements, with the language redolent of what Power (1997) has called the 'audit culture' as part of the new managerialism that accompanies broader neo-liberal policy reforms. Schools are ranked against each of these eight elements on a four-point scale from Outstanding to Low. In sum, these developments have signalled the end of what we have argued to be a 'moment' of progressive educational reform in Queensland, the New Basics.

Conclusion: From New Basics to teaching and learning audits and discipline-based curriculum

Our policy narrative has documented the move from the New Basics trial to the implementation in Queensland of the discipline-based Australian Curriculum in P-10. We must, of course, remember that the New Basics was only ever a trial – most Queensland schools continued with a Key Learning Areas Curriculum overseen by the Queensland Studies Authority. In Queensland, the P-10 Australian Curriculum in Maths, Science and English is being implemented in 2012, while History will be implemented in 2013. Other P-10 subjects will follow along with senior curriculum. Unlike other States, Queensland opted early to adopt in full the Australian Curriculum compared with other States such as Western Australia, which is yet to begin the implementation of the first tranche of P-10 subjects.

Both the New Basics and the Australian Curriculum were/are curriculum developments set against the context of all the changes evinced when we speak of globalization, confirming Bernstein's sociological observation that curriculum changes are signifiers of societal developments. And, as we have already noted, the New Basics was a genre of curriculum emerging at the time across the globe and evidenced also in CfE. The New Basics and the national curriculum are simply different responses to globalization, but both accept that the development of Australia's human capital through education is central to Australia's future, both economically and socially. A particular policy moment in Queensland of a social democratic Labor government, the pressing need for educational reform, a confident bureaucracy and leadership in education, good relationships between educational researchers and the bureaucracy, and research informing policy, allowed a moment of (rearticulated) progressivism in Queensland schooling, set against the pressures of globalization and related changes.

We do not pretend that the New Basics was without its challenges, particularly in respect to resourcing and education of teachers, but its demise followed swiftly as the trial ended. We contend that political imperatives being driven by national accountability agendas prevented its full realization. Indeed, it was Queensland's poor comparative performance on the 2008 NAPLAN test that closed the moment of progressivism in Queensland schooling. Through political interventions largely in response to widespread and critical media coverage, NAPLAN quickly became high stakes in Queensland government schools (Lingard and Sellar, 2013), with all of the effects indicated in research on the topic in other national settings (Lipman, 2004; Nicholas and Berliner, 2007;

Hursh, 2008; Darling-Hammond, 2010; Sahlberg, 2011). NAPLAN remains high stakes for the school system in Queensland and concerns about performance on it have taken on meta-policy status.

The Australian Curriculum now being implemented in P-10 in Queensland schools is a more traditional curriculum than the New Basics; one constructed more around disciplines and one which is very content rich, leaving little space for teacher mediation. Interestingly, one rationale for the New Basics, based on the productive pedagogies research, was (as with CfE) to 'unclutter' the curriculum and emphasize depth over breadth. In contrast, the new national syllabuses exhibit an apparent emphasis on breadth of content and coverage, rather than the more open-ended framework of the Queensland syllabus approach.

To be fair to the new Australian Curriculum, though, we need to acknowledge that there are two elements in addition to the subjects that are indicative of a changed approach to curriculum as manifested in the New Basics and CfE. These are the 'General Capabilities' and the 'Cross-curriculum Priorities'. These general capabilities are: Literacy, Numeracy, Information and communication technology capability; Critical and creative thinking; Personal and social capability; and, Ethical behaviour and Intercultural understanding. These are embedded across the subject curricula. Additionally, the Australian Curriculum comprises what are called 'Cross-curriculum Priorities'. The ACARA website provides this rationale: 'The Australian Curriculum must be both relevant to the lives of students and address the contemporary issues they face. Thus the curriculum gives special attention to three priorities to be addressed in each subject curricula: Aboriginal and Torres Strait Islander histories and cultures; Asia and Australia's engagement with Asia; and, Sustainability'. However, in our view, while both the General Capabilities and Cross-curriculum Priorities are laudable, to this point in Queensland schooling (and across Australia) most attention has been given to the implementation of the P-10 subjects of the Australian Curriculum and improving NAPLAN performance across the system. Sadly, in our considered view, the New Basics have passed into the dustbin of Queensland educational history.

Notes

1 The research upon which this essay is based has been developed from an Australian Research Council (ARC) funded Discovery Project (DP1094850), *Schooling the Nation in an Age of Globalisation: National Curriculum, Accountabilities and their Effects.*

2 Bjelke-Petersen was the longest serving, most conservative Premier in Queensland's history (1968–87). His National Party government collapsed in 1989 after a Royal Commission showed serious corruption across senior levels of government.
3 Cross-curricular higher order cognitive goals of senior syllabuses. These are called 'common curriculum elements'.
4 Official name of the national curriculum.
5 However, our congratulations to the Queensland Studies Authority (2009) for producing an excellent summary of the research on the effects of high-stakes testing on teaching and learning.
6 Specific vernacular manifestations of GERM display all or some of these features in particular assemblages.
7 For an informative history of Queensland curricula developments set against political context, see Gilbert (2011).
8 Labor was in political power in Queensland, 1989 until 2012, apart from a short conservative interregnum of the Borbidge government, 1996–8.
9 The QSRLS was commissioned during the Borbidge government to evaluate the impact of school-based management (*Leading Schools*) on equity and student learning. The election of Beattie Labor in 1998 saw this government abolish *Leading Schools*, but continue support for this research (costing $1.3 million), which evolved into a documentation of classroom practices and their effects on student learning.
10 For example, Glenn Milne columnist for the Murdoch Press's *Sunday Mail* observed regarding the *My School* website: 'As millions of parents put their mouse where their vote is, Julia Gillard can bask in the phenomenal success of one of the Rudd government's landmark initiatives' (31 January 2010, p. 62); and, an editorial (19 January 2010, p. 13) in the Murdoch national paper *The Australian*: 'Ms Gillard is to be praised for defying the education unions, and everybody who believes in equality of opportunity should endorse her determination to ensure schools account for their performance'.

References

Adie, L. (2008), 'The hegemonic positioning of "Smart State" policy'. *Journal of Education Policy*, 23, 251–64.

Allen, R. (1999), *Financial Crises and Recession in the Global Economy* (2nd edn). Cheltenham, UK: Edward Elgar.

Australian Bureau of Statistics (ABS) (2011), *Year 12 Attainment*. Online at www.abs.gov.au/AUSSTATS/abs@.nsf/Lookup/4102.0Main+Features40Mar+2011 (accessed 16/03/12).

Barcan, A. (1993), *Sociological Theory and Educational Reality: Education and Society in Australia since 1949*. Kensington NSW, Australia: University of NSW Press.

Bernstein, B. (1971), 'On the classification and framing of educational knowledge', in M. F. D. Young, (ed.), *Knowledge and Control: New Directions for the Sociology of Education*. London: Collier-Macmillan.

Bourdieu, P. (1984), *Distinction*. London: Routledge.

Connell, R. W. (1987), *Gender and Power: Society, the Person, and Sexual Politics*. Stanford, CA: Stanford University Press.

— (1993), *Schools and Social Justice*. Philadelphia: Temple University Press.

— (1995), *Masculinities*. St. Leonards, VIC: Allen and Unwin.

Cope, B. (1990), 'Facing the challenges of 'Back to Basics'. *Curriculum Perspective*, 10, 20–34.

Darling-Hammond, L. (2010), *The Flat World and Education How America's Commitment to Equity will Determine Our Future*. New York: Teachers' College Press.

Dewey, J. (1969), *The Early Works, 1882–1898*. Carbondale: Southern Illinois University Press.

— (2001), *The School and Society; & The Child and the Curriculum*. Minola, NY: Dover Publications, INC.

Education Queensland (2004a), *The New Basics Project*. Retrieved 9/3/12. http://education.qld.gov.au/corporate/newbasics/

— (2004b), *The New Basics Report*, Retrieved 14/2/2012. http://education.qld.gov.au/corporate/newbasics/html/research/research.html

— (2004c), *The Rich Tasks*. Retrieved 14/2/2012. http://education.qld.gov.au/corporate/newbasics/html/richtasks/richtasks.html

— (2007), *Essential Learnings and Standards: Position Paper*. Retrieved 16/3/12. www.qsa.qld.edu.au/downloads/early_middle/qcar_el_position_paper.pdf

Gilbert, R. (2011), 'Social context and educational change: innovations in the Queensland Curriculum', in L. Yates, C. Collins and K. O'Connor (eds), *Australia's Curriculum Dilemmas: State Cultures and the Big Issues*. Melbourne: Melbourne University Press, pp. 163–81.

Hall, S. (1996), 'The meaning of New Times', in D. Morley and K.-H. Chen (eds), *Stuart Hall: Critical Dialogues in Cultural Studies*. London: Routledge, pp. 223–37.

Hayes, D., Mills, M., Christie, P. and Lingard, B. (2006), *Teachers and Schooling Making a Difference*. Sydney: Allen and Unwin.

Hunter, L. (2001), 'The Queensland New Basics: an interview with Allan Luke'. *English in Australia/Literacy Learning: The Middle Years*, 9, 132–40.

Hursh, D. (2008), *High-stakes Testing and the Decline of Teaching and Learning*. Lanham, MD: Rowman and Littlefield.

Lingard, B. (2007), 'Pedagogies of indifference'. *International Journal of Inclusive Education*, 11, 245–66.

— (2011), 'Policy as numbers: ac/counting for educational research'. *The Australian Educational Researcher*, 38, 355–82.

Lingard, B. and Sellar, S. (2013), 'Catalyst data: perverse systemic effects of audit and accountability in Australian schooling'. *Journal of Education Policy*. DOI: 10.10.80/02680939.2012.758815.

Lingard, B., Mills, M. and Hayes, D. (2006), 'Enabling and aligning assessment for learning: some research and policy lessons from Queensland'. *International Studies in Sociology of Education*, 16, 83–102.

Lingard, B., Hayes, D., Mills, M. and Christie, P. (2003), *Leading Learning: Making Hope Practical in Schools*. Buckingham, UK: Open University Press.

Lingard, B., Ladwig, J., Mills, M., Bahr, N., Chant, D., Warry, M., Ailwood, J., Capeness, R., Christie, P., Gore, J., Hayes, D. and Luke, A. (2001), *The Queensland School Reform Longitudinal Study*. Brisbane, Australia: Department of Education.

Lipman, P. (2004), *High Stakes Education: Inequality, Globalization and Urban School Reform*. New York and London: RoutledgeFalmer.

Luke, A. (1999), *Education and New Times: Why Equity and Social Justice Still Matter, but Differently*. Online at http://education.qld.gov.au/corporate/newbasics/docs/onlineal.doc (accessed 15/03/12).

Masters, G. N. (2009a), *Improving Literacy, Numeracy and Science Learning in Queensland Primary Schools, Preliminary Advice*. Melbourne: Australian Council for Educational Research.

— (2009b), *Improving Literacy, Numeracy and Science Learning in Queensland Primary Schools*. Melbourne: Australian Council for Educational Research.

Newmann, F. and Associates (1996), *Authentic Achievement: Restructuring Schools for Intellectual Quality*. San Francisco, CA: Jossey-Bass.

Nichols, S. and Berliner, D. (2007), *Collateral Damage: How High Stakes Testing Corrupts America's Schools*. Cambridge, MA: Harvard Education Press.

Power, M. (1997), *The Audit Society: Rituals of Verification*. Oxford: Oxford University Press.

Priestley, M. and Humes, W. (2010), 'The development of Scotland's Curriculum for Excellence: amnesia and déjà vu'. *Oxford Review of Education*, 36, 345–61.

Queensland Studies Authority (QSA), *The QCAR Framework*. Online at www.qsa.qld.edu.au/downloads/early_middle/qcar_is_framework.pdf (accessed 16/03/12).

Rizvi, F. and Lingard, B. (2009), *Globalizing Education Policy*. London: Routledge.

Sahlberg, P. (2011), *Finnish Lessons: What Can the World Learn from Educational Change in Finland?* New York: Teachers' College Press.

Stobart, G. (2008), *Testing Times: The Uses and Abuses of Assessment*. London: Routledge.

Vygotsky, L. S. (1978), *Mind in Society: The Development of Higher Psychological Processes*. Cambridge, MA: Harvard University.

Walkerdine, V. (1990), *Schoolgirl Fictions*. London: Verso.

Weiler, K. (2004), 'What can we learn from progressive education?' *Radical Teacher*, 69, 4–9.

12

A Curriculum for the Twenty-First Century?

Gert Biesta and Mark Priestley

Introduction

The ambition of this book has been to provide an overview and critical analysis of new trends in curriculum policy and practice. We have taken the Scottish Curriculum for Excellence (CfE) as a 'case', and in the first part of this book the contributors have provided detailed discussions of the defining aspects and characteristics of the Scottish approach, particularly in relation to the four capacities that structure CfE. We have placed this discussion within a wider perspective, both by looking at broader themes and issues such as teacher agency and teacher development, and curriculum policy and development, and by placing the Scottish approach in a more international perspective. Thus we have been able to show that the shape and form of CfE is not unique, but is indeed part of wider trends in curriculum policy and practice. Admittedly our focus has been on developments in the English-speaking world. Nonetheless, we think that the contributions to this book provide ways of looking at and thinking about recent trends in curriculum policy and practice that may be useful in other contexts and settings as well. In this regard we hope to have made a contribution to the field of curriculum scholarship and research which, at least in some countries and settings, has over the past decades led a rather marginal existence.[1]

In the introduction to this book we have characterized the 'New Curriculum' in terms of three major trends: a (re)turn to child-centred and student-centred approaches, itself fuelled by constructivist theories of learning (for a critical discussion of the impact of the latter see Biesta, 2011; 2012); an emphasis on the teacher as a central agent in curriculum making; and a tendency to formulate curricula in terms of capacities and competencies, and hence more in terms of what children and students ought to become than in terms of what they should be learning (see also Chapter 3 in this volume). While these developments are steering the curricular conversation in one direction, we have also indicated that: at the very same time, curriculum policy and practice are strongly influenced by economic arguments; that policymakers at national and supra-national level continue to increase their grip on the educational system; and that there is an ongoing emphasis on (measurable) outcomes. This suggests that when we zoom in on what is happening at the level of curriculum practice and, to a certain extent, curriculum policy, we find trends going in one direction – focusing on children and students and their learning, on teachers and their agency, and on the promotion of wider capacities and capabilities – but when we zoom out to bring the wider sociopolitical context into view, we see things moving in a different direction – one of narrow aims, central control and measurable outcomes. This explains why the general picture emerging from the chapters in this book is one of tensions and contradictions, more than of a clear and unambiguous development in one direction. That the curriculum field is characterized by tensions and contradictions is, in itself, of course not a new phenomenon in the history of curriculum (see, for example, Kliebard, 2004). Yet what is new, and in our view does warrant the use of the phrase 'New Curriculum', are the particular trends and dynamics currently happening in curriculum policy and practice.

Wider sociopolitical trends shaping the curriculum field

If much of what has been discussed in the foregoing chapters has focused on trends and trajectories that become visible when zooming in, we wish, in this concluding chapter, to place the analyses conducted in this book in a wider context. We do this by making three observations about the wider dynamics of the sociopolitical field in which curriculum policy and practice emerge and evolve.

Curriculum as a concern of national governments

The first observation to make is that, whereas up until about three decades ago the idea of a national curriculum – understood as a curriculum defined and controlled by the state – was in many Western countries seen as a highly controversial idea (if not an unwarranted intervention in the education system), over time many countries have adapted more or less elaborate national curricula, some specifying intended inputs or outcomes in very general terms, but others being extremely detailed in terms of what is to be taught and/or what is to be learned or achieved. The idea that curriculum belongs to the jurisdiction of governments, rather than, say, to schools or teachers, is now commonly accepted. This signifies an important shift in the power dynamics of the 'struggle' over the curriculum. This shift is partly the result of the rise of a culture of accountability in education, stemming from the intention to make public services such as the school more accountable to the public it is supposed to serve. Yet accountability is a two-edged sword because, as many authors have shown, it can either have a democratic face or one that is technical-managerial (see, for example, Poulson, 1996; Charlton, 1999; Biesta, 2004; Hopmann, 2008). It can, in other words, either be an instrument for democratization or an instrument for control, and there are many examples where accountability in education has turned into the latter, forfeiting its democratic potential (see, for example, Gewirtz, 2002).

The (silent) acceptance of the fact that curriculum is indeed the 'business' of the government is therefore not only remarkable when looked at from a wider historical perspective, but also raises important questions about the particular interests that shape the way in which governments approach their involvement in curricular issues. While in principle governments could – and in our opinion: should – have the common good or public interest at the forefront of their considerations, in practice we can see, as several of the authors in this book have also highlighted, that many governments let their decisions about curricular policy be guided by economic concerns, particularly in terms of a concern for competitiveness in the global economy. That is one of the main reasons why many curricula emphasize the apparent need for the acquisition of a set of skills and competencies – such as literacy, numeracy, critical thinking, communication skills and the skill of learning itself – that allow young people to remain flexible in the face of the every changing demands of a global economic order (see, for an example of this line of thinking, the twenty-first-century skills movement; Trilling and Fadel, 2009; and for a critical discussion Biesta, in press). Surprisingly this economic order itself is only seldomly questioned and often figures only in very abstract terms, that is, as something that sets the 'demands' for education, rather than as something that should be critically scrutinized by responsible citizens.

The impact of supra-national organizations

This is connected to a second trend within the wider sociopolitical field in which curriculum development takes place and curriculum policy is set, which is the fact that increasingly decisions about curriculum and wider education policy are influenced by supra-national entities and organizations, such as, perhaps most notoriously, the Organisation for Economic Development and Cooperation (OECD). The impact of the OECD on national policies has particularly taken place through PISA, OECD's programme for international student assessment which, since 2000, has been running 'curriculum-independent' tests of reading, mathematics and science on a three-year cycles through a questionnaire-based study of a representative sample of 15-year-old students in participating countries. While PISA is presented as a system to provide countries with information about the performance of their education system so that, *in principle*, it does nothing more than producing information that governments might use in their policy considerations, *in practice* PISA has had, and is continuing to have, a significant impact on education policy in many countries (see, for a recent analysis and overview, Baird et al., 2011).

In several countries, the publication of PISA results has led to what is known in the literature as the PISA shock (see ibid.; see also, for example, Waldow, 2009) and has led governments to adjust their policies in such a way that it will generate better results in subsequent PISA cycles. This shows that, rather than that PISA being just an instrument for the provision of information, it has quickly turned into a definition of what good education is supposed to be. Surprisingly, the definition implied in PISA – one in which only three subjects are measured and thus only three subjects seem to 'count' – tends to be uncritically accepted rather than critically questioned. As Steiner-Khamsi (2003) argues, what we find here is therefore less a process of deliberate policy borrowing and lending and much more a process of 'cross-national attraction', where definitions of what should count in education such as those produced by PISA, become the centre around which national policies and priorities are defined. It is the logic of this process itself that is concerning, as it seems to be driven by information rather than that the information is one of the sources for decision-making. But what is perhaps more concerning is that organizations, which are beyond democratic control and accountability, have such a strong influence on national policies and practices and thus on the playing field within which curricular decisions are made.

The economic imperative and the question of democracy

These developments show how the economic imperative has become a major driver of decisions about the direction of education policy and practice (see also Bank, 2012). While the economic dimension is, of course, not without importance, there is first of all the question *how* the economic dimension is represented – there is, after all, an important difference between, for example, a focus on global economic competitiveness and a focus on global economic cooperation, just as there is an important difference between a focus on economic development or on ecological sustainability – and there is, secondly, also the question *to what extent* economic considerations should drive or determine education policy and practice. Perhaps the biggest question here is to what extent education should be driven by economic concerns, and to what extent it should be driven by wider human concerns, such as a concern for democracy, a concern for social and ecological justice and a concern for peaceful human coexistence. From an economic perspective, the latter are of course far more difficult to measure as 'returns' of an investment in education, not only because, in the economic lingo, they are 'soft outcomes' but also because they are *long-term* outcomes.

The question of (educational) return on (public) investment assumes that the reference point for curriculum policy and practice is that of public education, that is, education funded by public means and, in principle, orientated towards the common or public good. While in some countries this is (still) the default situation where it concerns education in schools, colleges and universities – we can see this particularly in countries with a strong social-welfare tradition – other countries have a relatively long-standing tradition of a privately funded education sector alongside publicly funded education.[2] The growth of privately funded education, both in countries with and countries without a social-welfare tradition, is therefore another dimension of the increasing influence of the economic imperative, particularly when privately funded education is explicitly positioned in terms of an investment in one's own future earning-power (an increasingly prominent argument where it concerns higher education) or where, *de facto*, privately funded education contributes significantly to the reproduction of social privilege and inequality. This is, of course, not necessarily what privately funded education is about, as many countries also have privately funded education that operates on an explicit democratic agenda; nonetheless this remains a minority within the privately funded sector. In addition to this, the economic imperative also plays a role in the more recent involvement of for-profit organizations in the educational field, which contributes to a further hollowing out of the democratic imperative of public education (see Ball, 2007, 2012).

Conclusion: A curriculum for the twenty-first century?

These observations suggest that one of the most important tensions within the wider sociopolitical field, in which curriculum policy and practice take shape, is that between education as a private good and education as a public good or, in more general terms, between education orientated towards economic concerns or towards democratic concerns. The analyses of the Scottish Curriculum for Excellence offered in this book, and the contributions that set these analyses within a wider context, show that the verdict is still open, in that there are trends within the New Curriculum that more clearly go in the direction of the economic imperative and trends that (still) provide opportunities for education orientated towards democracy and democratization. In which direction the New Curriculum will develop is still an open question, although we have indicated that there are powerful forces at work, some of them deliberately pushing education and the curriculum in a particular direction, others operating as more abstract and anonymous attractors. It is particularly in light of the latter that it remains important for all those involved in the theory and practice of curriculum to be aware of the possibilities as well as the tensions and threats. While this book offers no recipes for resolving the wider 'curriculum conflict', we hope that it will provide those involved in curriculum policy and practice with tools for a critical engagement with the direction of curriculum in and for the twenty-first century.

Notes

1 We are aware that this is a contentious claim that itself needs to be contextualized. Perhaps it refers first and foremost to the situation in the United Kingdom where, in the wake of the establishment of National Curricula in the late 1980s and early 1990s, curriculum scholarship seems to have occupied a far less prominent place within the wider field of educational research. The focus of such research appears to have shifted to, on the one hand, more micro studies of the dynamics of 'teaching and learning' (the phrase that seems to have replaced the notion of 'curriculum' – see, for example, the name of the United Kingdom's Teaching and

Learning Research Programme, a national research programme that has had a major impact on educational research in the United Kingdom in the first decade of the twenty-first century; see www.tlrp.org), and on the other hand to sociological studies of education policy and practice. In other countries the field of curriculum theory and research has developed in different ways. For an interesting insight in aspects of the discussion about curriculum scholarship in North America see the contributions by Wraga, Hlebowitsh, Urban and Reynolds in an issue of the *Journal of Curriculum Studies* from 2003 (Reynolds, 2003; Urban, 2003; Wraga and Hlebowitsh, 2003a, 2003b).

2 We resist calling privately funded education 'independent' education, because, unlike publicly funded education, privately funded education is always dependent on private funding streams that often come with particular ideological agendas.

References

Baird, J. A., Isaacs, T., Johnson, S., Stobart, G., Yu, G., Sprague, T. and Daugherty, R. (2011), *Policy Effects of PISA*. Oxford: Oxford University Centre for Educational Assessment.

Ball, S. (2007), *Education plc: Understanding Private Sector Participation in Public Sector Education*. London/New York: Routledge.

— (2012), *Global Education Inc.: New Policy Networks and the Neoliberal Imaginary*. London/New York: Routledge.

Bank, V. (2012), 'On OECD policies and the pitfalls in economy-driven education: the case of Germany'. *Journal of Curriculum Studies*, 44, 193–210.

Biesta, G. J. J. (2004), 'Education, accountability and the ethical demand. Can the democratic potential of accountability be regained?'. *Educational Theory*, 54, 233–50.

— (2011), 'Transcendence, revelation and the constructivist classroom; or: in praise of teaching', in R. Kunzman (ed.), *Philosophy of Education 2011*. Urbana-Champaign: PES, pp. 358–65.

— (2012), 'Giving teaching back to education'. *Phenomenology and Practice*, 6, 35–49.

— (in press), 'Responsive or responsible? Education for the global networked society'. *Policy Futures in Education*.

Charlton, B. G. (1999), 'The ideology of "accountability"'. *Journal of the Royal College of Physicians of London*, 33, 33–5.

Gewirtz, S. (2002), *The Managerial School. Post-welfarism and Social Justice in Education*. London/New York: Routledge.

Hopmann, S. (2008), 'No child, no school, no state left behind: schooling in the age of accountability'. *Journal of Curriculum Studies*, 40, 417–56.

Kliebard, H. M. (2004), *The Struggle for the American Curriculum, 1893–1953* (3rd rev. edn). New York: Routledge.

Poulson, L. (1996), 'Accountability: a key-word in the discourse of educational reform'. *Journal of Education Policy*, 11, 579–92.

Reynolds, W. (2003), 'Rejoinder'. *Journal of Curriculum Studies*, 35, 445–51.

Steiner-Khamsi, G. (2003), 'The politics of league tables'. *Journal of Social Science Education*, 1. Available online at www.jsse.org/2003/2003-1/tables-khamsi.htm (accessed 26/10/12).

Trilling, B. and Fadel, C. (2009), *21st Century Skills: Learning for Life in Our Times*. San Francisco, CA: Jossey-Bass.

Urban, W. (2003), 'Commentary'. *Journal of Curriculum Studies*, 35, 439–44.

Waldow, F. (2009), 'What PISA did and did not do. Germany after the 'PISA-shock''. *European Educational Research Journal*, 8, 476–83.

Wraga, W. and Hlebowitsh, P. (2003a). 'Toward a renaissance in curriculum theory and development in the USA'. *Journal of Curriculum Studies*, 35, 425–37.

— (2003b), 'Commentary'. *Journal of Curriculum Studies*, 35, 453–7.

Index

ability 9, 14, 21–3, 38, 40–1, 43–4, 54, 61, 66, 77, 80, 88, 92, 95, 104, 118–19, 123–4, 147, 153, 182, 193, 195
academies 27, 135, 143, 167
accountability 5, 9, 15, 20, 172, 176–7, 179, 195, 208, 210–11, 219–21, 223–4, 231–2
  agendas 210–11, 220, 224
achievement,
  achievement 2001 initiative 2
  of Agency 188–91, 198, 203–4
  educational 82, 94, 211
  equity Of 157
  outcomes-focused 154
  underachievement 54, 80, 143
adult education 52, 54–7, 60, 68, 84
agency,
  democratic 45, 47
  professional 176, 187, 197
  student 142, 152–3, 156
  teacher 3, 9, 18, 37, 182, 187–8, 190–1, 201, 203
Aitken, G. 3, 8, 35, 151, 156, 187
Alexander, R. 181–2
ambition 13, 26, 29, 36, 66, 120, 169, 171–3, 175–6, 179, 208, 229
anxiety 81, 83, 88, 90, 119, 166, 178, 194
ARF Pilot Study 219
Aristotle 38
Arnott, M. 100–1
aspiration 9, 19, 22–3, 35, 52, 56, 69, 79–80, 153, 156, 178, 188, 191–2, 196–7, 199, 218
assessment,
  formative 3, 58, 66, 69, 167
  international 220
  literacy 214, 219
  methods 80, 90
  peer 61, 66–7
  reform 178
  school-based 209, 219
  self 58, 69–70
  summative 167
  tasks 214, 217
Assessment Is For Learning Programme 25, 59, 63, 65, 69
attainment 14, 25, 27, 58–9, 63, 143, 166–8, 174, 177–8, 195–6
  agenda 25, 27, 177
attitudes 21–2, 41, 78, 80, 82, 115, 118, 146–7
attributes 21, 35, 37, 47, 60, 64, 76–7, 87, 94, 103, 105–6, 117–18, 216
audit 20, 27–8, 180, 211, 223–4
autonomy 3, 9, 18, 23, 25, 54, 60, 68–70, 153–7, 165, 171, 175–9, 182
  professional 18, 157, 171, 177–8

Baker, K. 2
Ball, S. 6, 23, 28–9, 166–7, 175, 191, 234
Beattie, P. 214, 226
Being Young In Scotland 124
beliefs 8, 9, 14, 17, 19, 24, 36, 52, 92, 99, 105, 109, 131, 150, 157, 188, 190–5, 197, 204
Bernstein, B. 4–5, 69, 207, 212, 216, 224
Biesta, G. 3–10, 17–18, 35, 39, 43–4, 46, 58, 87, 99, 110–11, 147, 155, 157, 181, 187–8, 194, 196, 229, 231
bildung 7, 39
Bjelke-Petersen, J. 208, 226
Black, P. 58, 63, 65
Bligh, A. 208, 211, 222
Bloomer, K. 24
Borbidge, R. 213, 226
Bourdieu, P. 207
Bruner, J. 53–4, 63

capabilities 35–7, 43, 46, 64, 76, 78–9, 86, 105, 117–18, 147–8, 230
  general 36, 147, 150, 225
  personal 46, 191

capacities 3-4, 6-7, 17, 19-20, 27, 30, 35-47, 49, 55, 76-7, 79, 99, 105, 115, 117-18, 130, 133-4, 147-8, 208, 229-30
capital,
  cultural 79, 93
  human 130, 224
Carr, M. 78, 147
case study 6, 126, 202
chartered teacher 169, 179
child,
  -centred 3, 54, 76, 133, 208, 229
  participation 8, 119, 121-3, 130, 134
Children's Plan, The 143
citizen,
  active 102, 106, 109-10, 214, 216
  democratic 100, 111-12, 114
  global 23, 108
  justice-oriented 112-13
  participatory 106-8, 112-13
  responsible 3-4, 8, 19, 35-6, 99, 101, 103, 105-9, 111-15, 117, 120, 148, 210, 231
citizenship,
  curriculum 110
  education 8, 99-106, 112, 114, 119, 120
  learning 106, 110
Claxton, G. 78, 81, 83, 147
collaboration 25, 57, 76, 78, 87, 151, 171-2, 220
  Social 79
Collaborative Professional Enquiry 180
colleges 22, 24, 31, 90, 173, 176, 233
Collins, C. 1, 3, 5, 40
Common Core Standards 141-2, 146, 152, 154
communication 23-4, 26-7, 32, 35-6, 62, 117, 122-3, 149, 199, 203, 216, 225, 231
competence,
  -based education, 36, 40-1, 44-5
  emotional 89, 92
competencies 7, 8, 36, 40-7, 86, 103, 118, 130, 142, 146-8, 152, 156, 158, 195, 230, 231
  Key, 3, 4, 5, 36, 45, 146-8
constructivism 3, 21, 52-60, 62, 64, 84-5, 208, 217, 229

contributor 61, 143, 215
  effective 3-4, 8, 19, 35, 105, 117-39, 148, 210
control 2, 9, 13, 16, 20, 52, 55, 58-9, 69, 130, 152-3, 155, 157, 165, 171-2, 182, 192, 208, 230-2
core values 175, 218-19
CPD 19, 30, 169, 176
critical thinking 36, 117, 173, 191, 194, 231
Cross, B. 124, 128
curricula 2-5, 76, 80, 85, 93, 141-8, 150, 152-3, 156-9, 187, 207-9, 211-13, 215, 217, 219, 220-1, 223, 225-7, 230-1
  -alternative 54
  national 141-2, 146, 150, 153, 156-8, 220, 234
curricular,
  cross- 24-5, 36, 65, 106, 147-8, 226
  reform 14, 20, 26, 118
curriculum,
  alternative 54
  Australia 36, 141, 143-5, 148-50, 172, 208, 210-15, 220, 224-5
  capacities based 37
  change 30, 174, 187, 212
  development 1, 3, 6, 9-10, 27, 125, 151, 169, 173-4, 179-80, 182, 199, 232
  England 23, 42, 66, 76, 87, 141, 143, 145, 149, 155, 165, 182
  Finland 172
  guidelines 17, 31
  Italy 131
  national 2, 4, 10, 36, 54, 86, 141, 143, 145, 147-8, 154-8, 208, 215, 220, 223-6, 230
  New Zealand 2-5, 36, 141, 144-5, 148-51, 154-6
  Northern Ireland 36, 141, 147, 150-1, 165
  principles 20, 151
  process-based 63, 75
  reform 142, 145, 209, 215
  Review Group 16, 118, 145
  United States 146, 152, 154, 172, 213
  Wales 151, 165
curriculum reform 2, 9, 31, 54, 141, 143, 165, 173, 220
curriculum values 218

Index

Davies, L. 128–9, 193
Dearing Review 2
democracy 17, 54, 59, 99, 101, 105, 110, 112, 114–15, 126, 129, 167, 233–4
democratic participation 108, 114
determination 35, 62, 68, 70, 103, 122, 226
development,
   cognitive 52–4, 57
   organizational 56–7
   self- 54, 65
   staff 15, 18
developmentalism 3, 7, 51–2, 54
devolution 14, 70, 101, 166, 171
Dewey, J. 52, 188, 207, 210, 217
discourse 3, 7, 13, 15, 18–21, 23, 26, 29, 51–3, 57–8, 60, 67, 69, 94, 118, 121, 166, 170, 192, 196, 204, 221
   Professional, 204
dispositions 7, 22, 26, 41, 57, 75–94, 102–9, 115, 120, 147–8
Donaldson, G. 22, 30, 168, 179–81

Ecclestone, K. 7, 27, 83–4, 88, 91–4
education,
   for citizenship 101–15, 120
   professional 40–1, 45
   progressive 3, 207–8, 217
   student-centred 54, 57, 79, 194, 213, 217, 229
Education Scotland 5, 18, 24, 26, 28, 37, 67, 101, 117–18, 135, 143, 180
educational,
   improvement 142–3, 156, 158
   values 196, 199
Elder-Vass, d. 197
emancipation 39, 46–7, 55, 147
Emirbayer, M. 153, 189–90
emotional,
   maturity 103
   regulation 79, 94
employment 15, 21–2, 144, 147, 175, 179
empowerment 86, 153
engagement,
   active 27, 106, 133, 180
   civic 79, 90
   professional 31
enterprise 15, 22, 102, 173, 175

equity 8, 142–4, 147, 150, 156–8, 208, 212, 214, 226
evaluation 18, 20, 27, 29, 31, 39–40, 76, 103, 125, 155, 167, 172, 174–5, 210–12, 218
   Self- 16, 61, 66, 172–3, 177
exam 92, 167, 182
Experience And Outcomes 37–8, 69

feedback 14, 24, 58, 67, 90, 124, 176, 219
fieldwork 124–6, 132
flexibility 118, 154–5, 157, 173, 175–8
focus groups 25–6, 119, 176–7
Ford C. 27
Freire, P. 55, 217

gender 82, 83, 207, 212
GERM *see* Global Education Reform
Gillard, J. 208, 221, 226
Gillies, D. 19, 150
Gillies, V. 84, 92
Global Education Reform
   Movement 210–12, 226
globalization 3, 118, 147, 210, 212, 214, 216, 224

Hall, S. 216
Hartley, D. 59
Haste, H. 43
Hayward, L. 178
Her Majesty's Inspectorate of Education 3, 6, 13, 31, 101, 105–6, 109, 173
HGIOS *see* How Good is Our School?
HMIE *see* Her Majesty's Inspectorate for Education
How Good Is Our School? 174
Howard, J. 208
Hulme, M. 9, 25, 119, 165, 168, 171, 173, 180, 187
Humes, W. 1, 6, 13–14, 16, 19, 26, 30, 38, 76, 77, 91, 133, 158, 167, 178, 195, 210

identity,
   national 14
   professional 26
IEA *see* International Association for the Evaluation of Educational Achievement

Importance Of Teaching, The 168
inclusion 8, 14, 75, 92, 99, 115, 151
independence 76, 80, 87, 167, 193
inequality 77, 83, 88, 92, 94, 143, 233
initiative 2, 6, 13, 27, 36, 54, 58, 103, 117, 119, 146, 173, 201, 213–15, 217, 219, 221
innovation 2, 6, 10, 22, 29, 31, 53, 134, 171–2, 175–6, 200, 214
inspection 24, 27, 58, 112, 177, 187, 203
instrumental 1, 4, 6, 144, 148, 191, 194–6, 199
International Association for the Evaluation of Educational Achievement 211, 220, 222
International Program of Reading Literacy Study 220

Jessup, F. W. 54
Journey To Excellence, The 20, 30, 174
judgement 18, 27, 38, 43–4, 46, 68, 105, 189
  normative 46, 93, 190
  professional 16, 178
  teacher 208
  value 46
justice 19, 47, 80, 105, 112–13, 115, 131, 144, 207, 233

Kahne, J. 112–15
Kelly, A. V. 2, 3, 39–40
Klafki, W. 39
knowledge,
  content 146–7, 218
  curriculum 84, 87
  disciplinary 85
  economy 166
  everyday 5, 84, 158
  personalized 76
  powerful 5, 88, 158
  procedural 22
  propositional 22
Knowles, M. S. 55

Lambert, D. 157
Lawton, D. 2
Leadbeater, C. 59
leadership 13, 20, 22, 23, 66, 119, 159, 200, 217, 224
  devolved 172, 175

learner 3, 5, 7, 19, 21, 23, 30, 35, 51–2, 55, 57–63, 64, 66–70, 78, 82, 84–5, 89, 105, 117, 120, 142–4, 146–7, 151–2, 155, 158, 167, 193–4, 210
  confident 78, 90
  effective 19
learning,
  active 3, 17, 30, 54, 64–5, 120, 132, 156–7, 177, 207
  collaborative 67, 173
  cooperative 3, 63, 132, 172, 202
  How To Learn 57, 61, 86
  identity 82, 91
  interdisciplinary 26, 27
  lifelong 7–8, 23, 40, 52–4, 57, 60, 118, 146
  logs 67
  organizational 52, 56
  outcome 23, 26, 38, 58, 209, 217
  personal 22, 51, 61, 66, 68–9, 124–5
  power 78, 81
  recommended 24
  self-directed 53, 62
  student-centred 54, 57
Learning And Teaching Scotland 7, 13, 17, 20, 24, 26, 29–31, 101, 124, 131, 175, 179, 202
Lewin, K. 52, 55, 56
Lingard, R. 3, 9, 23, 93, 141, 166, 182, 187, 207, 209, 212, 214, 217, 220–1, 224
literacy,
  emotional 79, 92, 94
  political 110
local authority 14, 24–8, 31–2, 70, 124, 126, 170–3, 176, 179–80, 198
Luke, A. 215–18
Lumby, J. 82–3
Lundy, L. 123, 128–9

McCrone, G. 15, 100, 169–70
McGregor, G. 9, 23, 187
MacKinnon, N. 27
MacLellan, E. 21
managerialism 20, 182, 223
Maslow, A. H. 54
Masters, G. 211, 222–3
Mead, G. H. 53, 188
mental health 82–3
Menter, I. 9, 25, 168–74, 180–1, 187

mentor 65, 172
  peer 93
Mische, A. 153, 189–90
modernization 118, 147, 165, 172
Moore, A. 1, 5
Moss, P. 130–4
motivation 35, 41, 54, 56, 60, 62–3, 80, 82, 86, 157
Muller, J. 144, 148
Munn, P. 15, 99–101, 111, 118
My School 211, 221, 226

NAPLAN *see* National Assessment Plan- Literacy and Numberacy
National Assessment Plan- Literacy and Numeracy 210–12, 220–5
new basics 9, 209–12, 215–20, 223–5
new curriculum 1, 2, 6, 17, 24–5, 27–8, 47, 52, 62–5, 69, 156–7, 193, 198–200, 209, 229–30, 234
Newmann, F. (and Associates) 213–14
numeracy,
  strategy 152, 168

Oates, T. 145, 157
observation 46, 188, 212, 224, 230
OECD *see* Organisation for Economic Co-operation and Development
oppression 55, 81, 83
Organisation for Economic Co-operation and Development 4, 15, 40–1, 45, 53, 57, 60, 79–80, 118–19, 130, 143, 147, 157, 166, 220, 232
outcome,
  learning 38
  measurable 88
  pupil 180
ownership 24, 56, 61, 67, 173

paideia 7, 38–9
parent,
  association 127
  council 127
  -Teacher Association 107
participation 8, 54–5, 59, 75, 78, 82–3, 85, 87, 102–7, 109, 112–13, 117, 120–5, 128–30, 132, 134, 143, 153, 173, 196
partnership 20, 24–5, 36, 65, 117, 153, 171–3, 179, 220, 223

PAThS *see* Promoting Alternative Thinking Strategies
pedagogy 3, 8, 21, 23–5, 31, 53, 55, 65, 68–70, 78, 84–5, 87, 92–3, 131, 134, 142, 146, 150–2, 156–8, 169, 178, 181–2, 207, 209–10, 214, 216–21
peer observation 173, 175, 199, 202
performance 10, 20, 40, 43, 44, 46, 52, 56–9, 62, 66, 80, 118, 143, 167–8, 174, 180, 182, 209, 211–12, 218, 221–6, 232
  management 52, 56–9, 66, 168
performativity 6, 182, 188, 203
personal qualities 37, 45, 103
Petrie, P. 130
philosophy 3, 5, 38, 176, 188, 194, 213
Piaget, J. 52
PIRLS *see* International Program of Reading Literacy Study
PISO *see* Programme for International Student Assessment
Plato 38
Plowden Report 54
Polikoff, M. S. 145
Porpora, D. V. 197
Porter, A. 143–6
Priestley, M. 1–3, 7, 9–10, 18–19, 23, 27–8, 30, 35, 38, 58, 76, 91, 122, 133, 154, 156, 158, 165, 167, 178, 180–1, 187–8, 210, 229
problem-solving 61, 63–4, 89, 151
Productive Pedagogies, The 209, 215, 225
professionalism 18, 23–4, 30, 89, 168, 171, 176–7, 179, 181–2, 187, 192, 211
Programme for International Student Assessment 4, 10, 40, 118, 166, 220, 232
Promoting Alternative Thinking Strategies 89
Pupil Voice 55, 122–3, 126, 128

QSRLS *see* Queensland School Reform
qualities 35, 37, 103–4, 120, 198, 203
quality assurance 52, 58, 70, 180
quality initiative In Scottish schools 58
Queensland School Reform Longitudinal Study 209, 214–18, 226
questionnaire 124, 170, 232

Ranson, S. 60, 68
Rata, E. 5, 82, 85–6, 88, 93
Reeves, J. 7, 58
reflection 61
reform 6, 8, 9, 13–31, 53–4, 101, 141–3, 145, 152, 165–7, 173, 175, 178, 194, 197, 209–11, 215, 217, 220–1
  educational 1, 23, 216, 223–4
Reggio Emilia 131–2
Reimer, T. 156
Reiser, B. J. 156
relationships 64, 68–9, 84, 88, 94, 107, 112, 126, 128, 130, 132, 134, 190–1, 197–204, 224
  professional 188, 197, 202
Research Engaged Schools Programme 171
resilience 36, 53, 68, 77–9, 89, 94, 117
respect 3, 9, 17, 36, 77, 99, 104–5, 108–9, 120–2, 150, 191, 196, 209, 211, 213, 216, 218–19, 221, 223–4
  self- 36
responsibility,
  personal 102, 109, 112–13, 115, 196
  professional 176–7, 192–3
rhetoric,
  policy 3, 6, 144
  political 91, 182, 216
rights 8, 17, 55, 102–8, 111, 114, 120–4, 133–5, 152, 207, 216
  human 94, 109
Rights Respecting Schools Programme 133
Robinson, S. 3, 9, 18, 58, 188
Rogers, C. R. 53–4
Rudd, K. 208, 210, 220–1, 226
Russell, M. 23, 197

Sahlberg, P. 6, 15, 17, 210–11, 225
school 1, 2, 6, 9, 16, 20, 22, 25–8, 37, 40, 51, 55, 58–9, 63–5, 67, 69, 78, 81–2, 86, 100, 106, 109–10, 112, 119–21, 124–30, 132–5, 143–4, 148, 150, 152–5, 157–9, 165–6, 169–77, 179, 188, 191, 195, 197–203, 208–11, 213, 215, 218–19, 221–3, 225–6, 231
  council 125–30, 135
  improvement 20, 59, 171–2, 176
School-Based Research Consortia Initiative 171

School Of Ambition 173–5
school survey 127
self,
  -actualization 54, 57, 69
  -awareness 53, 68, 78–9, 85
  -esteem 78–9, 84, 91–4, 103, 168
  -improvement 51, 57
  -management 57, 66, 170, 176
  -reliance 36, 79, 117
senior management 127, 198–202
sense-making 157, 196, 199
Shier, H. 153
Simon, B. 181–2
Sinnema, C. 3, 8, 36, 151, 155–6, 187
skills 3, 5, 15, 17, 21–2, 25–6, 36, 39–42, 44–5, 51, 54, 57, 61–7, 69, 75–80, 86, 89–91, 102–3, 106, 118, 129, 134, 144, 146–9, 158, 166–7, 170, 172–5, 191, 193–5, 202, 209, 213, 215–18, 231
  citizenship 105
  coping 68
  core 65, 103, 202, 208
  craft 90
  curriculum 174
  deficit 22
  democratic 108
  discrete 146–8
  discussion 170
  generic 5, 103
  key 77, 195, 219
  Learning To Learn 69, 78, 86, 89
  personal learning 22, 51, 61, 66
  self-management 57
  self and peer assessment 61, 66–7
  shortages 172
  teamwork 195
  thinking 22, 66, 86, 89, 148, 195
  transferable 7, 45, 61
Skills For Learning, Skills for Life and Skills for work 21, 65, 67, 195
smart state 214–15, 222
Smithson, J. 145
SoA see School of Ambition
Social,
  change 22, 79
  justice 17, 83, 90, 94, 105, 108–9, 113, 144, 191, 196, 217, 221
  skills 92–3, 194
socialisation 195

society 2, 5–6, 13–14, 17, 19, 35, 39, 45–7, 59, 79, 81, 104–9, 111, 113, 115, 118, 120, 135, 144, 148, 150, 212, 215
  democratic 107–8
Soden, R. 21
spaces 128, 134
  children's 131–2
Spillane, J. 156–7, 175
spiritual values 105, 107
standards,
  agenda 168
  professional 146, 159
Steiner-Khamsi, G. 232
Stenhouse, L. 3, 39, 53–4
Stephen, C. 122, 132
strategy 17, 31, 113, 168, 171–2, 175–6, 179, 214
subject,
  areas 17, 215, 220
  -based knowledge 84, 93
  content 8, 76, 80–1, 84, 87
  disciplines 75, 78, 81, 87
  knowledge 84–6, 89–91, 94
  teachers 26, 65
successful learner 7, 35, 51–3, 55, 57, 59–61, 63, 65–71, 73, 77, 148
survey 28, 118, 124–7, 129

Taylor, D. 6, 81, 191
teacher,
  agency 197, 229
  development 20, 169, 175, 178, 229
  education 22, 42, 159, 166–8, 179, 181
  engagement 9, 22, 28, 165, 178, 179, 182
  learning 175, 178–9
  performance 166, 168
  principal 25–6, 28, 31, 178, 183, 199
  professional Learning 159, 217
  professionalism 179–82
teacher assessment 219
Teacher Working Time Research Project 169–71
Teachers' Agreement 169
Teaching And Learning Audit 211, 223–4

Teaching Scotland's Future 168, 179, 181
Technical and Vocational Edcuation Initiative 54
technology 36, 47, 62, 115, 149, 173, 225
testing 4, 91, 187, 193, 203, 220, 226
  national 167, 210, 220–1
TIMSS see Trends in International Maths And Science Study
Tisdall, K. 8, 122, 125
transcripts 171, 175–7
Trends In International Maths And Science Study 211, 220, 222
trust 53, 112, 135, 173, 180, 190, 201, 211
TWTR see Teacher Working Time Research

uncertainty 76–7, 91, 94, 144, 158
UNCRC 120, 122–3, 128–9, 134–5
union 4, 28–9, 223
United Nations Convention On The Rights Of The Child 8, 55, 120, 152
universities 18, 24–5, 39, 88, 90–1, 126, 171–2, 176–81, 213, 215–16, 233

vocational 16, 22, 40–1, 44–5, 54, 75, 100, 167, 172–4
  education 44, 54, 100, 167
  learning 172
  programmes 173–4
Vygotsky, L. 53, 217

Walkerdine, V. 207
Watson, C. 4, 36
well-being 7, 18, 36, 64–5, 67, 76–7, 79, 81–3, 89–90, 118, 128, 147, 149, 174
Westheimer, J. 112–15
Wheelahan, L. 1, 4–6
White, J. 81, 87
Wiliam, D. 58, 63, 65
Williams, R. 166
wisdom 19, 27, 29, 44, 47, 105
Wolf, A. 42, 75

Yates, L. 1, 3, 5
Young, M. 3, 5, 82, 85–6, 88, 144, 148, 158